SOCIETY OF BIBLICAL LITERATURE

MONOGRAPH SERIES 19

IMPERIALISM AND RELIGION:

Assyria, Judah and Israel in the Eighth and Seventh Centuries B.C.E.

Morton Cogan

SOCIETY OF BIBLICAL LITERATURE

AND

SCHOLARS PRESS

Distributed by

SCHOLARS PRESS

University of Montana

Missoula, Montana 59801

IMPERIALISM AND RELIGION

ISBN: 0-88414-041-5

Library of Congress Card Catalogue Number: 73-83723

PRINTED IN THE UNITED STATES OF AMERICA

PRINTING DEPARTMENT, UNIVERSITY OF MONTANA, MISSOULA, MONTANA 59801

Editor's Preface

Various minor inconsistencies in footnote style and related aspects have been allowed to remain in the interests of economy. A generous subvention provided by the UNIVERSITY OF THE NEGEV helped defray a portion of the typesetting and printing costs. We are all in their debt. I hope that they (and the author) will be generous in overlooking the abovementioned matters of detail.

Robert A. Kraft
Editor, SBL Monograph Series
(1967-1972)

Acknowledgments and Dedication

The present monograph is a revised edition of my doctoral dissertation, originally submitted to the Faculty of Oriental Studies at the University of Pennsylvania (April, 1971). It has benefited from the advice and criticism of many of my teachers, foremost among them Professor Moshe Greenberg, chairman of my dissertation committee. His erudite counsel and penetrating analyses gave valuable direction to my investigation. He gave unstintingly of his time and effort, often at great personal inconvenience, for which I am most indebted.

To Professors Erle Leichty and Barry Eichler, members of my committee, I express my gratitude for their many valuable comments on cuneiform problems. Professor Leichty also kindly collated several texts for me in the British Museum, London, during the summer of 1970.

To Professor Hayim Tadmor of the Hebrew University I owe a special note of appreciation for his guiding my initial steps into the realm of Neo-Assyrian civilization during my stay in Jerusalem, 1968-69, and for his critical reading of a semifinal draft. That year of study and research was made possible, in part, by a generous grant from the Memorial Foundation for Jewish Culture.

To the editor of the SBL Monograph Series and his associates I also extend my personal thanks for their assistance in bringing this work to publication.

Lastly, to my parents, for their constant support and encouragement, and for their instruction in "the mainstay of knowledge" (Prov 1.7), I affectionately offer this dedication.

Philadelphia
April, 1972

Morton Cogan

Contents

List of Illustrations

INTRODUCTION

FOR the sister states of Israel and Judah, the eighth and seventh centuries B.C.E. proved to be a crucial age, testing their capacity for continued national existence. The Neo-Assyrian empire, having renewed its thrust toward the Mediterranean coast, was quick to engulf northern Israel and, for over a century, posed a constant threat to the independence of southern Judah. Over and above this external peril, Israelite moral and religious traditions were threatened from within, as a result of the precipitate adoption of pagan practice by the citizenry of both states.

Biblical prophets and historians viewed these developments with alarm. To their thinking, national weal was inextricably interwoven with and conditioned upon Israelite fidelity to YHWH's covenant, so that apostasy could only lead to misfortune. The book of Kings, therefore, justified Samaria's destruction and exile by Assyria in an exhaustive indictment, listing violations by Israel of "all the commands of YHWH, their God" (cf. 2 Kgs 17:7-23). Judah's exile, as well, was seen as "surely YHWH's decree . . . to remove (them) from his sight," because of Manasseh's abominable misdeeds (cf. 2 Kgs 24:3; 21:10ff.; Jer 15:4).

Historians have sought repeatedly to elucidate the origins and character of Israelite apostasy during the Neo-Assyrian era. Late nineteenth-century studies adhered closely to the biblical viewpoint: the religious struggles of that age were a phenomenon peculiarly Israelite. Julius Wellhausen wrote of Judah's king, Manasseh:

> Assyrian suzerainty appears at that time to have made but little impression; since the time of Ahaz Judah had been accustomed to this relation. The Book of Kings speaks only of internal affairs under the reign of Manasseh. According to it, he was a bad ruler, who permitted, and even caused, innocent blood to flow like water. But what was of greater consequence for the future, he took up an attitude of hostility towards the prophetic party of reform, and put himself on the side of the reaction which would fain bring back to the place of honor the old popular half-pagan conception of Jehovah, as against the pure and holy God whom the prophets worshipped.[1]

Ernest Renan went as far as to declare that the ruling Assyrians "did not exercise any restraint upon religious liberty" within Judah; the reign of Manasseh was one of "toleration," when everyone "was allowed to worship after his own fashion."[2]

[1] J. Wellhausen, "Israel" in *Prolegomena to the History of Ancient Israel* (repr. Cleveland: Meridian Books, 1957) 485; *idem, Israelitische und jüdische Geschichte* (7th ed.; Berlin: Georg Reimer, 1914) 125.

[2] E. Renan, *History of the People of Israel* 3 (Boston: Roberts Brothers, 1894) 11-12, 106-7. Cf. the earlier statement to the similar effect by Heinrich Ewald, *The History of Israel* 4 (London: Longmans, Green, 1871) 168ff.

At the same time, the recovery and decipherment of the cuneiform inscriptions of ancient Assyria prompted other historians to revise their judgments concerning the effects of Assyrian imperial rule. Writing in 1875, George Rawlinson described the imposing figure of Ashur, the tutelary deity of Assyria, who marched at the head of Assyria's armies, granting them victory over all enemies: "It is to spread his worship that they carry out their wars. Finally, when they subdue a country, they are careful to 'set up the emblems of Ashur,' and teach the people his laws and his worship."[3] Since "some formal acknowledgement of the presiding deities of Assyria on the part of subject nations may not improbably have been required in most cases," biblical reports of pagan introductions during the reigns of Ahaz and Manasseh took on new perspective.[4] The new altar, commissioned by Ahaz for the Jerusalem temple (cf. 2 Kgs 16: 10ff.), was most likely of Assyrian provenance, and, including the Assyrian cultus connected with it, was adopted by Ahaz "in deference to his Assyrian suzerain."[5]

Not everyone, however, spoke of Assyrian imperialism in such categorical terms; some thought it "the fashion to swim with the stream and to prove one's culture by imitating Assyrian customs."[6] Heinrich Graetz described Ahaz, "in his timidity," as making himself the vassal of the king of Assyria. He "had, therefore, to pay homage to Tiglath-pileser. Instead of feeling humiliated, he was seized with admiration for the Assyrian customs, and determined to imitate them in his own country"—evidence the worship of sun and stars.[7] Rudolf Kittel thought the imitations to be the result of a tacit understanding: Assyrian vassals were "expected" to render praise to their overlord by adopting the worship of his god, Ashur.[8]

If there were any lingering doubts as to the necessity of adopting an Assyrian cult by Assyria's subjects,[9] they were dispelled by A. T. Olmstead. In 1908, in discussion of Sargon II's administration, Olmstead took note of the monarch's

[3] Rawlinson, *The Seven Great Monarchies of the Ancient Eastern World* 1 (New York: A. L. Burt, [1875]) 342.

[4] Rawlinson, *Monarchies*, 505.

[5] Rawlinson, *Monarchies*, 505 and n. 770. Rawlinson repeated his explication of the Ahaz incident in *The Kings of Israel and Judah* (New York: Anson D. F. Randolph [1889]) 173.

[6] Karl Budde, *The Religion of Israel to the Exile* (New York: Putnam, 1899) 164.

[7] H. Graetz, *History of the Jews* 1 (Philadelphia: Jewish Publication Society, 1891) 260. (Note that according to the text of 2 Kings [cf. 16:3-4 and 21:3ff.], Manasseh was the first to sponsor astral cults in Judah.)

[8] R. Kittel, *Geschichte des Volkes Israel* 2 (2nd ed.; Gotha: F. A. Perthes, 1909) 483-84; cf. 518-19.

[9] Cf., e.g., the indecision of J. R. Lumby, *Kings* (Camb. B., 1909), who noted that the Ahaz altar reforms were undertaken "either from inclination or because policy required him to acknowledge the deities of his superior lord" (at 2 Kgs 16:10). Hugo Winckler, in *The History of Babylonia and Assyria* (New York: Charles Scribner's Sons, 1907), omits all mention of Assyrian religious impositions. He claimed that tributary states were no more than tax-gatherers for Assyria's ruling class, and, as such, suffered no interference

religious policies: "Each newly organized province was at once given its images of the king and of Ashur, a curious anticipation of the provincial worship of 'Rome and Augustus.' "[10] The idea that the "whole organization" of the Assyrian provincial system "centered around the worship of Ashur, the deified state and reigning king,"[11] was popularized in much of Olmstead's subsequent work. In his *History of Assyria* and *History of Palestine and Syria*, this construct was asserted *a priori*.[12] Frequently, Olmstead summoned biblical examples to illustrate specific religious impositions, when the otherwise informative Assyrian sources fell silent. Thus, we read of the "Pro-Assyrian" Manasseh:

> Manasseh himself made his sons pass through the fire, the sacrifice in Tophet to the god king Melech. As a loyal servant of Ashur, his worship was reintroduced with that of the Assyrian king, and this in turn added to the prestige of Melech. Altars were built on the roof of the upper chamber of Ahaz in connection with the stepped sun dial, altars for the sun, moon, zodiacal signs, and all the host of heaven were to be found in the temple and its court. There were processional chariots dedicated to the sun under the charge of the chamberlain Nathan Melech, whose father had thus designated his son as the gift of the king god. Ishtar, the Babylonian mother-goddess, appeared as the Queen of Heaven, whose obscene images were produced in great numbers, her son and lover Tammuz was bewailed by the Jerusalem women. (2 Kgs 21:5; 23; Jer 7:17ff., 44:15ff.; Ezek 8:14)[13]

Sidney Smith's description of Assyria's "gloomy religious fanaticism" closely resembled the earlier remarks of Olmstead, except that for Smith "the fact that their national god was, in essentials, similar to the gods of the peoples whom they had to govern enabled them to impose on their subjects with the more ease a worship which did not interfere with ancient rites."[14] Assyria's Ashur was worshipped as "a counterpart of the Ba'alim," in a cult "entirely dependent upon

in their internal affairs. "Assyria expected to receive from her provinces, she had nothing to give them" (see 291-95). Contrast C. F. Lehmann-Haupt, *Israel* (Tübingen: J. C. B. Mohr, 1911) 93, 126 and 142.

[10] Olmstead, *Western Asia in the Days of Sargon of Assyria, 722-705 B.C.* (New York: H. Holt, 1908), p. 171. The deification of Augustus and his successors was originally a practice foreign to Rome, having spread from the East and been adopted in Rome because of its practical political value sometime after 40 B.C.E. See *CAH* 10 (1934) 208ff., 481ff. Deification has been traced to the earlier Hellenistic ruler cults, those "spontaneous creations of citizen communities" which conferred divinity upon great men; so, V. Ehrenberg, *The Greek State* (New York: Barnes and Noble, 1960) 168ff. Whether the Egyptian worship of the divine Pharoah or the Persian "proskynesis" served as the model for the hellenistic cults is still disputed. Cf. Ehrenberg, p. 261, and L. R. Taylor, "The 'Proskynesis' and the Hellenistic Ruler Cult," *Journal of Hellenic Studies* 47 (1927) 53-62.

[11] A. T. Olmstead, "Oriental Imperialism," *American Historical Review* 23 (1917-18) 758. Cf. *idem*, "Assyrian Government of Dependencies," *American Political Science Review* 12 (1918) 72.

[12] See, e.g., Olmstead, *History of Assyria* (Chicago: University of Chicago Press, 1923) 614, and 66f., 103f., 198f., and 601; and his *History of Palestine and Syria* (New York: Charles Scribner, 1931) 452, 464 and 485.

[13] Olmstead, *Palestine-Syria*, p. 482; cf. his *Assyria*, pp. 378f., and 212-14, 632.

[14] Smith, *CAH* 3 (1929) 91f.

military accomplishments." With the retreat of the Assyrian army from the conquered provinces, Assyrian religion withdrew as well.[15]

Most biblical handbooks written in the last half-century have embraced Olmstead's reading of Assyrian history. The paganization of the Judahite cultus during the reigns of Ahaz and Manasseh is regularly reported to have been "part of the obligation of subject states to the empire."[16] John Gray claims to have found evidence of Assyrian cults in north Israel during its final years of independence.[17] Although W. F. Albright called attention to the composite nature of the "new Aramaic culture, composed of Canaanite and Neo-Assyrian elements with the latter dominant," which spread over the West in the eighth and seventh centuries B.C.E., he, too, maintained that Assyrian military power "strongly supported" the spread of that culture.[18] The current scholarly consensus might best be epitomized by citing part of the discussion in Martin Noth's authoritative *History of Israel*:

> In the ancient Orient political suzerainty required the adoption of the official religion of the ruling power, not in place of, but alongside, the native hereditary religions. . . . In the provinces in the territory of the former kingdom of Israel, there existed . . . the official Assyrian religion, especially that of the imperial god Ashur. This was also true of dependent vassal states. When king Ahaz of Judah surrendered to Tiglath-pileser, he had to make room for the Assyrian religion in the official sanctuary in Jerusalem. . . . When Hezekiah abandoned his dependence on Assyria in 705 B.C., he quite consistently abolished this Assyrian religion and thereby "reformed" public worship in Jerusalem.[19]

Of all recent biblical investigators, only Yehezkel Kaufmann doubted the universality of an Assyrian policy of religious coercion. He found the Assyrio-

[15] Smith expressed this same idea in his *Early History of Assyria to 1000 B.C.* (New York: E. P. Dutton and Co., 1928) 337. If religion is imposed by the force of arms, it is "generally shaken off when that dominance ceases."

[16] J. A. Montgomery, *Kings* (ICC 1951) 520, cf. 460.

[17] Gray, *Kings*² (OTL, 1970) 648.

[18] Albright, *Archaeology and the Religion of Israel* [= ARI⁵] (5th ed., Garden City: Doubleday Anchor, 1969) 156.

[19] Noth, *The History of Israel* (2nd ed.; New York: Harper and Row, 1960) 266, and cf. also, 272. Corresponding views have been expressed by: L. W. Fuller, *The Historical and Religious Significance of the Reign of Manasseh* (Leipzig: W. Drugulin, 1912) 72ff.; G. Smith, *Deuteronomy* (Camb. B., 1918) 65; T. H. Robinson, *A History of Israel* 1 (Oxford: Clarendon Press, 1932) 377 and 419; J. Bright, *A History of Israel* (Philadelphia: Westminster Press, 1959) 259, 290 and 298; H. B. MacLean, IDB 1, 65, *s.v.* "Ahaz;" IDB 2, 997, *s.v.* "Josiah;" IDB 3, 254, *s.v.* "Manasseh;" and J. Gray, *Kings*², 635, 706.

Fohrer's latest discussion of Israelite religion during the Ahaz-Manasseh age deviates but little from the standard exegesis outlined above. He would seemingly credit the apostate Judahite kings with well-advised political sense in that they chose Assyrian "vassalage which was tied to the introduction of the cult of the overlord," rather than incorporation into the empire and deportation. See Georg Fohrer, *Geschichte der israelitischen Religion* (Berlin: Walter de Gruyter, 1969) 126-28.

logical evidence scant — one citation from the annals of Ashurbanipal.[20] "But that list, which mentions only three countries (Kaldu, Aramu, and the Sea-lands-southern Babylonia) cannot serve as proof that the custom was regularly practiced in every locality"; it is crucial, argued Kaufmann, that biblical sources are silent on the issue of the political necessity of pagan cult adoption — the gods of Assyria not being mentioned in the Bible at all.[21] Rather, a psychological crisis among the upper class of Judahite society, brought on by Judah's political subjugation to Assyria, accounts for the foreign introductions during Manasseh's age.[22]

Kaufmann's doubts had been anticipated by Hugo Gressman some years earlier. Gressman had called for "an accurate study of the relation of Assyrian politics to foreign religions. . . . We would like to know exactly what religious cultic demands the Assyrian state as such imposed upon subjugated peoples."[23] It is this issue, never systematically tackled, which the present study undertakes to investigate.

Inasmuch as Nineveh issued no "white paper" on religious policies within the Assyrian empire, data will be gathered by asking a set of leading questions of the Neo-Assyrian historical corpus (i.e., royal inscriptions, state letters, legal and business documents):

1) Did Assyrian conquest and rule affect the on-going native cults of defeated nations? In what areas?

2) Was it imperial policy to impose the worship of Assyrian gods? What specific cultic demands were made? Was such policy enforced in all territories?

All Assyrian texts will be treated chronologically, so as to note thematic origins and developments. Occasionally, reference to Middle Assyrian materials helps provide the requisite historical perspective.[24] Throughout, particular attention will be paid to the works of A. T. Olmstead, insofar as Olmstead may be considered to have been the leading proponent of the notion of Assyrian religious

[20] Asb. Rm. IV:103-7.

[21] Kaufmann, *Tōlᵉdōt Hāʾemūnā Hayyisrᵉʾēlīt* 1 (Tel-Aviv: Dvir, 5720 [=1960]) 95.

[22] Kaufmann, *Tōlᵉdōt* 2, p. 234. Kaufmann's objections were directed in the main against the view which interprets the Josianic cult reform (2 Kgs 22-23) as an anti-Assyrian move, one element in a broader political revolt. The most detailed elaboration of this thesis is by T. Oestreicher, *Das Deuteronomische Grundgesetz*, BFCT 27/4 (1923) 9ff.; 37-58; *idem, Reichstempel und Ortsheiligtümer in Israel*, BFCT 33/3 (1930) 35-37. Cf. also, A. C. Welch, *Jeremiah, His Times and Work* (Oxford: Blackwell, 1951) 4f., 17; and S. Smirin, *Josiah and His Age* (Hebrew) (Jerusalem: Mosad Bialik, 1952) 28ff., and 50f.

[23] Gressman, "Josia und das Deuteronomium," *ZAW* 1 (1924), 234. Gressman satisfied himself with the single Assyrian annal citation (cf. n. 20 above) as proof of religious coercion.

[24] According to the current periodization of Assyrian history, the Middle Assyrian (=MA) era extends from the reign of Ashur-uballit (1365-1330 B.C.E.) to *ca.* 1000 B.C.E.;

imperialism. It should also be noted that in contradistinction to previous studies which treated Assyrian and biblical sources in complement — the result being a blurring of the witness each source provides — our study allows each source to speak for itself.

Only with an account of Neo-Assyrian religious policy in hand, arrived at in isolation from the biblical record, do we turn to restudy specific Israelite problems from the period of Assyrian domination over Palestinian affairs, i.e., *ca.* 750-625 B.C.E.[25] To the biblical data we address the following questions:

1) What pagan innovations in the Israelite cult were peculiar to the Neo-Assyrian age? Can their introduction be traced to Assyrian imperial policy?

2) What were the immediate and long-range effects of Assyrian policy upon traditional Israelite religion?

In this section of our study, the affairs in Israel and Judah will be set out separately, for, as argued below, the disparate conduct of each state led to distinct Assyrian responses in each case.

One final word of introduction. The Deuteronomistic historiographers, in their anxiety to censure Manasseh's apostasy, left much unreported in 2 Kgs 21 concerning daily life in Judah; modern historians, however, have not hesitated completing the lacunae, often adding to Manasseh's burden. Some of the phenomena traced to the seventh century include: the displacement and the ultimate disappearance of the covenantal ark from the Jerusalem temple;[26] the importation of "the standard [Mesopotamian] terminology of the sun-god literature," for use by Judahite psalmists;[27] and the composition of Deuteronomy, based on an "Assyrian 'Vorlage.'"[28] All such scholarly observations must ulti-

the two-phased Neo-Assyrian (=NA) era, from Ashur-dan II (934-912 B.C.E.) to Shalmaneser III (858-824 B.C.E.) and from Tiglath-pileser III (744-727 B.C.E.) to Ashurbanipal (668-627 B.C.E.).

Recent historical surveys of these periods can be found in A. L. Oppenheim, IDB 1, 272-274, *s.v.* "Assyria and Mesopotamia;" H. W. F. Saggs, *The Greatness that was Babylon* (London: Lidgwick and Jackson, 1962) 83-139; E. A. Speiser, *At the Dawn of Civilization* vol. I of *World History of the Jewish People* (New Brunswick: Rutgers University Press, 1964) 217-28; and H. Tadmor, *En. Miq.* 5, cols, 83-103, *s.v.* "Mesopotamia."

The dates employed throughout our study are those given by J. A. Brinkman in Oppenheim's *Ancient Mesopotamia: Portrait of a Dead Civilization* (Chicago: University of Chicago Press, 1964), Appendix: Mesopotamian Chronology, pp. 335-52.

[25] Our Biblical dating follows the scheme worked out by H. Tadmor in *En. Miq.* 4, cols. 245-310, *s.v.* "Chronology."

[26] See M. Haran, "The Disappearance of the Ark," IEJ 13 (1963) 46-58.

[27] See N. Sarna, "Psalm XIX and the Near Eastern Sun-god Literature," *Proceedings of the Fourth World Congress of Jewish Studies* 1 (Jerusalem, 1967) 171-75.

[28] So, R. Frankena, "The Vassal-Treaties of Esarhaddon and the Dating of Deuteron-

mately be examined in the light of the exact political-religious relationship which obtained between the Neo-Assyrian empire and the Israelite states. It is the nature of this fundamental relationship which the present study sets out to probe.

omy," OTS 14 (1965) 150-54. Cf. M. Weinfeld, "Deuteronomy—The Present State of Inquiry," JBL 87 (1967), 254: ". . . a series of maledictions in Deuteronomy 28 . . . can be proved to have been transposed directly from Assyrian contemporary treaties into the book of Deuteronomy."

1. THE ASSYRIAN EMPIRE AND FOREIGN GODS — THE MOTIVE OF DIVINE ABANDONMENT

THE propensity of Assyrian historical literature for martial descriptions, glorifying the victories of god and man, is well known. Whether destined for public display or for divine perusal,[1] these scribal productions never tired of rehearsing the aid offered the Assyrian monarch by his gods. For example, Esarhaddon claimed:

dIštar bēlet qabli (u) tāḫazi *rā'imat šangūtīya idāya tazzizma* *qašassunu tašbir tāḫazašunu* *raksu tapṭurma*[2]	Ishtar, the Lady of War and Battle, who loves my priesthood, stood at my side, broke their bow, and undid their battle formations.

Victory over the Arab Uate', said Ashurbanipal, was due to allied divine assistance.

dNinlil rīmtu illilatu šaqītu . . . *unakkip nakrēya ina qarnēša gašrāti* *dIštar āšibat āl Arba-ilu išāti lithušat* *melammē našāta eli māt Aribi izannun nabli* *dIrra qardu anuntu kuṣṣurma* *urassipa gārīya . . .*[4]	Ninlil, the wild cow, exalted goddess . . . gores my enemies with her powerful horns. Ishtar, who resides in Arba-il, clothed in fire, bedecked with *melammū*,[3] rains flames upon Arabia. Irra, the warrior, organized for battle, cuts down my foe. . .

Not only on the field of battle, but behind the scenes as well, Assyria's gods worked to disrupt the enemy's plans. The king of Elam met disaster at the hands of Ashurbanipal because

[1] A. L. Oppenheim holds that royal inscriptions, buried as foundation deposits or displayed in the dark recesses of Assyrian palaces, were "not intended for reading" by the public. Formally, they were reports to the gods of "the king's victories and his piety and demand blessings in return"; see *Ancient Mesopotamia*, p. 148. Cf. the remarks of E. A. Speiser in *Idea of History in the Ancient Near East*, ed. by R. C. Dentan (New Haven: Yale University Press, 1955), pp. 60-69, establishing a link between the annals and letters to the god. To the foreign visitor in Assyria, bold Assyrian palace reliefs, rather than the written word, narrated the royal exploits. On this early use of "psychological warfare," see H. W. F. Saags, "Assyrian Warfare in the Sargonid Period," *Iraq* 25 (1963), 149f.

[2] Borger, *Die Inschriften Asarhaddons Königs von Assyrien*, AfO Beiheft 9 (1956), § 27, ep. 2, 74-76.

[3] *Melammū* is the awe-inspiring radiance which surrounds divinity; see AHw 643. Oppenheim, "Akkadian *pul(u)ḫ(t)u* and *melammu*," JAOS 63 (1943), 31-34, would have us understand *melammū* in a very literal sense, viz. a mask and/or head-gear worn *(našū)* by the gods. Cf. also, ANET, p. 300.

[4] Asb. Rm. IX. 75ff.

ša balu ilāni itbā[5]	he set forth without (the consent of) the gods.

His plan seemed so foolhardy and lacking in reason that the writer spoke of him as

ša [d]*Ištar ušannū melik ṭēmēšu*[6]	one whose mind Ishtar has deranged —

the goddess purposefully leading him to his destruction.

At times, Assyria's foe was thought to be the object of divine imprecation; e.g.,

[m]*Tarqu šar māt Muṣur u māt Kūsi nizirti ilūtīšunu rabīti*[7]	Tarqu, king of Egypt and Ethiopia, cursed by their [i.e., Ashur and the great gods] great divinity.

In one striking instance, the god Ashur is pictured as intervening on behalf of Ashurbanipal by sending a dream to a foreign king, which proved sufficient inducement for him to seek a protective alliance with Assyria.

[m]*Guggu šar māt Luddi nagū ša nēberti tāmti ašru rūqu ša šarrāni abbēya la išmū zikir šumīšu nibīt šumīya ina šutti ušabrīšuma* [d]*Aššur ilu bānū'a umma šēpā* [md]*Aššurbānapli šar māt* [d]*Aššur*[ki] *ṣabatma ina zikir šumīšu kušud nakrēka*[10]	Gyges, king of Lydia, a district on the other side of the sea,[8] a far-away place whose name my royal ancestors had never heard, the god Ashur, my creator, revealed my very name[9] to him in a dream: Take hold of the feet of Ashurbanipal, king of Assyria. By (acknowledging) his name, conquer your enemies.

That the entire world served as the arena for Assyria's gods in no way inhibited the participation of foreign divinities in the determination of destinies. Occasionally, one can discern reference to non-Assyrian gods extending aid to the imperial cause, albeit circumscribed and indirect aid. It is the development and use of this motif we now proceed to trace.

[5] Asb. B.V.19.

[6] Asb. B.V.22. For the expression *melik ṭēmēšu*, see AHw 652b.

[7] Borger, *Asarhaddon*, § 65, rev. 37-38 and note to line 38.

[8] Or, "by the passes of the sea"; cf. AHw 773.

[9] Oppenheim, WZKM 44 (1937), 179, and *The Interpretation of Dreams in the Ancient Near East, Transactions of the American Philosophical Society*, N.S. 46/3 (1956), 202, attempts to explain away the unlikelihood "that Gyges knew enough cuneiform to be able to read the name of the Assyrian king," by rendering *nibīt šumi* as "phonetic transcription of an Assyrian name in another system of writing." Oppenheim's conjecture will not hold for the reference in Borger, *Asarhaddon*, § 27, ep. 14, 14, where the inscribing of Esarhaddon's name on statues returned to Arabia is termed *šiṭir šumi*. Should we not expect the use of a "foreign writing system" in this case as well, considering that the purpose of the Esarhaddon inscription was to give prominent display to the name of the Assyrian king among the Arabs?

[10] Asb. Rm. II. 95-99.

Mesopotamian historiography, almost from its inception, had considered that the displeasure of a deity with the behavior of his subjects could cause natural disaster and/or national destruction.[11] Misfortunes suffered at the hands of an enemy were rationalized as one's abandonment by his own gods.

Late Neo-Assyrian texts, recasting the familiar motif of divine abandonment, present the first examples in which the conqueror, rather than the conquered, invokes this motif in order to justify his ravages. The earliest suggestion on the part of the Assyrian conqueror that his enemy's gods were instrumental in predetermining the outcome of battle in Assyria's favor is found in the inscriptions of Sennacherib.[12] Twice Sennacherib describes the abandonment of the foe by their own gods preceding their downfall. Referring to seven rebellious cities on the border of Qummuḫ, Sennacherib wrote:

ilānīšun īzibūšunūtima ušabšū rēqūssun[13]
Their gods abandoned them, rendering them helpless.

In like manner:

mKirua bēl āli ša āl Illubri ardu dāgil pānīya ša īzibūšu ilānīšu[14]
Kirua, ruler of Illubru, a faithful vassal of mine, whom his gods had abandoned.

Study of the several documents related to Sennacherib's conquest of Babylon affords insight into the unique Assyrian application of the divine abandonment

[11] See recent survey of evidence in Bertil Albrektson, *History and the Gods* (Lund: CWK Gleerup, 1967), esp. chs. 1, 2, and 6; cf. E. A. Speiser in *Idea of History*, pp. 55-60. The newly-published "Lamentation over the Destruction of Sumer and Ur," translated by S. N. Kramer, in ANET *Supplement*, pp. 175-83 contains further examples of divinely-decreed destruction and abandonment, and should be added to Albrektson's citations.

[12] Although Sargon had earlier claimed that he had been called by Marduk to punish Merodach Baladan, with whom the Babylonian god was angry (cf. Lie, *The Inscriptions of Sargon II, King of Assyria. Part I: The Annals* [Paris: Geuthner, 1929], lines 267-273), Sargon neglected to make use of the abandonment motif. This neglect is patent, when we consider Sargon's Eanna inscription (YOS 1, no. 38), appropriated by Sargon's scribes from an earlier Merodach Baladan text (*Iraq* 15 [1953], 123-34). In the Merodach Baladan text, the tale of Marduk's previous anger with Babylon which had led to Assyrian rule (lines 8-11), did not mention abandonment by Marduk of his city. So, the Sargon text could not take over, nor did it introduce, the adandonment motif.

[13] OIP 2, 64.22-24. The reading of the last word has been disputed ever since the first publication of the text by L. W. King, PSBA 35 (1913), pl. 16 (=OIP 2, 64). King opted for the reading *talkūtu*, rather than *rēqūtu*, considering that the gods had brought "their path into adversity" (p. 88 n. 90). Luckenbill in OIP 2, chose *rēqūtu*, followed by CAD E, 417b, translating "and brought about the loss of their power." Other recent suggestions include Borger, *Asarhaddon*, p. 41, note to line 24, *ri-kil-tú* (cf. *ibid.*, § 11, ep. 3c[3], 5) "eine Verschwörung anzettelten." CAD B, 157, corrects the text: *re-šu* (!)*-ut-su-un*, "and let them enter slavery." But if King's copy of this rock inscription be true, the remaining wedges can only be read as *qú*. On *rēqūtu*, cf. GAG, 147b; ARM 15, 250.

[14] OIP 2, 61.62-63.

motif. Sometime after the battle of Ḫalule in 691 B.C.E.,[15] Sennacherib pursued his policy of decisively subduing Babylonian unrest by "another campaign"[16] to the south. Much space is given over in his Bavian inscription to describing the thoroughgoing destruction of the city, its sanctuaries and their gods.[17] No special reason is offered for this severe treatment, but it seems that "the patience of Sennacherib was exhausted."[18] Interestingly, the sacking of Babylon did not occasion a new edition of the royal annals, as was so often the case upon completion of an important campaign.[19] We suspect that this official silence stemmed from an attempt to avoid notoriety being given a particularly sensitive issue: the violation of a religious center respected by Assyrians and Babylonians alike.[20]

In the inscriptions of Esarhaddon, on the other hand, we find prominent attention given to the sacrilege of Sennacherib. The anger of Marduk, Babylon's own god, and his subsequent abandonment of the Esagila were invoked as the cause for Babylon's destruction:

īgugma ᵈenlil ilāni ᵈMarduk *ana sapān māti ḫulluqu nišēša* *iktapud lemuttim . . .* *arrat marušti iššakin ina pīšu*[21]	The lord of the gods, Marduk, was angry. He planned evil; to wipe out the land, to destroy its inhabitants . . . an evil curse was on his lips.
ilāni ištarāti āšib libbīšu iṣṣūriš *ipparšūma ēlū šamāmiš* *šēdē [. . . ippar]siddūma ittanamgišū* *aḫāti*[22]	The gods and goddesses who dwell in it (i.e., the temple Esagila) fled like birds and went up to heaven. The protective gods [. . . ran] off and withdrew.

This widely discussed "apologia" sought to appease and win back Babylonia to the camp of Assyria, by implying that the deeds of Sennacherib were undertaken at the command of the Babylonians' own god, Marduk. Earlier, Babylon

[15] An exact date is difficult to determine, because our information is dependent upon an undated dedicatory inscription (Bavian Inscription = III R 14). The last edition of the Sennacherib annals was edited in 691 B.C.E. (=Taylor Prism) and was recopied in similar fashion until 689 B.C.E. (=Chicago Prism), without detailing Babylon's destruction. See the discussion of Grayson, AfO 20 (1963), 84, and AS 16, p. 342 n. 45.

[16] The term *ina šanī girrīya* (OIP 2, 83.43) need have no chronological significance. It simply notes that sometime following the year mentioned in line 34, this campaign was undertaken. Cf. Olmstead, *Assyria*, p. 295.

[17] OIP 2, 83.43-54.

[18] Olmstead, *Assyria*, p. 295.

[19] See above, n. 15. One further reference to the Babylonian action is known. Cf. OIP 2, 137.36-37 (=KAH 2, 122). Note the variant reading in CAD I, 102b.

[20] At the very least, the influence of Babylonian circles at the court of Sennacherib must have been minimal. Tadmor, "The 'Sin of Sargon' " [Hebrew], EI 5 (1958), 161f., suggests that a policy shift towards Babylonian appeasement took place before the death of Sennacherib. Note his appointment of Esarhaddon, "a Babylonian sympathizer," as successor. Cf. our remarks below, pp. 38-39.

[21] Borger, *Asarhaddon*, § 11, ep. 5, A + B.

[22] Borger, *Asarhaddon*, § 11, ep. 8, A + B. (On the translation, cf. AHw 710.)

itself had likewise rationalized its subjugation to Tiglath-pileser III as due to the anger of Marduk.[23] The favor which this explanation enjoyed in later Babylonian[24] and Babylonian-oriented[25] sources suggests that originally it was the product of a Babylonian priesthood and/or party,[26] which urged acceptance of this interpretation of history upon the Assyrian court, as part of its price for rapprochement. At the same time, it was in Assyrian self-interest to accede to such Babylonian rationalizations, inasmuch as they legitimized the Assyrian conquest.

Were the Babylonian affair the only instance of Assyrian acknowledgment of divine abandonment, we would hesitate proceeding further; for ever since the reign of Tilgath-pileser III, Assyria had exhibited ambivalent respect for "the religious and psychological sensibilities" of Babylon's governing classes.[27] But other Neo-Assyrian texts apply the abandonment motif to territories far and wide.

According to Esarhaddon,

ᵐSanduarri šar āl Kundi u āl Sissû . . .	Sanduarri, king of Kundu and Sissu . . .
ša ilāni umaššírūma[28]	(was one) whom the gods had forsaken.

Ashurbanipal, too, spoke of divine abandonment. The Ashurbanipal annals report that during the last Assyrian campaign against Elam, the goddess Nanā

[23] See inscriptions of Merodach Baladan: BA 2 (1891), 258f., col. I, 17-19; *Iraq* 15 (1953), 123, lines 8-11.

[24] See VAB 4, Nab. 8, I, 18-25:
kīma uzzi ilimma ītepuš māti ul ipšur [ki]miltašu rubû ᵈMarduk 21 *šanāti qereb Aššurᵏⁱ irtame šubassu*
He [Sennacherib] treated the land in accord with the anger of the god. Prince Marduk did not relax his anger; for 21 years he took up residence in Assyria.

[25] See Ashurbanipal Inscriptions P^1, 8-9 (=Streck, VAB 7, p. 232); S^2, 24-26 (= Streck, VAB 7, p. 242).

E. Reiner (JNES 17 [1958], 45), citing the Era Epic as evidence, traced this theme back to the MB period. "Any calamity befalling Babylon was always explained in the Babylonian literature as the result of a voluntary or enforced absence of Marduk." The newly reconstructed "Marduk prophecy" text, datable to the reign of Nebuchadnezzar I (1124-1103 B.C.E.), affirms this position. Therein, the god Marduk, in a first person address, tells of three self-imposed exiles (to Ḫatti, Assyria and Elam), complete with sufferings wrought in Babylon due to his absence and good fortune bestowed upon his temporary foreign abodes. For text and discussion, see R. Borger, "Gott Marduk und Gott-König Šulgi als Propheten. Zwei prophetische Texte," BiOr 28 (1971), 3-24.

[26] Cf. the remarks of Landsberger, *Brief des Bischofs von Esagila an König Asarhaddon*, in *Mededelingen der Koninklijke Nederlandse Akademie van Wetenschappen, Afd. Letterkunde Nievwe Reeks* 28/6 (1965), 14-16. Albrektson, *History and the Gods*, p. 102, incorrectly attributes this "marketable" work to Esarhaddon's own court politicians.

[27] See the full comments of Speiser, *Dawn of Civilization*, p. 224; and Oppenheim, *Ancient Mesopotamia*, pp. 65f., and 166.

[28] Borger, *Asarhaddon*, § 27, ep. 6, 22. This same phrase occurs in ep. 2, 24, to which Borger (p. 41) appended a long note rejecting the suggestion that "the gods" be considered the object of abandonment by the subject. The consistent use of plural verbs, even when the object is singular, indicates that an interchange cannot be suggested without

was brought back to her city, Uruk, after a self-imposed exile of 1,635 years, as had been previously predicted:[29]

^{d}*Nanā ša* 1635 *šanāti tasbusu* *talliku tūšibu qereb māt Elamti* *ašar lā simātēša u ina ūmēšuma* *šī u ilāni abbēša tabbū šumī ana* *bēlūt mātāte tayyārat ilūtīša* *tušadgila pānū'a*[30]	Nanā, who for 1,635 years was angry, went to stay in Elam, a place not fit for her. But at the time that she and the gods, her fathers, spoke my name for rule of all the countries, she entrusted me with the return of her divinity.

While the Elamite wars were undertaken for purely political motives (cf. Asb. Rm.V. 92), at least one NA text makes the restoration of Nanā the chief issue. In this text, K.1364,[31] Ashurbanipal asks the Elamite Ummanaldasi to return the captive goddess and is refused:

šūt alāk ^{d}*Nanā ultu qereb āl Šušan* *ana Uruk*^{ki} *a*[*na māt Elamti*] *ana Ummanaldasi šar māt Elamti* *ašpuršuma ul i*[*š-menni?*][32]	I wrote to Ummanaldasi, king of Elam in Elam, about the return of Nanā from Susa to Uruk. But he did not [listen to me(?)]

Following this rebuff, a separate campaign—a "third" one[33]—was undertaken to retrieve the goddess.[34]

textual emendation. Nevertheless, Borger's translations remain ambivalent. Support for our translation is found in ep. 2, 43, where the same actors, who have been abandoned by the gods, are said to have proceeded *balu ilāni*, "without the help of the gods."

[29] Variations in this date occur. For discussion, see Nassouhi, MAOG 3/1-2 (1927), 34f.

[30] Asb. Rm. VI.107-112.

[31] Streck, VAB 7, p. 175; Bauer, *Das Inschriftenwerk Assurbanipals* [=IWA] (Leipzig: J. C. Hinrichs, 1933), p. 51. Cf. K.2644, 5 (Bauer, p. 64).

[32] Rev 7-8. The reading LÚ *mār šiprī-ia* at the end of line 6 in Streck's edition is to be eliminated, as a result of Bauer's collation. Cf. Bauer, p. 64.

[33] The use of *šalšiānu*, "for a third time," may not have strict chronological significance, but may represent the final and concluding item in an ascending sequence. See H. Tadmor, AS 16, pp. 353-54, for similar usage in NB texts of *ina šalulti šatti.*

[34] A number of texts seem to suggest that ^{d}Nanā was not alone in her return from Elam: see K.2631 + K.2653 + K.2855, rev. 16-17 (=Streck, VAB 7, p. 186); K.3065, rev. col. III, 7-8 (=Bauer, IWA, p. 58); K.2524, obv. 1ff. (=Bauer, pp. 73f.); K.7673, lines 13ff. (=Bauer, p. 78); on K.3101a+ (=Streck, VAB 7, pp. 219ff.) see, for correction, Bauer, p. 34 n. 1. At least two, if not three, other goddesses are said to have entered Eanna after release from Elam. These are ^{d}Uṣuramatsa/u and ^{d}Arkaītu (^{d}Urukaītu), and seemingly, ^{d}Ištar of Uruk. Most opinions see these deities as "by-names" of Nanā (so, Streck, VAB 7, p. clxviii n. 2; Tallqvist, *Akkadische Götterepitheta*, StOr 7 [1938], 481; BIN 2, p. 48). The Ashurbanipal texts cited do, indeed, speak of all three goddesses in the third person fem. sing., as does the main annal edition with reference to Nanā alone. But the identity of Nanā as ^{d}Ištar of Uruk must be ruled out for the late NA period. In ABL 476, a work-report on temple repairs in Uruk, all three goddesses are spoken of as distinct entities (obv. 12-13, 24-26). See also, A. Falkenstein, *Literarische Keilschrifttexte aus Uruk* (Staatliche Museen zu Berlin, 1931), p. 51 nn. 2 and 3. This does not preclude the possibility that at some earlier date various manifestations of Nanā

In the case of Nanā of Uruk, Assyria appeared, not as the conqueror and exiler of the goddess, but as the redeemer of her divinity; for the divine abandonment had taken place in times long past. Nevertheless, one wonders whether behind this exhibition of concern by Ashurbanipal for the welfare of a Babylonian goddess did not lay political considerations, i.e., securement of Urukian loyalty and aid to Assyria during the Elamite wars.

Turning now to an Ashurbanipal dedicatory text (K.3405), we meet with an account of divine abandonment of the enemy described in the context of the persistently strained relations between Assyria and the Arabian tribes. The occasion for this inscription was Ashurbanipal's victory over the Uate', son of Bir-dadda, king of the Arabs (rev. 3).[35] The Assyrian king dedicates a star-emblem (*kakkabtu*) to an Arabian goddess, thanking her for helping him defeat and capture Uate', as she had previously helped his grandfather, Sennacherib. Since an up-to-date transcription of the obv., taking into account the cuneiform text first published by Theo Bauer, is not available, we present a new transliteration and annotated translation of the entire text.

may have become separated and hypostatized. Cf. Edzard in WM 1/1, *s.v.* Nanāja, p. 108; and the remarks of Brinkman, WO 5 (1969-70), 44.

[35] This appears certain, for the rev. 8-12 find their best parallel in the concluding description of Asb. Rm. IX.104-110. Which Uate', of the two Arab leaders who bear this name, is meant was not clear to the author of the Rassam edition of the annals. I. Eph'al, *The Nomads on the Border of Palestine in the Assyrian, Babylonian and Persian Periods* [Hebrew] (Ph.D. dissertation, Hebrew University, Jerusalem, 1971), pp. 39f., by identifying the various orthographic traditions of this name, traces the confusion to the "Letter to the Gods" (K.2802 +). The composite nature of the Rassam annals, i.e., its composition from multiple sources, added to the confusion. Note that VIII.1-2 reintroduces Uate', known already from VII.83.

K.3405: TEXT[36]

obverse

1. *a-na* ^{d}x x[37] [^{f}*Te-'-el-ḫu-nu ku-*]*mir-tu šá* KU[R! *A-ri-bi*]
2. *ša it-ti* ^{m}*Ḫa-z*[*a*-DINGIR MAN] KUR *A-ri-bi tas-bu-*[*su*[38]]x *it* [ ]
3. *ina* ŠU^{II} ^{md}30.PAB.MEŠ.SU AD.AD DÙ-*ia tam-nu-šu-*[*ma ta*]*š-ku-na* ŠI.[ŠI-*šu*]
4. *la a-šá-ab-šá it-ti* UKU.MEŠ KUR *A-ri-bi taq-bu-ú a-na* KUR AN. ŠÁR.KI *ta-as-ba-*[*ta ḫar-ra-na*]
5. ^{m}AN.ŠÁR.PAB.AŠ MAN KUR AN.ŠÁR.KI AD *ba-nu-a mi-gir* DINGIR.MEŠ [GAL.MEŠ]
6. *šá ina pa-laḫ* DINGIR.MEŠ *u* ^{d}15.MEŠ *ik-šu-du-ni* [ ]
7. AN.ŠÁR *ù* ^{d}UTU *ina* GIŠ.GU.ZA AD *ba-ni-šú ú-šé-*[*šib-u-šu-ma*]
8. DINGIR.MEŠ KUR.KUR *šal-lu-tu ú-tir-ru áš-r*[*u-uš-šu-un*][38]
9. ^{m}*Ḫa-za-*DINGIR MAN KUR *A-ri-bi it-ti ta-mar-ti-*[*šú ka-bit-ti*]
10. *a-di maḫ-ri-šú il-lik-am-ma ú-na-áš-šiq* [GÌR^{II}-*šu*]
11. *áš-šú na-dan* ^{d}*iš-tar-šú im-ḫur-šú-ma ri-e-mu ir-ši-šu-ma im-gu-*[*ur-šu*]
12. ^{f}*Te-'-el-ḫu-nu* ^{f}*ku-mir-ta-šá maḫ-ri-tu a-na ub* (?)-[ ]
13. *ina* UGU ^{f}*Ta-bu-a* ^{d}UTU *iš-al-ma um-ma ši-i* x [ ]
14. *it-ti* ^{d}*iš-tar-šú ú-tir-ma* [*id-din-šú*][43]
15. *ú-še-piš-ma* MUL.*tu* GUŠKIN ḪUŠ.A *ša ni-siq-ti* NA$_{4}$.MEŠ *za-'-na-at ša* [ ]
16. ⌜*a-na* TI.LA ZI.MEŠ-*šú* GÍD.DA UD.MEŠ-*šú šá-lam li-pi-šú ka-*[ ]
17. *šul-bur* LUGAL-*ti-šú sa-ḫap* LÚ.KÚR.MEŠ-*šú* [ ]
18. DINGIR.MEŠ KUR.KUR *šá-a-tu-nu šá áš-ra-te-šú-nu ú-šak-bi-su dam-qa-ti* [*ēpuššunūti*]
19. *ik-rib* UD.MEŠ SUD.MEŠ *lik-tar-ra-bu* EGIR-*su* UGU *ṣal-mat* SAG.DU [ ]
20. *a-*⌞*na-ku* ^{m}AN. ŠÁR.DU.IBILA MAN KUR AN.ŠÁR.KI DINGIR.MEŠ GAL.MEŠ [ ]

[36] Bauer published K.3405 in IWA, plate 38. A transcription and translation of the rev. was given on p. 45; while obv. 1-20 was left on the whole unworked, with reference given only to the earlier work of Streck, VAB 7, pp. 222f.

K.3087, more or less a duplicate of K.3405, was also copied by Bauer, plate 34. Slight variations in scribal transcription of the two texts are evident, e.g., *šar/šar*$_{4}$ (obv. 5); *u/ù* (obv. 6); *-utu/uti* (obv. 8). But to assume a word identity of the two texts would produce several inordinately crowded lines; see particularly, lines 4 and 11. Moreover, K.3087 lacks the dedication to the unknown goddess of obv. 1. K.3405 may represent a variant recension of K.3087, which was somewhat abbreviated for the present dedicatory text. In this eclectic text, those elements restored from K.3087 are underscored; brackets, [], represent conjectured restorations.

[37] The name of the goddess is no longer legible. See Bauer's comment, IWA, p. 45, n. 1. Streck's reading ^{d}*dil-bat* (VAB 7, p. 222, n. 3) was apparently based on George Smith's copy in *History of Sennacherib* (London: Williams and Norgate, 1878), p. 138. The signs were not included in Winckler's text edition. ^{d}*dil-bat* would not be an inappropriate appellation for an Ishtar figure within the context of a jeweled "star" dedication (see below). Cf. VAB 7, p. 188, K.2652, obv. 1, 5. See also Tallqvist, *Götterepitheta,* p. 282 and the etymology of the name—"the brightly shining or flaming one"—proposed by A. Poebel, AS 14 (1947), pp. 86f. (This last citation was called to my attention by Dr. Sol Cohen of the University Museum, Phila.)

[38] Collation (courtesy of E. Leichty) indicates that Bauer's copy of the text is correct. Streck's readings, *tas-bu-su* [and *aš-ru-uš-*[(line 8), simply followed Winckler, *Keilinschriftliches Textbuch zum Alten Testament* (Leipzig: Pfeiffer, 1892), p. 38; but "there is no evidence that there was a fresh break between the time of the two copies" (Leichty).

K.3405: TRANSLATION

obverse

1. To the goddess x x [, beloved of (?) Telḫunu, priest]ess of the land of [Arabia],
2. who, angered at Hazail, king of Arabia [ ]
3. handed him over to Sennacherib, my own grandfather, and caused his defeat.
4. She (i.e., the goddess) determined not to remain with the people of Arabia and set out for Assyria.[39]
5. Esarhaddon, king of Assyria, my own father, favorite of the great gods,
6. who had achieved [ ] because of his reverence of the gods and goddesses,
7. Ashur and Shamash install[ed him (i.e., Esarhaddon)] upon the throne of his own father.[40]
8. He returned the captured gods (i.e., images) of all lands to their sanctuaries.

9.-10. Hazail, king of the Arabs, came before him with [his rich] gifts, kissed his feet,

11. and appealed to him[41] concerning the return of his goddess. He (i.e., Esarhaddon) had mercy upon him and agreed.
12. Telḫunu, her former priestess, to [ ].[42]
13. As for Tabua, he (i.e., Esarhaddon) inquired of the Shamash oracle: Is she [ ]?[44]
14. Then he gave him back [Tabua] together with his goddess.
15. He had a star of red gold made, which was studded with precious stones, [ ].

16.-17. [and presented it][45] for a healthy life and long days, the prosperity of his decendants, the constancy of his rule, and the overthrow of his enemies.

18. [He showed] kindness towards the captured gods of all lands, whose sanctuaries had been trampled,
19. (so that the gods) might grant him the blessing of long life and [permit] his offspring [to rule] over mankind.
20. I, Ashurbanipal, king of Assyria, the great gods [ ]

[39] Ashurbanipal's dedicatory inscriptions often begin with a descriptive phrase glorifying the attributes of the god named; e.g., cf. Streck, VAB 7, p. 234 (L[6]); 272; 276; 286. The terminology and imagery of our text follows that of the several texts adduced above — all referring to the anger of the gods. To take Telḫunu, the priestess-queen, as the subject of the verbs in lines 2-4, as has been done in all previous studies (cf. Streck, VAB 7, pp. 216-17; Oppenheim in ANET, p. 301), is unwarranted. The goddess to whom the dedication was made is the subject. Not only foreign gods, but Assyrian gods as well, were on occasion similarly described:

(1) Sharrat Kidmuri in Ashurbanipal annal C.X.49-50:

dšarrat kidmuri ša ina uggat libbīša atmanša ēzibu ūšibu ašar lā simātīša

Sharrat Kidmuri who in her anger left her cella and stayed in a place not fit for her . . .

(Streck's restoration of line 48, *dIštar ša Ninua*ki, is not borne out by R. C. Thompson, *The Prisms of Esarhaddon and Ashurbanipal* [London: British Museum, 1931], II.9; nor by the duplicate in Knudsen, *Iraq* 29 [1967], ND.5413 +, ii, 23);

(2) An unnamed god in a bi-lingual penitential prayer, dated to Ashurbanipal, IV R 10, 16 (=OECT 6, pp. 39ff.): *ilu ša elīya isbusu ana ašrīšu litūra* "May the god who is angry with me return to his place."

[40] Oppenheim reads line 7 differently: "who had reinstalled [Hazail] upon the throne of his own father [upon a command given by] Ashur and Shamash." No text from the reign of Esarhaddon preserves information concerning the return of Hazail to his ancestral throne. Moreover, Hazail appeared before Esarhaddon at the outset as the recognized ruler of the Arabs (cf. line 2). Our suggestion views the line as an allusion to the role of the gods in the successful struggle for the throne waged by Esarhaddon himself at the start of his reign (see Borger, *Asarhaddon*, § 27, ep. 2).

reverse

1. [*ù ina* Á[11]]-*a il-lik-ú-ma ú-šak-m*[*i-su ajābī šaplanūa*(?)][46]
2. LÚ.KÚR.MEŠ-*ia i-ni-ru ú-šá*[-*zi*]-[*zu-in-ni ṣīr gārīya*][47]
3. *iš-ni-ma* [m]*Ú-a-a-te-'* MAN KUR *A-ri-bi ša* [ ]
4. *ša* MUN *e-pu-šu-uš la iṣ-ṣu-r*[*u*]
5. *ia-a-ti ú-maš-šir-an-ni it-ti* [md]GIŠ.[ŠIR.MU.GI]
6. [d]*iš-tar be-el-tu šá-qu-tu* [ ]
7. *ina a-mat qí-bi-ti-šá ṣir-ti a-na-ku* [m]AN.ŠÁR.DÙ.IBIL[A]
8. *ina qí-bit* AN.ŠÁR [d]*Nin-líl* [d] x x x x x x [ ]
9. *šá-a-šú bal-ṭu-us-su ina* ŠU[11]-*i*[*a*]
10. UZU.ME.ZÉ-*šú ap-lu-uš ina la-a*[*ḫ-ši-šu*]
11. *ina* KÁ.GAL *ṣi-it* [d]UTU-*ši ša* M[UŘ]
12. *na-bu-u zi-ki*[*r-ša*][48]
13. *ina* UD-*me-šú* MUL.*tu šu-a-*[*tu*]
14. *mim-ma*] DINGIR-*ti-šá* GAL-[*ti*]
15. *ni-iš* ŠU[11]-*ia* [ ]
16. *e-ma* [ ]
17. UD.MEŠ [ ]
18. x x [ ]

[41] For this meaning of *maḫāru*, see AHw, 578a, *sub* 2, "sich wenden an jmd., angehen." The parallel Esarhaddon text (Borger, *Asarhaddon*, §27, ep. 14, 9) reads *uṣallānnima*, "he entreated me." (The text is quoted in full below, p. 35)

[42] Had Telḫunu voluntarily exiled herself, as assumed by previous translations, we should expect an indication of her own reconciliation with Hazail at this point in the text. Rather, it is not the anger of Telḫunu (so, Oppenheim) but that of the goddess which must be assuaged; accomplished here by the recognition of the Assyrian king (lines 9-10). The only way to make Telḫunu the subject in K.3405, obv. 2-4, is to suppose that the author has identified the fortunes of the goddess with that of her priestess, interchanging the two without affecting the meaning (cf. W. Hallo, *Exaltation of Inanna* [New Haven: Yale University Press, 1967], pp. 6ff.); so, Olmstead, *Assyria*, p. 310. The possibility might also be considered that the anger of the goddess was directed both at Telḫunu and the king. The broken passage in VAS 1, 77, rev. 22ff., may tell of the defeat of [Telḫ]unu, queen of the Arabs, along with Hazail (see K.8544, obv. 5ff., in Winckler, *Altorientalische Forschungen* 1 [Leipzig: Pfeiffer, 1893], pp. 532ff.). If so, perhaps the first line of the obv. in our text K.3405 should be read: *ana* DINGIR xx [*ša itti Telḫunu ku*]*mirtu ša mā*[*t Aribi u*].

[43] Cf. Borger, *Asarhaddon*, § 27, ep. 14, 14.

[44] On the identity of Tabua, and her relation to Hazail and Telḫunu, see J. Lewy, HUCA 19 (1945/46), 420f. and n. 86.

[45] Cf. K.2630 + K.4436, 17 (=Bauer, p. 44), BA-*eš lim-ḫu-ra* ("I presented, may she accept it").

[46] See AHw 431-32, and Borger § 27, ep. 2, 49.

[47] Cf. Asb. Rm.V.30. *ú* is read from K.3087, rather than the erroneous *ga* of K.3405.

[48] Lines 10-12 may be restored in their entirety from Asb. Rm.IX.106-111.

reverse

1. [who accom]pany me, who force [the enemy] to his knees [before me,]
2. who destroy my adversaries, who raise [me up over my foe,]
3. Uate', king of Arabia, had a change of heart[ ]
4. The favor I had done for him he disregarded [ ]
5. He forsook me and [joined forces] with Shama[sh-shum-ukin . . .]
6. Ishtar, exalted mistress [ ]
7. by whose august command, I, Ashurbanipal [ ]
8. By the word of Ashur, Ninlil, [ ]
9. [I captured] him alive. [ ]
10. I pierced his jaw [and put a rope through his] jawbone.
11. In front of [Nineveh's] east gate, [ ]
12. which is named: [I sat him.]
13. At that time, this star-emblem [ ]
14. Whatever her great divinity [ ]
15. My prayers [may she receive (?)].[49]

(The remainder is too fragmentary for translation.)

The identification of the unknown goddess, honored by Assyrian royalty, as an Arabian goddess is crucial to our understanding the divine abandonment motif. We note: the third fem. sing. verbal forms *tasbusu* (obv. 2);*tamnušuma, taškunu* (obv. 3); *taṣbata* (obv. 4), as well as the pronominal suffix *ša*, "her" (obv. 4 and 12), consistently refer to the deity invoked at the outset of the inscription. That we are dealing with an Arabian goddess can clearly be shown from the fact that the Arab queen Telḫunu is said to have been *kumirtaša maḫrītu* (obv. 12), "her former priestess," i.e., of the goddess referred to in obv. 1.

Streck had followed the suggestions of earlier studies and read the now lost name of the deity as *ᵈdilbat*. The evidence of the Ashurbanipal annal account of Asb. B.VII.93-98 establishes the identification of this goddess as the Arabian *Atarsamain*. Referring to the appearance of Uate', Hazail's son, in Nineveh, we read:

[aššu ilānī]šu imḫurannima . . . ᵈAtarsamain utīrma addinšu[50]
He appealed to me concerning his gods . . . . I gave him back Atarsamain.

Oppenheim noted that the star-emblem of obv. 15 is a gift appropriate to an Ishtar figure.[51] This is confirmed by rev. 6 of our text, which addresses Atarsamain as:

[49] Cf. AHw 797, 3ᵇ.

[50] Asb. B. VII.93-98: Streck, VAB 7, pp. 130-32, read these lines differently (89-92, in his numeration):

aššu ilānīšu ša abu banū'a išlulu . . . ᵈAtarsamain utīrma addinšu.

On p. 832, Streck reports his use of K.30 (later published by Bauer, IWA, pp. 35f., plate 18) for the completion of the B prism. K.30 is a building inscription and displays variant(s) from the standard B text. K.30 was apparently overlooked (for this reason?) by Peipkorn in his edition in AS 5. The text we have quoted, from AS 5, is now partially completed by ND.5518, col. VI, published by Knudsen, *Iraq* 29 (1967), plate 23.

[51] Oppenheim, ANET, p. 301 n. 2, "star." The star is mentioned on rev. 13, as well.

ᵈIštar bēltu šaqūtu . . . ina amat qibītīša ṣīrti . . .
Ishtar, exalted mistress . . . by whose august command. . . .

This goddess, therefore, was an Ishtar manifestation, "a feminine deity or at least considered to be one by the Assyrians."[52]

From this text it seems clear that both Esarhaddon and Ashurbanipal acknowledged the role of the Arabian Atarsamain in the determination of Arabian affairs. We may assume that a prime factor motivating Assyrian consideration of the Arabian goddess was the positive propaganda value of such a move in Arabian territories. This use of the divine abandonment motif in relation to the Arabs is significant in that it points to Assyrian recognition of national gods in territories outside the immediate Assyro-Babylonian cultural sphere.

Beyond the political advantage obtained by use of the divine abandonment motif with reference to foreign gods, Assyria did not lose sight of its own gods, whose strength was manifest in Assyrian victories. On occasion, these two considerations were linked, producing a new composition: Foreign gods abandoned their faithful in submissive recognition of the might of Assyria's god, Ashur.

The clearest expression of this idea may be found in Sargon's flattering characterization of the god Ashur, presented before narrating the battle of Muṣaṣir.

ᵈAššur ab ilāni bēl mātāti šar
kiššat šamē erṣetim ālid <gimri>[53]
bēl bēlī ša ultu ūm ṣāti ilāni māti
u šadē ša kibrat arba'i ana šutuqqurīšu
lā naparšudi manama itti išittīšunu
kitmurti ana šūrub Eḫursaggalkurkurra
išrukuš illil ilāni ᵈMarduk[54]

Ashur, father of the gods, lord of all countries, king of all heaven and earth, progenitor <of all>, lord of lords, to whom Marduk, the foremost of the gods, has granted from olden times, the gods of lowland and mountains, from the four quarters of the world, that they, with no exceptions, might ever honor him, bringing their heaped treasures into (the temple) Eḫursaggalkurkurra.

It was the duty of every god, said Sargon, to honor Ashur. Thus, when Assyria's enemies were defeated, it was not merely because they had been abandoned by their own gods, angered at some unspecified wrong; rather the enemy was overcome because his gods had left their homes to journey to Assyria in order to dutifully praise Ashur. Prefacing the tale of Assyria's victory over Muṣaṣir and the subsequent removal of its divine images by these lines suggests that they voice a rationale for the army's action. The journey of the gods to

[52] Streck, VAB 7, p. 222 n. 3. Is it possible that a strict differentiation between the Arabian and the Assyrian Ishtar figures was not pressed? We note that the Arabian goddess is addressed simply as *ᵈIštar* (rev. 6) without any local or national designation, as is often the case (e.g., Ishtar of Nineveh, Ishtar of Arba-il). This non-differentiation may, in part, account for the liberal Assyrian conduct. See S. Smith, CAH 3, pp. 91f., for a differing view.

[53] This reading was suggested by Thureau-Dangin in TCL 3, p. 48 n. 2.

[54] TCL 3, 314-316.

Assyria was concretely expressed in the actual physical transfer of their images to Assyria. Would not such action on the part of the gods require the residents of conquered territories to follow suit?

We are now in a position to understand Esarhaddon's laconic remark describing the divine images he is about to send home:

ilāni mātāte ša ana māt Aššur iḫīšūni . . . ana ašrīšunu utīršunūtima[55]
The gods of all the countries who had hurried to Assyria . . . I returned to their shrines.

Esarhaddon, as had Sargon before him, depicted the gods as abandoning their faithful by rushing to Assyria to take up temporary residence.[56] These gods remained in Assyrian exile until repatriated by Esarhaddon.

In sum, we have observed that Neo-Assyrian royal inscriptions tell of victories by Assyria's armies accomplished through the intervention of foreign as well as native Assyrian gods. Boastfully, the claim is put forward that the enemy's gods had abandoned their faithful in submission to Assyria's Ashur.

Before the NA period, no conqueror had thought to enlist this thesis in justifying his conquests. What seems to have been a purely personal attempt by the subdued to rationalize the misfortunes suffered at the hands of Assyria was adopted by Assyrian court scribes to political advantage. By utilizing the divine abandonment motif, Assyrian scribes avoided depicting foreign gods as taking the field in defense of their adherents, thus sparing these gods humiliating defeat at the hands of the superior Assyrian gods.

In practical terms, the motif of divine abandonment resulted in the deportation of divine images from foreign lands to Assyria. We turn now to study this practice.

[55] Borger, *Asarhaddon*, § 47, 22-23. Goetze's suggestion (JCS 17 [1963], 131) to render passively, "who had been rushed to Assyria," is not supported by usage; the lexicons indicate only intransitive use of the verb *ḫâšu/ḫiāšu*, "to hurry." See AHw 343; CAD Ḫ, 146.

[56] CAD Ḫ, 146b, in rendering this passage, adds a parenthetic amplification: "the gods . . . who had rushed to Assyria (for protection)." But in no NA text do the gods appear in need of protection.

2. ASSYRIAN SPOLIATION OF DIVINE IMAGES

THE idea of divine abandonment did not remain a motif limited to scribal productions. It found practical application in the conquest and administration of an empire; its main expression being the oft-mentioned capture of the gods of defeated nations.[1]

Terminology and Description of Practice

Assyria was assuredly not alone among the ancient conquerors in despoiling divine images;[2] but the repeated mention of Assyrian spoliation in the sources permits study of its practice in particular. Table 1 compiles the evidence from MA and NA royal inscriptions on the incidence and terminology of Assyrian spoliations.[3]

The carrying-off of the gods of defeated nations as booty is regularly described in brief formulaic language. We are afforded little idea of the details of this

[1] Scholars have viewed this practice variously. M. Streck, in a long note in which he collected many of the NA references, held that the pillage of cities included "idols, not so much for their highly important metal and art value, but more in order to rob the inhabitants, thereby, of the protection of their native deities" (VAB 7, p. cccxl n. 3). According to Forrer, the "conveyance of the gods to Kalḫu (was) the formal sign of incorporation of a subjected land" (*Die Provinzeinteilung des assyrischen Reiches* [Leipzig: J. C. Hinrichs, 1920], 47). H. Schrade thought that deportation would alienate conquered peoples from their national gods, preventing restrengthening against Assyria (*Der Verborgene Gott* [Stuttgart: W. Kohlhammer Verlag, 1949], 78). Wiseman has stated, specifically with regards the gods of the Arabs, that they were taken "in an effort to obtain control over them" (*Iraq* 18 [1956], 121). Assyrian kings, in this manner, were able "to keep a hold of these nomads" and use the gods "to bargain" for more peaceful relations (Wiseman, *Chronicles of Chaldaean Kings* [*626-556 B.C.*] *in the British Museum* [=CCK]; [London: British Museum, 1961], 31-32). Only B. Meissner had supposed that capture was symbolic of the anger of the god at his native land — anger which permitted the enemy to destroy the land and bring his statue to a foreign country. Meissner referred to the Esarhaddon narrative of Babylon's destruction (cf. above, pp. 12f.) as typical (*Babylonian und Assyrien* 2 [= BuA]; [Heidelberg: Carl Winter, 1920], 128).

[2] To Streck's source listings of non-Assyrian spoliations (cf. above, n. 1) add: Babylonian spoliations of Assyrian gods, ABL 1000, 12-14; BM 21901, obv. 8 and 9 (=Wiseman, CCK, 54); of Arab gods, BM 21946, rev. 10 (= Wiseman, CCK, 70). Hittite spoliations by Hattushilis, see, Heinrich Otten, MDOG 91 (1958), 73-84; Hittite invocation of enemy gods before their return home, KUB 7, 60.II, 22ff., discussed by J. Friedrich, AO 25/2 (1925), 22. Biblical references are treated in Appendix 1.

[3] See pp. 119-121.

practice, only that "x number of gods were taken from GN and brought to Assyria." The terms employed by the scribes varied, with synonymous phrases freely interchanged. The verbs of spoliation and transfer, listed here in order of frequency, are: *šalālu*, "to despoil"; *ana šallati/šallatiš manū*, "to count as spoil";[4] *ištu* GN *ana āli/māt Aššur wabālu*, "to bring from GN to Assyria"; *našū*, "to carry off"; *šūṣū*, "to bring out"; *nasāḫu*, to deport"; *turru*, "to turn back"; *ana māt Aššur warū*, "to lead to Assyria"; *ḫarrān* GN *šēpū šuškunu*, "to set on the road towards GN" (in Assyria; see below, p. 26); *abāku*, "to lead away"; *ḫabātu*, "to rob" or "take away"; *ekēmu*, "to take away (by force)".

A single literary instance affords us a glimpse of the procedure of spoliation. Sargon's Letter to the Gods (TCL 3) tells how Assyrian troops entered the town of Muṣaṣir unhampered. Once inside, the first order of business in the plundering was:

ša [d]*Ḫaldia tukulti māt Urarti* *aqtabi šūṣāšu meḫret abullīšu* *šaltiš ušēšibma*[5]	Respecting the god Ḫaldia, in whom Urartu trusted, I gave orders to take him out. I, as victor, placed him in front of his town gate.

The chief deity of Urartu, thus seated before the town's market center, publicly oversaw the carrying-off of his treasures. His worshipers were given to understand that through his divine approval Muṣaṣir fell to the mighty Sargon. Once the tally was complete, Ḫaldia himself left for Assyrian exile.[6]

In addition to this Sargon inscription, we have a palace relief, dating from the reign of Tiglath-pileser III, depicting the spoliation of an unknown town.[7] Assyrian soldiers are shown carrying the statues of various deities, all of whom are resplendently seated upon their thrones. This stately and respectful portrayal of the gods' procession to Assyria seems to suggest that Assyria sustained in practice the literary motif of the gods voluntarily abandoning their faithful and flocking to Assyria to praise Ashur.

While all areas of the Near East were raided by Assyrian forces at some time during the MA and NA periods, not every battle report ends with the capture

[4] This phrase is the only item in the entire list peculiar to Sargonid inscriptions.

[5] *TCL* 3, 346-47.

[6] *TCL* 3, 367-68.

[7] A. H. Layard, *Monuments of Nineveh* 1 (London: J. Murray, 1849), 65. Barnett and Falkner, *Sculptures of Tiglath-Pileser III* (London: British Museum, 1962), 29-30, suggest assigning the relief to the 743 B.C. north Syrian campaign. Note the fragmentary panel (Barnett, pl. 7), showing south Babylonian gods in transit to Assyria; cf. also the remarks on pp. xvif. and 17.

From the reign of Sennacherib, scenes of three additional transfers survive. See A. Paterson, *The Palace of Sinacherib* (The Hague: M. Nijhoff [1915]), plates 38, 80 and 91. (On the identity of the gods in pl. 91 as those removed from Ashkelon during Sennacherib's third campaign, see M. Falkner, "Die Reliefs der assyrischen Könige," AfO 16 [1952-53], 26-28.)

and transfer of the gods to Assyria.[8] Does this mean that some areas were spared this humiliation?[9] The following evidence would indicate this to have been so; but these areas, in turn, suffered other calamities.

The detailed letter of Sargon's eighth campaign records the seizure and deportation of Urartu's gods, Ḫaldia and Bagbartu, from the Muṣaṣir temple (TCL 3, 368 and 423); but for hundreds of other defeated towns and villages nothing of the sort is noted. On the other hand, a Khorsabad relief depicting the battle of Muṣaṣir shows a divine image being smashed and its precious plate being weighed out—evidently some god other than Ḫaldia or Bagbartu.[10] Likewise, the wrecking of a temple to Ḫaldia in Arbu, reported in this same Sargon letter (TCL 3, 279), implies the destruction of the god (i.e., his statue) along with the cult center.

From the reports of two additional campaigns, whose descriptions go beyond the ordinary stock phraseology, evidence for similar differential treatment of divine images is retrievable. In the Sennacherib account of the sack of Babylon the destruction of Babylonian gods and their shrines is reported.[11] But while this annal report emphasizes the anger of the king and the resultant desecration, in reality a twofold policy must have been practiced, for post-Sennacherib inscriptions tell of many objects, sacred as well as profane, saved from the pillage.[12] Included in the spoil were the statue of Marduk, his throne, and his ritual bed. As in Sargon's campaign, here too some items were given over to the soldiers for looting; others were collected for transfer to Assyria.

Ashurbanipal acted in the same way. During his Elamite campaigns he deprived the Rashu district on the Babylonian-Elamite border of its gods (Asb. Rm.V.59-62); an earlier defeat of this same territory at the hands of Sennacherib had ended with no such spoliation (OIP 2, 39.56-81). Much clearer is the report that the statues of gods from the environs of Susa were destroyed (Asb. Rm.V.119ff.), while from the city itself nineteen gods were deported (Asb. Rm.VI.33-47).

This information provides the background of Ashurbanipal's (?) inquiry into the violation by Assyrian soldiers of an interdicted temple. The fragmentary opening lines do not permit us to locate the scene or to name the gods whose temple was involved.[13] But, clearly, the place was not given over to general pillage.

[8] If we were to assume that this absence is due to the abbreviated nature of the accounts, in which not every detail, particularly not routine detail, is repeated, then only scribal caprice would account for the mention of any particular spoliation.

[9] With reference to the Medes, König notes that the Assyrians never took their gods captive, for their religion was imageless (AO 33/3-4 [1934], 17f., 58).

[10] See P. E. Botta, *Monument de Ninive* 2 (Paris: Imprimerie nationale, 1849), plate 140, panel 3. Cf. H. Tadmor, JCS 12 (1958), 86 n. 269; contra, Meissner, BuA 2, 129.

[11] OIP 2, 83.43-54.

[12] Cf. Landsberger, *Bischof*, 25.

[13] See Waterman, *Royal Correspondence of the Assyrian Empire* 3 (Ann Arbor: University of Michigan Press, 1931), 346f., for bibliographic information and suggested sites.

[ša šarri] išpura umma ṣābēka kī
tašpura nikasi ana libbi āli kī
unakkisū šiltaḫū igār bīt ilāni
undellū ṣābēya ša ṭēma iškunū umma manma
manma lā imaḫḫaṣ u qassu[15] *manma lā*
idekkū ul ana šumi ša ilāni iplaḫūma
ṭēma aḫāmeš iškunū u innamdan ana nišē
[ ] *u šiltaḫū ana igār bīt ilāni*
[ ] *šū ṣābēya ša išḫiṭūma itti*
ig[ār] *izzizū ina libbi ušezzi[zma*
] *akka'i qišta ana igār bīt*
[ilāni] liṣbatū[18]

[Concerning that which the king] wrote (in inquiry): "After you dispatched your troops and they broke into the city, they flooded[14] the temple wall with arrows!" My soldiers, who had agreed among themselves not to harm or threaten anyone, had no respect for the name of the gods. They made their own agreement, and it was given to the people [ ] and the arrows [that were sent] against the temple wall; it was my unit that mounted the attack[16] as they stood beside the wa[ll], where I ordered them to stand. That is how[17] the bows were drawn against the temple wall!

The evidence points to a policy of selective capture of statues. It seems clear that many small shrines and their images were irreverently destroyed, while other religious objects were spared and taken off to Assyria. Presumably the treatment of each god and statue accorded with the importance attached to them by the Assyrian conqueror and his advisors; those items most revered by the vanquished nation were exiled.

Deposition of captured statues inside Assyria is described in terse, summary terms (cf. Table 1). MA texts specify that the statues were brought *ana ālīya Aššur*, "to my city Ashur." This specification holds true at least down to the reign of Tukulti-ninurta II, at which time Nineveh is first mentioned. From the middle of the ninth century onward, the earlier phrase *ana ālīya Aššur* is gradually replaced by *ana (qereb) māt Aššur*, "into (the midst of) Assyria," which becomes the standard term in all NA inscriptions. Even though no NA text explicitly states the place within Assyria to which the statues were transferred, the change in language may be significant. Had the city of Ashur continued to be the sole location, we would be at a loss to explain the introduction of new and less specific terminology.

Some information on this question can be obtained from the chronicle literature. In BM 25127, reference is made to the booty taken by Ashurbanipal from Elam.

ilāni ša māt Šušan ša māt Aššur
ībukūnimma ina Uruk^{ki} *ušēšibū*
ilānīšunu ^{md}*Nabû-apal-uṣur ana*
Šušan ultaḫḫis[19]

The gods of Susa which Assyria had carried off and deposited in Uruk, their gods Nabopolasar returned to Susa.

[14] Lit. "filled." Cf. AHw, 598, "pour out;" CAD I, 37a, "shower."

[15] Collation of the text at this point (courtesy of E. Leichty) corrects Waterman's readings. The signs ("quite clear" — Leichty) are: *ù* ŠU^{II}-*su*. Cf. CAD D, 127a. On *qātē dekû*, see A. L. Oppenheim, "Idiomatic Akkadian," JAOS 61 (1941), 269.

[16] For *šaḫātu*, "to raid/attack," see ARM 15, 259; TCL 3, 4, n. 5; OIP 2, 36.5 and the comments of Ungnad, ZA 38 (1928-29), 197.

[17] Cf. *CAD* A 1, 273a, *s.v. akka'i.*

[18] ABL 1339, obv. 3-14.

[19] Wiseman, CCK, 50, obv. 16-17.

This Babylonian witness to Assyrian activity in Elam permits us to reinterpret the passage in the annal literature, where this same transfer is termed *ana māt Aššur* (Asb. Rm.VI.3-47). This phrase should now be understood as meaning "into Assyrian territory," for the Elamite gods were evidently brought only as far as Uruk.

New light is also shed on the notice concerning the victory of Ashurbanipal over the Arabs in his ninth campaign.

ilāni mala ina tukulti ᵈ*Aššur u* ᵈ*Ištar bēlēya ikšudā qātāya ḫarrān māt Dimašqa ušaškina šēpūšun*[21]	I had the gods, as many as I had captured through the help[20] of Ashur and Ishtar my lords, take the road to Damascus.

This information, from the latter days of the empire, indicates that locations on the fringes of the realm received captured gods. There is no suggestion in either of the texts that this procedure was innovative or temporary. Moreover, as we shall see, throughout the late NA period spoils of war were divided up among various centers — the capital and its temples, the army, and outlying provincial districts.[22] The founding of new cities required this kind of endowment. The possibility, therefore, suggests itself that with the expansion of the empire and official recognition of new capitals and sacred precincts, provision was made for the reception of statues, along with other booty, in many locations throughout Assyria and its provinces.[23]

NA texts provide us with little information on the treatment of captured gods once they were brought to Assyria. This silence may be due to the continu-

[20] Oppenheim's ANET translations offer varying renditions of *tukultu* (GIŠ.TUKUL-*ti*): "trust-inspiring oracles" (p. 275); "trust (-inspiring) oracle" (pp. 277, 287, 294, 295); "trustworthy oracles" (p. 293); "trust (-inspiring oracle given by)" (p. 286). Oppenheim elaborated: *tukultu* is a "sign," not based on an omen, but on a legal argument, conveyed to the king in a mysterious manner (JNES 19 [1960], 136); interpreted as "direct divine interference" (ANET, 298 n. 7). Cf. A. Walther (LSS 6/4-6 (1917), 206 n. 3) who had suggested equating *tukultu* with *qibītu*, *amatu*, "word, command," and the oracular function of the divine weapon — *kakku*; and the remarks of Landsberger, WO 3 (1964), 75f.

[21] Asb. Rm. 9.3.8; K. 2802, III, 5-10 (= Streck, VAB 7, 199).

[22] See below, pp. 28f.

[23] If this be so, then the long-standing difficulty with Sennacherib's use of [Eridu] (?) for the storage of the gods of Uruk taken during the sixth campaign need cause no further wonder (cf. Baby. Chron., col. 2.47–3.1-3, 29 [= CT 34, 46f.]). Unfortunately, the crucial signs in line 29 are no longer legible and the question must await further discovery for solution. The suggested restoration of Borger, *Handbuch der Keilschriftliteratur* 1 (Berlin: Gruyter, 1967), 232 [KUR.ELA]M (see earlier proposal of Delitzsch in ASAW 25/1 [1906], 29) is to be rejected on internal grounds. Elam did not pillage Babylon, as is proven by the Nebi Yunus Inscription (OIP 2, 87:31-33); and correctly translated by Oppenheim in ANET, 302. S. Smith (JRAS [1925], 65f.) doubted the proposed "Eridu" on account of its southern location, supposing that all spoil had to be moved northward into Assyria. But Eridu may have been a convenient spot for deposit within Babylonian territory already under Assyrian control.

ation of customs considered by the scribes too well known to be worthy of remark.[24] So we must fall back upon the practices evidenced in the MA period.

The earliest information comes from the reign of Tiglath-pileser I, who, after several successful campaigns, is reported to have presented captured statues to his own gods. Not every case of spoliation and deportation was followed by a dedication.[25] But where dedications are described, we learn that several Assyrian deities were honored by presentations of items from the rich spoil, including exiled gods.

itti ilānīšunu ana ^{d}*Adad rā'imīya ašruk*[26]	(Copper vessels from Qummuḫ) along with their gods, I presented to Adad, who loves me.
25 *ilānīšunu* [*a*]*na* (?)[27] *ilāni ša ālīya* ^{d}*Aššur u* ^{d}*ištarāte ša mātīya aqīš bušū*[*šunu*] *ana* ^{d}*Adad bēlīya ašruk*[28]	25 of their gods (of Lulumē), [ ] I dedicated to the gods of my city Ashur and to the goddesses of my country. Their property I presented to Adad, my lord.
ilāni ša mātāti šinātina kišitti qātāya ša alqā ana utu'ūt bīt ^{d}*Ninlil ḫīrti rabīte namaddi* ^{d}*Aššur bēlīya* ^{d}*Anim* ^{d}*Adad* ^{d}*Ištar aššurīte ekurrāt ālīya* ^{d}*Aššur u* ^{d}*ištarāt mātīya lū ašruk*[30]	The gods of those countries, which I myself took captive, for . . .[29] to the temple of Ninlil, the greatly beloved wife of Ashur my lord, to Anu, Adad, the Assyrian Ishtar, the temples of my city Ashur and the goddesses of my country, I presented.

The choice of recipient deities seems to have been dictated by the ranking in the divine hierarchy, for Adad played a prominent role at this time.[31] The juxtaposition of the statues of the gods and the other spoil makes one wonder whether

[24] Note, however, that it is characteristic of Assyrian royal inscriptions not to include information on life within Assyria; rather, they focus attention upon praise of the gods and the pious deeds of the Assyrian monarchs in war and building. For literary studies of NA inscriptions, see S. Mowinckel, "Die Vorderasiatischen Königs-und Fürsteninschriften, eine stilistische Studie," in *Eucharisterion: Festschrift H. Gunkel* (Göttingen: 1923) 278-322; W. Baumgartner, "Zur Form der assyrischen Königsinschriften," OLZ 27 (1924) 313-17.

[25] E.g., AKA, 41, 2.31-32; 57, 3.81; 58, 3.102; 79, 6.8-9; KAH 2, 71.37-38.

[26] AKA, 44, 2.61-62.

[27] Borger, *Einleitung in die assyrischen Königsinschriften* 1, *Handbuch der Orientalistik* 1/5 (Leiden: E. J. Brill, 1961) 115, completes the break: [*ana Ninlil, Anum, Adad u Ištar aššurīt*]*e*; by reading K.2806 *a*]*na* as *t*]*e*.

[28] AKA, 117, obv. 5-7 + Assur 22251(b), AfO, 18 (1957-58) pl. xxx, 360.

[29] The crucial *utu'ūtu* seems, unfortunately, to be a *hapax legomenon*. The noun *itūtu*/*utūtu* (CAD I, 317; AHw, 407b) from the verbal root *atū*, "to discover, search for," describes the gods' selection of rulers, rather than the rulers' note of the gods, as would be the case in the present passage. Besides problems of context, the writing with *aleph* is unexpected.

[30] AKA, 62f., 4.32-39.

[31] Cf. Olmstead, *Assyria*, 67-69. Adad's sacred precinct received not only gods, but also precious stones from Nairi, AKA, 101, 8.11-16.

any distinction was made between them. Both seem to have been presented to the temples designated, and appropriate use made of each. This would mean, as we will see from NA texts, that the material spoil was used to enhance the shrines and their accessories.[32] As for the gods, we can only speculate as to the possibility of their participation in ceremonies of submission.[33]

The early Neo-Assyrian ruler Adad–nirari II reports the dedication of captured gods exclusively to Ashur, in a short notice which adds little detail.

ilānīšunu kī qīšūte ana Aššur bēlīya aqīš[34]
I dedicated their gods as gifts to Ashur, my lord.

From this point on, however, NA texts continue to report dedications of spoil without the accompanying presentation of captive gods. For example, while Tiglath-pileser III's inscriptions refer to dedications of numerous sheep, horses, oxen, gems, and even a royal bed, to Ishtar of Nineveh and to Ashur, the gods go unmentioned.[35]

Two badly damaged Esarhaddon texts detail the course of such dedications. The first text, a letter to the gods, reads:

[ ] x *ša eli eribī ma'adū*	[ ] more numerous than locusts,
[*u*]*ltu qereb māt Šubria ana māt Aššur ašlula*	[f]rom out of Shupria to Assyria I carried off.
[*rīšēti*][36] *ana* ^{d}*Aššur* ^{d}*Ninlil* ^{d}*Šerua*	[The best] to Ashur, Ninlil, Sherua,
[ ] ^{d}*Ninurta* ^{d}*Gula* ^{d}*Nergal* ^{d}*Ištar ša Ninua*^{ki} ^{d}*Ištar ša Arba-ili* ^{d}*Nusku*	[ ] Ninurta, Gula, Nergal, Ishtar of Nineveh, Ishtar of Arbail, Nusku
x [*idā*]*ya ittallakūma inārū gārīya*	[who] go at my si[de] and slay my enemies,
x [ ] x *mušamṣū mal libbīya ana širikti ašruk*[37]	[ ] who respond to all my desires, I presented as a gift.

The first portion of the booty, of choice quality, was given over to the gods. According to the second Esarhaddon text, it could be used for repair and improvements of their temples:

[32] Cf. remarks by Lambert, AfO 18 (1957-58) 41 on devotion of spoil taken by Tukulti-Ninurta from Kashtilliash.

[33] It may be noted, however, that when Tiglath-pileser I exacted oaths of allegiance from defeated kings, their own national deities were not present. See, e.g., AKA, 69f., 5.12-22 (where the oath is taken before Shamash); 70, 5.22-29.

[34] KAH 2, 83.16-17. Weidner, "Die Annalen des Königs Aššurdan II. von Assyrien," AfO 3 (1926) 158, restores an Ashurdan II annal text on the basis of our present citation. [*ilānīšunu*] *kī qīšūte ana Aššur bēlīya lū aqīš* (Assur 4312a, rev. 13), "I dedicated [their gods] as gifts to Ashur, my lord." However, Weidner inaccurately speaks of setting up the statues in the Ashur Temple as the usual MA procedure (p. 158 n. 11).

[35] P. Rost, *Die Keilschrifttexte Tiglat-Pilesers III* (Leipzig: Pfeiffer, 1893) 15-16, 46-47, 73.

[36] Cf. Ashurbanipal's dedications of Elamite spoil epitomized: *rīšēti ana ilānīya ašruk* (Asb. Rm. 7.1), "I dedicated the choice items to my gods."

[37] Borger, *Asarhaddon*, § 68, III, 8-13.

[*ina lil*]*met ḫurāṣi kaspi abnē kišit*[*ti qātēya*(?)] *u šallat māt Muṣur u māt Kūsi*	[shin]ing gold, silver, gems, boo[ty] and spoil of Egypt and Ethiopia, [which
[*ša ina tu*]*kulti* ᵈ*Aššur bēlīya ikš*[*udā qātāya*]	by the he]lp of Ashur, my lord, I, myself, took; [the shrines] of Sumer and Akkad
[*māḫazi*][38] *māt Šumeri* (*u*) *Akkadi uḫḫizma kīma ūme unammir*	I decorated and made them shine (as bright) as daylight.
[ ] *ēpušma attadi qerebšun*[39]	[ ] I fashioned and deposited in it.

As a rule, select elements of the captive population were then inducted into the Assyrian army and skilled craftsmen distributed for work within Assyria.[40] Finally, the remainder of the booty[41] was apportioned among the officialdom, both in the capital and outlying royal cities.[42] Throughout each step of booty distribution, the whereabouts of captive gods is unspecified.

The lack of specific information on the NA treatment of the gods adds nothing substantial to the data gleaned from MA texts. All that we can say is that the statues must have been brought to the capital and/or found their way to other centers. If they were not marked for quick repatriation (see below, pp. 37ff.), little care seems to have been given them during their stay in Assyria. This was certainly the case while Sennacherib reigned; for when Esarhaddon undertook to restore imprisoned gods to their former shrines, he boasts of extending the following courtesy:

ša ilāni mātāte šallūti ultu qereb māt Aššur / u māt Elam /[43] *ana ašrēšunu utirruma ušēšibu šubtu nēḫtu adi ekurrāti ušakliluma*[44]	(I am he) who returned the pillaged gods of the countries from Assyria / and Elam / to their shrines, who let them stay in comfortable quarters until he completed temples (for them).

The phrase *šubtu nēḫtu*, "comfortable quarters," is often used to contrast a former

[38] On the completion of this lacuna, cf. Borger, *Asarhaddon*, § 27, ep. 20, 38.

[39] Borger, *Asarhaddon*, § 64, obv. 28-30.

[40] Borger, *Asarhaddon*, § 68, III, 14-20; cf. Asb. Rm. 7:2-5.

[41] Borger, *Asarhaddon*, § 68, III, 21. The text at this point reads *sit*[*tūti*] (line 21) and is understood by several commentators to refer to human rather than material spoil. E.g., *sittūti . . . uza'iz* (Asb. Rm. 7.6-8), "I divided up the remaining (prisoners)," CAD Ṣ, 129b; *sitti šallati nākiri kabittu* (OIP 2, 61.60, 63.22), "I distributed the rest of the many enemy prisoners," CAD Z, 82. But it may be that *šallatu* refers to material objects; cf. the very quotation cited in CAD. E.g., *nakru aḫū lizāza mimmūkun* (Iraq 20 [1958] 430), "May a hostile foe divide your possessions;" // *nakru aḫū liza'iza* (!) *šal*[*latkunu*] (Borger, *Asarhaddon*, § 69, IV, 19). Cf. *šallat nākiri gimir mimma šumšu*, "enemy booty of every sort," (Borger, *Asarhaddon*, § 27, ep. 21, 44).

[42] Cf. Asb. Rm. 7.6-8.

[43] The phrase occurs only in the version preserved in Borger, *Asarhaddon*, § 11, ep. 36, 5-11.

[44] Borger, *Asarhaddon*, § 27, ep. 3, 23-26. Similar references are shortened: *ibid.*, § 21, 7; § 53, obv. 37; § 65, rev. 4-5. Cf. below n. 105.

state of desolation,[45] hunger,[46] or disturbance.[47] Prior to Esarhaddon's restoration order, then, these gods had been situated throughout Assyria and Elam in what seem to have been inappropriate conditions. Apparently upon their arrival in Assyria they had been simply packed away until further disposition. Permanent display of these gods as trophies of war in any temple and/or public building seems unlikely.

Only the journeys of Babylon's Marduk statue, carried off by Sennacherib, can be followed in any detail; the unique position enjoyed by Babylon and its chief deity made it a frequent topic of report. Streck, somewhat hesitantly, had supposed that the statue, along with other cultic furniture, was brought to Assyria, dedicated to the "service of Ashur," and so found a place in the Ashur Temple.[48]

But the fate of the statue seems to have been little different from that of lesser statues. As Landsberger has shown, two conflicting views can be distinguished in the sources; one tending to mollify Babylon, referring to Assyria as a place "not worthy" of Marduk's stay; the other, pro-Assyrian, reducing Marduk to the role of the son of Ashur.[49] Landsberger concludes:

> Sennacherib, whether because of a tinge of religious awe, or because of its material worth, did not surrender the staue of Marduk and his four paredroi to the rage of the soldiers, but secretly brought it to Ashur and hid it away.[50]

Consequently, Esarhaddon's reported attempt to fashion a new Marduk statue was but a "pious (?) fraud," which allowed delay in the return of the original statue to Babylon. In reality, therefore, the ultimate disposition of the Marduk statue, like others, had to await political decisions.

Effects of Spoliation upon the Enemy and His Cult

The enemy was not always content to submit passively to abandonment by his gods. He often tried to prevent the physical transfer of the statues to Assyria, for their seizure would be a sign that the gods had deserted.

Initial information comes from the annals of MA ruler Tiglath-pileser I, which report of the enemy survivors of his Qummuḫ campaign

ana šūzub napšātēšunu ilānīšunu iššū ana gisallāt šadī šaqūti kīma iṣṣūrī ipparšū[51]	To save their lives, they took their gods and, like birds, fled to the ridges of the high mountains.

A similar account, four centuries later, from Sargon's second campaign against

[45] AKA, 240, rev. 40.

[46] AKA, 92, 7.32-35.

[47] VAB 3, 6:36.

[48] See Streck, *VAB* 7, 232 n. 4; 292 n. 8.

[49] Landsberger, *Bischof*, 20-27. This discussion includes full bibliographic citation of post-Streck studies.

[50] Landsberger, *Bischof*, 24f.

[51] AKA, 42, 2.39-42.

Merodach Baladan (709 B.C.E.), tells of the latter's preparations for war, which included:

ullānū'a ^{md}*Marduk-apla-iddina* *ālānīšu ašbūti u ilāni āšib libbīšun* *upaḫḫirma ana āl Dūr-Yakina ušēribma*[52]	Furthermore, Merodach Baladan gathered together the residents of his towns (lit. "his inhabited towns") and the gods that were in them, and brought them into Dūr-Yakin.

The Babylonians placed their confidence in the gods, hoping that the physical presence of the statues in Dūr-Yakin would be able to insure their protection.[53] This act must be understood as one of desperation, for the authorized cult at traditionally sanctified sites was stopped. After victory, Sargon piously affirms:

u ilānīšunu šallūti ana māḫazīšunu *utīrma sattukēšunu baṭlūti utīr*[54]	I returned the pillaged gods to their cult centers and restored their interrupted regular offerings.

This same Merodach Baladan later appears as the foe of Sennacherib. At the end of his sixth campaign, Sennacherib tells of the flight of his enemy.

šū ^{md}*Marduk-apla-iddina . . . ilāni* *mārak*[55] *mātīšu ina šubtīšunu idkīma* *qereb elippēti ušarkibma ana* GN *raqqi* *šā qabal tāmti iṣṣūriš ippariš*[57] *aḫḫēšu zēr bīt abīšu ša umašširu* *aḫi tāmtim adi sitti nišē mātīšu* *ušēṣamma šallatiš amnu*[58]	That Merodach Baladan . . . removed the gods of the entire country from their shrines, and loaded them upon ships, and made off like a bird to GN of the lagoon,[56] which is in the middle of the sea. His brothers of royal lineage, whom he had left on the seashore, together with the rest of the people of his country, I brought out and counted as spoil.

This passage makes abundantly clear the reason behind this hurried pack-up and

[52] *Iraq* 16 (1954) 186, 6.27-30. Shortened version, Winckler, *Die Keilschrifttexte Sargons* (Leipzig: Pfeiffer, 1889), 73.126; and Lie, *Sargon*, 58, 17 and 404. The latest study of the career of Merodach Baladan, along with a complete catalogue of primary sources of his reign is given by J. A. Brinkman, "Merodach-Baladan II," in *Studies Presented to A. Leo Oppenheim* (Chicago: University of Chicago Press, 1964), 6-53.

[53] This is evident from the later Assyrian remark in this same campaign: *u ilāni tiklīšun ištēniš ašlulamma* "The gods, in whom they trusted, I pillaged, one and all" (Gadd, *Iraq* 16 [1954] 186, 6.61-62).

[54] Lie, *Sargon*, 64, 11-12.

[55] *Mārak* is the reading adopted by CAD E, 342 and AHw 608b, replacing the original suggestion by Luckenbill, *mašal*. See Borger, *Asarhaddon*, p. 24 note to lines 4-9.

[56] On *raqqu*, see Ungnad, ZA 38 (1928-29) 197.

[57] The expression *kima iṣṣūri ipparšu* / *iṣṣūriš ipparšu* is found in the MA inscription of Tiglath-pileser I (AKA, 42), in a description of escape with gods. It was apparently reintroduced in NA royal inscriptions by Sargon. Cf. Albert Schott, "Die Vergleiche in den akkadischen Königsinschriften," MVAG 30/2 (1925) 92-93 and 96.

[58] OIP 2, 35.59-65. Secondary reports, *ibid.*, 38.34f.; 78.26f.; 85.7ff.; 86.22. The account in 85.8 adds: *itti eṣmēti abbēšu maḫrūti ultu qereb kimaḫḫi iḫpirma*, "together

transfer of gods. The nearness of the god and his aid was eagerly sought, even in retreat, despite the cost in human lives left behind.[59]

In line with the preceding picture are the several passages in Babylonian chronicle material. In 626 B.C.E. several Babylonian cities sent their gods to Babylon in the face of the rapid advance of the Assyrian army under Sin-shar-ishkun.

ina araḫ Tišrīti, ilāni ša Kiš ana Babili illikū . . . ᵈŠamaš u ilāni ša Šapazzu ana Babili ittalkūni . . . ilāni ša Sippar ana Babili itta[*lkūnimma*].[60]	In the month of Tishri, the gods of Kish came to Babylon. . . . Shamash and the gods of Shapazzu came to Babylon. . . . The gods of Sippar came to Babylon.

Sippar's action, moreover, seems to have preceded the Assyrian siege of a neighboring city by just one day.[61]

Even after the close of the NA period, this practice of "ingathering" is attested. NB examples shed light on the older sources. With Cyrus close to final victory over Babylon, Nabonidus gathered the gods of outlying districts into the capital:

[*il*]*āni ša Marada, Zababa u ilāni ša Kiš, Ninlil* [*u ilāni ša*] *Ḫarsagkalamma ana Babili ērubūni adi qīt Ulūli ilāni ša māt Akkadi* [ ] *ša elān* IM *u šaplān* IM *ana Babili ērubūni*[62]	[The gods] of Marada, Zababa and the gods of Kish, Ninlil [and the gods of] Ḫarsagkalamma entered Babylon. By the end of Elul, the gods of Babylonia [ ] from north and south (?) entered Babylon.

The meaning of these "entries" by the gods into Babylon is not to be sought in ritual or ceremonial practice requiring their presence in the capital.[63] Nabonidus wanted to keep the statues from falling into the hands of the enemy; from their safe abode, the gods would protect him from defeat.

But the propagandistic Cyrus cylinder, issued soon after Cyrus' entry into Babylon, preserves another view of this episode:

with the bones of his ancestors, which he dug up out of their sepulchers." (On this translation, we note that *iḫpirma* is rendered "collect, assemble" by CAD Ḫ, 170 [following Luckenbill] and "ausgraben [bildlich]" by AHw, 340a. But in this passage, the verb *iḫpir* simply means "dig up" as the root *ḫepēru* normally does; while the one other instance cited in both dictionaries, CT 22, 1.10, means to "search for, hunt up." Cf. the semantic range of the cognate Hebrew *ḥāpar*, "dig, search for," BDB, 343b). Brinkman, "Merodach-Baladan II," 27 n. 153, notes the respect shown ancestral remains in Mesopotamia. We add that this act of Merodach-Baladan prevents the possible desecration of these bones at the hands of the invading Assyrians (cf., Asb. Rm. 6.70-76) by prior removal to safe ground. This act of piety must be seen as one which would also produce effective aid and intercession on his behalf during his escape by his ancestors' spirits.

[59] OIP 2, 35.65f.

[60] Wiseman, CCK, 50-52; rev. 19, 21; obv. 6.

[61] Wiseman, CCK, 9.

[62] S. Smith, *Babylonian Historical Texts* (London: Methuen, 1924), Nabonidus Chronicle col. III, 9-11.

[63] So, Dougherty, YOS, *Researches* 15 (1929) 168-69. Cf. the remarks of Millard, *Iraq* 26 (1964) 17, as regards the removal of Anu from the city of Der.

ilāni āšib libbīšunu īzibū atmanšun *ina uggati ša ušēribi ana qereb Babili*[64]	The gods, who lived among them (i.e., the Babylonians), left their abode, angry that he had brought them into Babylon.

The gods reacted with displeasure over their removal to Babylon, and thus abandoned the city. Only later did Cyrus "make them happy" by restoring the gods to their former sanctuaries.[65] The attempt by Nabonidus to guarantee the gods' presence at his side had failed to produce effective results, for the priesthood attendant upon those gods had become disenchanted with Nabonidus. They openly supported Cyrus, and welcomed him into the city.[66] The loss of support from the religious establishment is expressed as the gods' displeasure at entry into Babylon. Forcing the hands of the deities did not prove efficacious; for once abandonment had been decreed by the gods, no means were available to thwart their action.[67]

Nevertheless, when spoliation of divine images did occur, the loss of these palladia does not seem to have proved fatal to the native cults. Meissner conjectured that if the return of the gods from captivity was delayed, new statues were fashioned and the cult resumed.[68] His supposition can be validated in part.

[64] VAB 3, 2, 9-10.

[65] VAB 3, 6, 33-34.

[66] See H. Tadmor, "The Historical Background of the Cyrus Declaration" [Hebrew], *ᶜOz Lᵉ David: Studies Presented to David Ben Gurion* (Jerusalem: Kiryat Sefer, 1964) 461ff., especially pp. 466-68. Disaffection seems to have spread to other sacred precincts as well. The gods of Borsippa, Cutha and Sippar had not come to Babylon (Smith, *Babylonian Historical Texts*, Nab. Chron., col. III, 11-12); and Sippar, it is noted, was taken by Cyrus without a battle.

[67] M. Weinfeld has suggested that Nabonidus sought to make the cities from which the gods were taken "religiously dependent upon the capital . . . and thereby strengthen their determination to defend it" ("Cult Centralization in Israel in the Light of a Neo-Babylonian Analogy," *JNES* 23 [1964] 205). He rejects the view that the gods were "brought to Babylon so as to prevent them from falling into the hands of the enemy" (so, S. Smith, *Babylonian Historical Texts*, p. 103), for the action is branded sinful.

But there is clear evidence that the removal of gods to other places was for their safekeeping (cf. above pp. 30ff.). Moreover, Nabonidus' hurried act, interrupting the cult of those gods relocated in Babylon, would only have demoralized the countryside. Nabonidus' act is most naturally interpreted as an attempt to insure the protection of Babylon by all the gods whose statues he brought into the city. The priests of Marduk, who were bitterly hostile to the king on other grounds (cf. Tadmor, above, n. 66), considered his collecting of the gods as another of his sacrilegious acts; it was they who produced the negative evaluation preserved in the Cyrus cylinder.

Second Isaiah may illuminate still further the excitement in Babylon over the appearance of Cyrus and the preparations taken to meet his attack. In Isa 41.5-7, the prophet describes how the idolators bolster their spirits by fastening and nailing their statues so as not to topple (41.7). Might this passage be a description of the last-ditch effort made by Nabonidus to insure the "strength" and sturdiness of his gods? For a different interpretation of this passage, see S. Smith, *Isaiah XL-LV* (London: Schweich Lectures of 1940, 1944) 159f. n. 8.

[68] Meissner, BuA 2, 128.

Our only information comes from the city of Uruk and the history of Nanā's exile in Elam. Ashurbanipal's annals speak of Nanā's angry departure from Uruk, 1,635 years earlier,[69] but the absence of her statue did not put a stop to her cult. Sennacherib removed another statue of Nanā during his raid upon Uruk.[70] Esarhaddon led a statue of Nanā in procession into the rebuilt Eḫilianna temple in this same city.[71] Even Ashurbanipal himself, who speaks of the statue as staying in *ašar lā simātīša*, "a place not fitting her" divinity, received an oracle from Nanā.[72] When Ashurbanipal sent the Marduk statue home, a statue of Nanā was present, along with those of other gods, on Babylon's wharf, greeting the returning Marduk.[73] Nanā is continually invoked in blessing formulas in the Harper correspondence,[74] and sacrifices to her are twice mentioned.[75] Loss of the image did not, therefore, mean the end of religious practice; it is inferable that a new image was fashioned. The fashioning of a new Nanā statue was most probably accompanied by priestly appeasement of the angered goddess, whose divine blessing would have been required before replacing the original statue still in Elamite exile.[76]

If this was the case in Babylonia, it may well have been standard procedure elsewhere. Did the Assyrians object to the replacement of deported statues? Apparently not; the transfer of the divine images to Assyria was but the formal aspect of submission and did not imply the abrogation of native cults. At the same time, great value, both historical and sentimental, continued to be attached to the original, time-honored cult statue whose return was highly desirable and sought after.

[69] Asb. Rm. 6.107.

[70] OIP 2, 87.31-33.

[71] For dedicatory inscription, cf. Borger, *Asarhaddon*, § 49 and § 50.

[72] Asb. Rm. 6.113ff.

[73] L⁴, col. 3, 12-13 (= Streck, VAB 7, 266).

[74] See listings in Waterman, *Royal Correspondence* 3, index *s.v.* Nanā.

[75] ABL 23, rev. 5; ABL 1202.

[76] Cf. Esarhaddon's invitation to Marduk to sanction the fashioning of a new Marduk statute for Babylon, Borger, *Asarhaddon*, § 53, rev. 9bff. The tale of Sippar's Shamash statue discloses part of the restoration procedure. Soon after the destruction of the statue by Sutu invaders in the mid-eleventh century B.C.E., the Shamash cult was reinstituted in the presence of a surrogate Shamash symbol. L. W. King, *Babylonian Boundary-stones* 1 (London: British Museum, 1912), no. 36, tells of king Simbarshipak: *nipḫa ša pan ᵈŠamaš ušatriṣamma sattukēšu ukīnma*, "He set up a *nēbeḫu*/*nipḫu* before Shamash and established regular offerings" (1.18-20; AHw 773 reads *nēbeḫu*, "belt"; *AnOr* 43, n. 917, *nipḫu*, "sun disk image"). It was not until the reign of Nabu-apal-iddina, some 200 years later, that the loss was made good. The fortuitous finding by the banks of the Euphrates of an *uṣurti ṣalmīšu ṣirpu ša ḫaṣbi šikinšu u simātīšu*, "a baked clay drawing of his statue (showing) his appearance and regalia" (3.19-21) prompted Nabu-apal-iddina to underwrite the refashioning of the Shamash statue and to confirm existing priestly endowments. According to Lambert (AfO 18 [1957-58] 399), "nothing could be done to replace" the lost statue until the original clay model in the round was discovered. Without the original, any new statue "would not have been Shamash." In the case

Repatriation of Images and Cult Restorations

Two patterns for the repatriation of the original cult statues to their shrines are discernable: one developed out of initiatives taken by the vanquished, whose gods were exiled; the other was initiated by the Assyrians.

Foreign initiatives are detailed in information available from reports of the successive campaigns undertaken by Assyria to contain the desert tribes harassing the fringes of the empire. Tiglath-pileser III carried off "countless gods,"[77] and Sennacherib in turn took "the queen of the Arabs, together with her gods" captive.[78] Subsequently, during the reign of Esarhaddon, the Arab king Hazail appeared before the Assyrian ruler, bearing rich gifts, to plead for the return of his lost gods.[79]

^{m}*Ḫaza-ilu šar māt Aribi itti tāmartīšu kabittu ana Ninua* ^{ki} *āl bēlūtīya illikamma unaššiq šēpēya aššu nadān ilānīšu uṣallānnima rēmu aršišuma* ^{d}*Atarsamain* ^{d}*Daya* ^{d}*Nuḫaya* ^{d}*Ruldayau* ^{d}*Abirillu* ^{d}*Atarqurumā ilāni ša* LÚ *Aribi anhūssunu uddišma danān* ^{d}*Aššur bēlīya u šiṭir šumīya elīšunu ašṭurma utīrma addinšu*[82]

Hazail, king of Arabia, came before me with his rich gifts to Nineveh, my royal city. He kissed my feet and besought me to return his gods. I had pity on him and, so, Atarsamain, Daya, Nuḫaya, Ruldayau, Abirillu, Atarquruma, the gods of the Arabs,[80] I refurbished. Upon them I inscribed the strength of Ashur, my lord and my name,[81] and gave them back to him.

A long interval of some twelve years had elapsed between the capture of the gods by Sennacherib and the plea of Hazail.[83] The Arab ruler, somewhat belatedly,

of Esarhaddon, on the other hand, an oracular instruction was sufficient for the production of a new Marduk statue. Cf. Borger, *Asarhaddon*, § 53, rev. 20ff.

[77]]*ana la manī ilāni* [, *Iraq* 18 (1956), 136, rev. 18.

[78] K.8544, obv. 5, *šar*]*rat* LÚ *Arabi adi ilā*[*nīša* (= Winckler, *Forschungen* 1, 523ff.) is the contemporaneous report, later repeated by Esarhaddon (Borger, *Asarhaddon*, § 27, ep. 14) and Ashurbanipal (K. 3405, K. 3087). On the title *apkallatu*, "the wise one," for the Arab queens, see Borger, "Assyriologische und altarabistische Miszellen," Or 26 (1957) 8-11. *Apkallatu* is incorrectly given as a personal name in CAD A 2, 171a.

[79] Esarhaddon offered no reason for the delay in the return of these statues, after the apparent empire-wide restoration shortly after his rise to power (cf. p. 38 below). Are we to understand that such returns were contingent upon acts of submission by the ruling monarchs?

[80] On the identification of these gods, see Borger, Or 26 (1957) 10-11.

[81] Literally "an inscription with my name." Cf. the hendiadyl construction *šiṭrīya u šumīya* (e.g., Lie, *Sargon*, 82, 16-17); a phrase regularly used to describe the inscriptions written upon palace reliefs and steles; and above, p. 10 n. 9.

[82] Borger, *Asarhaddon*, § 27, ep. 14, 6-16.

[83] This figure is arrived at by dating VAS 1, 77 (= OIP 2, 89-93) to *ca.* 690 B.C.E., i.e., post-Ḫalule campaign, but prior to the final destruction of Babylon. According to Hirschberg (*Studien zur Geschichte Esarhaddons König von Assyrien* [681-669] [Ohlau in Schlesien: Herm. Eschenhagen, 1932] 53f.), the submission of Hazail and the Arabian campaigns occurred in *ca.* 679-78 B.C.E.

took up an outstanding claim before Esarhaddon and was favorably received.[84] The Arabian gods were sent off upon one condition: that an inscription be engraved upon the repatriated statues, serving as a visible reminder of the overlordship of Assyria.[85] In this manner the superiority of Ashur, Assyria's god, was assured prominent display in the Arabian cult rejuvenated upon the return of its gods. Notably, the Arabian statues were repaired before their return — a sign of respect to Arabian gods.

The gods of the Arabs were taken captive a second time by Esarhaddon, during a punitive raid against Uate', son of Hazail, who had broken his father's oath of loyalty:

ina tāḫaz ṣēri abiktašu iškun išlulū ilānīšu[86]	In a battle in open country, he (i.e., Esarhaddon) defeated him, and his gods were carried off.

Much later, Ashurbanipal restored them, and the description of this return recalls the earlier Esarhaddon episode:[87]

[*Iauta'*] *mār* ᵐ*Ḫaza-ilu šar māt Qadari* [*epēš ardū*]*tīya* [*aššu ilānī*]*šu imḫurannima uṣalla šarrūti ina šum ilāni rabūti uša*[z]*kiršuma* ᵈ*Atarsamain utīrma addinšu*[88]	[Uate'], son of Hazail, king of Qedar, my [vassal], appealed to me [concerning] his [gods], and he praised my majesty. I had him take an oath by the great gods, and gave him back Atarsamain.

A final capture is reported by Ashurbanipal (Asb. Rm.IX.3-8), after which

[84] I. Eph'al sees in this event "a clear gesture on the part of Esarhaddon aimed at quieting the western edges of Babylonia," noting that Hazail had earlier submitted as tributary to Sennacherib (*Nomads*, 91).

Against this interpretation, it can be argued that Esarhaddon increased, albeit in small measure, the tax payments imposed upon Hazail. Furthermore, the Arabian gods experienced extended confinement in Nineveh, beyond that of all other imprisoned deities. Cf. above, n. 79. Our text, presenting Hazail as the initiator of negotiations, may mean that some undeterminable pressure urged him to submit anew to Assyria at this juncture.

[85] To place inscriptions upon looted objects is not the usual practice. The suggestion that Esarhaddon inscribed a memorial to his "victorious achievement" (*lītu kišitti qātāšu*) upon the 55 statues of Egyptian kings taken over during the conquest of Egypt is based upon an erroneous completion of a lacuna in K. 3083, 6-7. Borger, *Asarhaddon*, § 65, rev. 52, shows that separate stela were erected upon which the inscription was placed. (The error seemingly originated with Streck, VAB 7, 216, followed by ARAB 2, 937, and ANET, 296, without indicating the state of preservation of text.)

[86] VAT 5600 I, 9 (= Streck, VAB 7, 376). The fragmentary text from Til-Barsip tells of the revolt of Uabu against Uate' (cf. Borger, *Asarhaddon*, § 27, ep. 14, 23-31; § 66, 18-19; § 72) and may contain information of still another deportation of Arabian gods (ll. 18-19). It is hard to connect this notice with VAT 5600 I, 9, for Uabu is completely absent there, and punishment is directed only against Uate'.

[87] This similarity caused early historians to doubt the integrity of the text. Cf. Streck, VAB 7, cclxxxi n. 3.

[88] Asb. B. 7.93ff. Completed, in part, by Knudsen, *Iraq* 29 (1967) pl. 23, ND. 5518, col. VI.

the annals run out. It is likely that restoration of the Arabian gods followed shortly after victory, perhaps on the occasion of Ashurbanipal's presentation of gifts to the Arabian Ishtar.[89]

Esarhaddon and Ashurbanipal showed consideration to others besides the tribe of Hazail. The reported return of captured gods of the territory of Bāzu[90] repeats, almost verbatim, the Hazail account. The defeated Layalē, king of Yadi', a "distant, forgotten wasteland," arrived in Nineveh and pleaded for mercy before Esarhaddon:

aqtabīšu aḫu[lap] ilānīšu ša ašlula danān Aššur bēlīya elīšunua ašṭurma utīrma addinšu[92]	I said to him: "Enough!"[91] I inscribed upon his gods, which I had carried off, the strength of Ashur, my lord, and gave them back to him.

From all these texts, a partial picture of Assyrian administrative policy emerges. With regard to areas too vast to control, no matter how great their economic or strategic value,[93] Assyria contented itself with exacting oaths of loyalty from defeated rulers.[94] At times, a *qēpu*-official[95] may have been assigned to the territory to protect Assyrian interests.[96] The captured gods were held hostage until the defeated ruler begged for their return, a public sign of his submission to Assyria. The gods were then returned, and their cults restored with no interference, except the inscriptions placed upon them. But at best, this policy was one of temporary restraint, for strife dominated the relations between such uncontrollable areas and the Assyrian empire throughout much of the NA period.

Another set of texts describes some of the considerations which motivated Assyria, on its part, to initiate cult statue restorations. The Assyrian monarch

[89] See the discussion of K. 3405 above, pp. 15-20.

[90] E. Forrer in RLA 1, 440-441, contests the identification of Bazu with the town Bazzu in Bab. Chron. IV, 5 (= Esar. Chron. 13), located by S. Smith in the territory of the Upper Zab (*Babylonian Historical Texts*, 17f.; cf. Landsberger and Bauer, ZA 37 [1926] 74-75), and argues for an area in the heart of the Arabian desert. See now Eph'al's comprehensive review of the geographical problems in *Nomads*, 93-99.

[91] CAD A 1, 213f.; AHw, 22f.

[92] Borger, *Asarhaddon*, § 27, B III, ep. 12, 46b-48.

[93] Arab cooperation with Assyria in the important South Arabian trade and in border defense is discussed by I. Eph'al in "Arab Penetration into the Border districts of Israel in the 8th Century B.C.E." [Hebrew], *Fifth World Congress of Jewish Studies* (Jerusalem, 1972), 145-51.

[94] In the case of Arabs, these were often queens. See, Rosemarin, "Aribi und Aribien in den Babylonisch-Assyrischen Quellen," JSOR 16 (1932) 8 n. 24; VAB 7, 217 n. 11.

[95] On the *qēpu*, see Godbey, AJSL 22 (1905-06), 81-88; Opitz, RLA 1, 459, § 6; J. J. Finkelstein, JCS 7 (1953) 124f.; and for the Neo-Babylonian period, see San Nicolò, SBAW 2/2 (1941) 24 n. 24; and now, Brinkman, WO 5 (1969-70) 46.

[96] So, within the territory of Queen Shamshi of Arabia; Rost, *Tigl. III*, III R 10, no. 2, 26.

often undertook prompt return of statues removed in war, hoping to profit from the goodwill thus engendered.

Sargon's defeat of Merodach Baladan included the capture of the gods his enemy had collected in Dūr-Yakin:

ilāni tiklīšun ištēniš ašlulamma[97]
The gods, in whom he trusted, I despoiled one and all.

No extended transfer to Assyria followed. Immediately upon the end of hostilities, Sargon reports:

ilāni šallūti ana māḫazīšunu utīrma sattukēšunu baṭlūti utīr[99]

I returned the pillaged gods to their cult centers[98] and restored their interrupted regular offerings.

The populations of the cities from which Merodach Baladan had originally taken these statues had surrendered to Sargon and pledged their loyalty to him. Babylon itself had welcomed the Assyrian king into the city, inviting him to partake in the ritual meal of Marduk.[100] Consequently, the necessity for deportation of the gods had been obviated. By the return of the gods to their shrines, a display of respect and concern for the Babylonian cult, Sargon thought to win support for his rule over Babylonia.[101]

At the start of his reign, Esarhaddon undertook to reconcile and consolidate the varied elements of his empire. He sought to erase the effects of the repressive rule of Sennacherib, which had apparently led to the latter's violent death. Plans were undertaken for the reconstruction of Babylon and its temples, work which lasted down through the reign of Ashurbanipal.[102] But the statue of Marduk

[97] *Iraq* 16 (1954) 186, 6.61-62. Cf. above, p. 31.

[98] See W. Moran in AnBib 12 (1959) 258-59, for reconsideration of the term *māḫazu*, in which he concludes that *m.* "must be a part of, or within, the temple, not the entire complex, or even less a city." E. Y. Kutscher studied the cognates of *māḫazu* based on a new Ugaritic vocabulary in "Ugaritica Marginalia" [Hebrew], *Lĕšonénu* 34 (1969) 5-18.

[99] *Ibid.*, 78. Cf. Lie, *Sargon*, 64, 12-13.

[100] Lie, *Sargon*, 371-75; cf. discussion by Oppenheim in *Ancient Mesopotamia*, 189.

[101] Sargon similarly reinstated the gods of the defeated Ḫarḫar rebels:

[ ] *ušaklil ekurrātēšu epu*[*š*] *ilānīšu ana ašrīšunu utīr*

[ ] I completed. His temples I rebuilt; his gods I returned to their shrines. (See L. D. Levine, *Two Neo-Assyrian Stelae from Iran, Royal Ontario Museum Art and Archaeology*, Occasional Paper 23 [1972] 40 line 44.) But whether it was Sargon himself or the mutinous citizenry who had displaced the gods in the first place cannot be determined.

Reconciliation with Muṣaṣir may have included the return of the Ḫaldia statue a year after its removal. See H. Tadmor, JCS 12 (1958), 85ff., for proposed reconstruction of C^{b}4 Eponym Chronicle, 11; followed by Oppenheim, JNES 19 (1960) 137.

[102] The final return of the couch of Marduk and his chariot did not take place until 654-53 B.C.E. The latest discussion is by Millard, "Another Babylonian Chronicle Text," *Iraq* 26 (1964) 19-23.

was not immediately returned to its shrine, indicating perhaps continued anxiety over relations with the south.[103] A general amnesty was declared, however, for all other imprisoned gods:[104]

ša ilāni mātāti šallūti ultu māt Aššur / u māt Elam / ana ašrēšunu utirruma ušēšibu šubtu nēḫtu adi ekurrāti ušakliluma ilāni ina parakkēšunu ušarmū šubat dārāti / ina kullat māḫazi aštakkanu simāte[105]	(I am he) who returned the pillaged gods of the countries from Assyria / and Elam / to their shrines, who let them stay in comfortable quarters until he completed temples (for them), and could set the gods upon daises as a lasting abode. / In all cult centers, (it was) I, who established the necessary accessories. /

Esarhaddon provided accommodations for the gods befitting their divinity, pending their return.[105a] In this case he made no requirements upon the renewed cults in their native lands, such as the display inscriptions set on the statues of the Arabian gods. But the generous outfitting and endowment had too obvious a political value to be considered entirely gratuitous.

Votive gifts by the Assyrian king to non-Assyrian gods were looked upon as accruing goodwill on the king's behalf, which might be of benefit sometime in the future. The inscriptions which accompany royal dedications frequently conclude with an explicit request for the divine blessing of the recipient deity. Ashurbanipal's text relating the gift of a star-emblem to the Arabian Atarsamain (K.3405, discussed above)[106] exemplifies the petitionary formula. Not only the gods, but their faithful as well, might be expected to respond favorably to Assyrian gener-

[103] Not until the inauguration of Shamash-shum-ukin in 668 B.C.E. was it sent home by Ashurbanipal. See Landsberger, *Bischof*, 23, for citation and discussion of sources.

[104] Cf. Borger, *Asarhaddon*, 122, for chronicle reports of these events.

[105] Borger, *Asarhaddon*, § 27, ep. 3, 23-26; / . . . / = Borger, *Asarhaddon*, § 11, ep. 36, 5-8. Other text-forms (from Uruk and Nippur inscriptions) substitute suitable equivalents: *šukuttašunu uddišma . . . ukinnu isqušun*, "he renewed their treasures . . . and (re-)established their income" (Borger, *Asarhaddon*, § 47, 22-23; JCS 17 (1963) 130, 11).

[105a] This gesture may well have extended over a number of years, during which time the new king sought to stabilize relations with his subjects. The gods of Agade, for example, were sent home from Elam only six years later. See Borger, *Asarhaddon*, § 109, year 674/3, C. (Agade's images were not taken during the Elamite raid upon Sippar reported for year 675/4, so, Smith, CAH 3, 81; but were, more likely, part of the hoard of Babylonian gods in Elamite custody which was periodically released, following political accommodation. Esarhaddon credits himself with having cared for these far-off gods.)

[106] Obv. 16-17 (cf. above, p. 16). The Ashurbanipal gift, spoken of in the fragmentary conclusion of this same inscription, must have asked similar blessing. Rev. 13ff. reads:

> *ina ūmēšu kakkabtu šuā[tu*] *mimma š[a] ilūtīša rabī[ti*] *nīš qātēya* [ ]
>
> At that time [I presented] this star-emblem. Whatever her great divinity [ ]. My prayers [to her . . . may she receive(?)].

osity. We know that the inhabitants of Ur greatly esteemed Assyrian gifts to the Sin and Nergal temples in their city.[107]

A singular allusion in the Ashurbanipal annals may testify to yet other votive offerings. The king reported that Shamash-shum-ukin, in open revolt against Assyria,

epēš niqēya lapān ᵈBēl mar ᵈBēl nūr ilāni ᵈŠamaš u qurādi ᵈIrra iklāma ušabṭila nadān zībīya[108]	prevented the performance of my (i.e., Ashurbanipal's) sacrifices before Bel, son of Bel, the light of the gods Shamash, and the warrior Irra; and interrupted the presentation of my food-offerings.

Our text tells of sacrificial gifts by Ashurbanipal to Babylonian gods. This seems to refer to a practice, well-attested in the Persian period,[109] in which the king would enhance himself with gods and men by endowing offerings by governors and foreign allies to their own gods in his name.

It is likely, then, that the restored cults continued uninterruptedly, with no change in their ritual save the requisite prayer on behalf of the Assyrian king.[110]

Summary

To recapitulate: NA spoliation of divine images was meant to portray the abandonment of the enemy by his own gods in submission to the superior might of Assyria's god, Ashur. Accordingly, foreign gods were not treated as captives nor displayed in Assyrian temples as trophies, but were held, at times not far from their homes, for as long as it took Assyria to secure guarantees of loyalty from the defeated.

Local cults were in no way suspended during the stay of the cult statues in

[107] ABL 1241, rev. 10-12; ABL 1246, rev. 3-5.

[108] Asb. Rm. 3.112-14.

[109] See reports from provincial centers of Elephantine (cf. B. Porten, *Archives from Elephantine* [Berkeley: University of California Press, 1968] 111, 114) and Jerusalem (Ezra 6:9f.).

[110] Several dozen gods of foreign origin, some of whom had shrines in the temples of main Assyrian cities, are called upon during the annual Tākultu ceremonies to bestow their blessing upon the NA king. See R. Frankena, *Tākultu* (Leiden: E. J. Brill, 1954), 77-119, for detailed listing of divine participants in the Tākultu. It would seem that native gods in provincial territories were accomodated within an extended Assyrian pantheon, under the rule of Ashur; thus explaining the role assigned non-Assyrian gods in Assyrian ritual. See provisionally Weidner's observations in "Subärische Gottheiten im Assyrischen Pantheon," AfO 15 (1945-51) 82-84.

Whether the fashioning of a gold statue of the god ᵈArmada — patron deity of the Mediterranean coastal city Arwad (?) — by Shalmaneser III for the Ashur Temple (KAH 2, 103) evidences this same phenomenon remains clouded. See E. Michel, WO 1/2 (1949), 268f. n. 23.

Assyria; if excessive delay was encountered in their return, new ones might be fashioned. Upon public acknowledgment of Assyrian suzerainty by the subdued, the exiled gods were promptly repatriated, with no substantive demands made upon their native cults by the overlord. Often Assyria appears as benefactor of sacrificial endowments and new constructions for foreign gods, hoping to win, thereby, support of both god and men for Assyrian rule.

Yet despite this exhibition of regard for native religious sensitivities, it is claimed that Assyria did at times impose service to Assyrian gods. A study of the nature and incidence of such impositions follows.

3. ASSYRIAN IMPOSITIONS IN PROVINCES AND VASSAL STATES

THROUGHOUT A. T. Olmstead's *History of Assyria*, one can read statements based upon the author's *a priori* assumption that conquered nations were obliged to serve Assyrian gods. Thus, for example:

> When kings are set free they are forced to swear the oath of the great gods for servanthood forever, and a captive king on whom Tiglath-pileser has mercy is sent home to be a worshipper of the great gods (p. 67).
>
> Dur Tukulti-apal-esharra was built, and the captives settled in his "Wall" were commanded to worship the royal image which his lord Ashur had ordered him to set up "as a sign of victory and might" (p. 177).

Close study of the pertinent texts, however, will not confirm Olmstead's assumption. The following survey will show that Assyrian imperial authorities did not follow a thoroughgoing policy of religious coercion. While all nations were obliged to acknowledge Assyria's god, the extent of this obligation depended upon the extent of subjugation to Assyria.

Late Neo-Assyrian documents provide a fairly detailed picture of Assyrian imperial organization, which distinguished between vassal states, i.e., allied foreign countries which paid tribute but were independent; and Assyrian provinces, i.e., formerly independent countries annexed to and governed by Assyria.[1] H. W. F. Saggs refines these categories to include an intermediate stage: occasionally, Assyria "would intervene in the internal affairs of the state to replace the unreliable ruler" who had rebelled, by another prince "acceptable to Assyria." This pro-Assyrian ruler "would now be bound by oath . . . [and] an Assyrian official, probably backed by a small military force, would be left within his territory."[2]

Adū — *Political Oaths of Loyalty*

This inquiry into the obligations demanded by Assyria of its subjects will begin with the *adū* documents. The very name and nature of this widely used category of pacts have been the subject of renewed debate ever since the publi-

[1] Cf. Meissner, BuA I, p. 138.

[2] H. W. F. Saggs, *Greatness*, p. 242. Cf. the remarks of H. Donner, "Neue Quellen zur Geschichte des Staates Moab in der zweiten Hälfte des 8. Jahr. v. Chr.," MIO 5 (1957), 163f.

cation of the Esarhaddon *adū* texts, the longest examples of *adū* unearthed to date in Mesopotamia.[3] The term *adū* was introduced in the NA period,[4] entering Akkadian, it seems, from the then current Aramaic usage.[5] *Adū* were not "vassal treaties," in the sense that they established vassalage, for the inferior status of the bound party was neither stressed nor indicated in the texts. During the NA era no party or power was equal to Assyria, and so every *adū* was by definition an imposition from above.[6] Furthermore, it needs to be emphasized that *adū* were imposed upon all administrative areas of the empire. Individuals and states,[7] both within Assyria and its provincial system and without, undertook *adū* obligations of loyalty to the sovereign.[8] Most often, recognition of the

[3] D. J. Wiseman, *Vassal Treaties of Esarhaddon* [=VTE] (originally published as ***Iraq*** 20/1 [1958]). Texts of other *adū* include: Shamshi–adad — AfO 8 (1932-33), 28; Ashurnirari — AfO 8 (1932-33), 24ff.; Naqia — ABL 1105, 1239; Esarhaddon — Borger, *Asarhaddon*, § 69; and Ashurbanipal — Or 37 (1968), 464ff.

[4] The two items listed by AHw, 14a, as evidence for MA usage have been re-interpreted by CAD A 1, 134a. Although the same AHw entry indicates MB usage, no citations of such are given. Lambert, AfO 18 (1957-58), 48, would interpret *a-de-e* in the fragmentary BM 98731, rev. 8, as "oath," but throughout this text "oath" is rendered *māmītu* (obv. B 33; rev. B 29, 38, and 40) as expected in a MB text.

[5] Fitzmyer, JAOS 81 (1961), 187, reviews etymological difficulties in relating Aramaic *ʿDYʾ* to *adū* ("we normally expect the *a*-vowel to shift to *e* because of the *ʿayin* in Accadian"), and so proposes a "loanword from Northwest Semitic." To Fitzmyer's bibliography cited there, add D. B. Weisberg, *Guild Structure and Political Allegiance in Early Achaemenid Mesopotamia* (New Haven: Yale University Press, 1967), pp. 32-40; and J. A. Fitzmyer, *The Aramaic Inscriptions of Sefîre* (*Biblica et Orientalia* 19; Rome, 1967), pp. 23-24.

[6] Instructive in this regard is the unique passage in Asb. Rm.I.123ff., containing the message sent by the rebel Egyptian princes to Tarqu:

eli ᵐ*Tarqu šar māt Kūsi ana šakān*	They sent their messengers to Tarqu,
adē u salīme uma'erū LÚ *rakbēšun umma*	king of Ethiopia to establish an *adū*
sulummu ina birinni liššakinma	of friendship: "Let friendly relations
nindaggara aḫāmeš māta aḫennā nizūzma	be established between us. Let us agree
ay ibbaši ina birinni šanūmma bēlum	to divide the country among ourselves.
	No foreigner should be lord over us."

In order to make the intent of the rebels clear, the Assyrian scribe had to gloss the term *adū*, which ordinarily signified implicit lordship, by the phrase "No foreigner should be lord over us." This was not to be a real *adū* agreement, for the Egyptian princes meant to remain equal, independent rulers. (This approach to the problem was suggested to me by Prof. H. Tadmor of the Hebrew University, Jerusalem, in an oral communication in November, 1968.)

Cf. identical terminology in Asb. B.VIII.59 — *ana šakān adē sulumme epēš ardūtīya*, "to establish an *adū* of friendship to do obeisance to me [i.e., Ashurbanipal]."

[7] ABL 33: 13 and 1239 contain listings of private persons, as well as state officials, obliged to *adū*. Cf. Borger, *Asarhaddon*, § 27, ep. 2, 50f., 80; Asb. Rm.I.18-22; and the comments by Klauber, *Assyrisches Beamtentum*, LSS 5/3 (1910), pp. 44-45; and Weidner, AfO 17 (1954-56), 4.

[8] Stressed by I. J. Gelb, "Review of Wiseman, *VTE*," BiOr 19 (1962), 162.

Assyrian monarch as sole ruler and active support and cooperation with him and his descendants against all acts of treason, sedition, and rebellion constituted the stipulations of the *adû*.

Assyria on its part may have undertaken to protect certain state interests of its subjects — e.g., defending threatened loyal rulers. After his capture of Urartian fugitives hiding in Shupria, Esarhaddon asserts that as regards "Urartian fugitives, I did not keep (even) one; a single person did not remain (behind). I returned them to their country in keeping with the *adû* (*[aš]šu adê naṣārimma*)."[9]

These "pacts of loyalty," as I. J. Gelb termed the *adû*,[10] specified obligations of a wholly political nature. Nowhere do the *adû* documents ever include cultic impositions. NA historical inscriptions, as well, mention *adû* only in political contexts. While the inscriptions never detail the terms of the pacts, we can reconstruct these terms by collecting the historical references to *adû* violations. Table 2 sets out a catalog of *adû* violations, all of them considered treasonable acts which invariably prompted Assyrian military reprisals.[11]

This survey of *adû* violations as reported in NA historical inscriptions, in complement with the *adû* texts themselves, provides ample evidence of the political loyalties expected of Assyrian subjects. Nowhere in this survey is a sacrilegious act mentioned, for specific religious obligations were not part of these loyalty oaths. Nonetheless, D. J. Wiseman opined: "Occasionally, the religious obligations accompanying a treaty are detailed in a tablet other than that in which the main agreement between the two parties is outlined."[12] The proof text cited by Wiseman, however, is not an *adû* document, but an OB Alalakh text, containing otherwise unknown ritual instructions.[13] It is of little purport in a discussion of NA *adû* oath stipulations. Since *adû* were solely concerned with political matters, we neither expect nor find any NA *adû* or *adû*-related texts specifying religious obligations.

Yet one might argue that even though the *adû* texts specify no religious obligations, the very fact that they are termed *adê* ᵈ*Aššur u ilāni rabûti*, "the *adû* of Ashur and the great gods," implies obligatory recognition of Assyrian gods. No such claim, however, can be made simply on the basis of this expression. *Adê ša* DN, "the *adû* of DN," indicates that divine sanction had been invoked to back *adû* obligations. Non-performance would immediately move the wit-

[9] Borger, *Asarhaddon*, § 68, III, 32ff. Cf. Sefiré treaty III, 19, for similar stipulation of mutual return of refugees (see Fitzmyer, *CBQ* 20 [1958], 448). Other examples of obligations binding Assyria to action are unavailable from the present corpus of *adû* (cf. above, n. 3).

[10] Gelb, BiOr 19 (1962), 162.

[11] See below, pp. 122-25.

[12] Wiseman, VTE, p. 27 and n. 211.

[13] See D. J. Wiseman, *The Alalakh Tablets* (London: British Institute of Archeology at Ankara, 1953), text 126. In the original publication of AT 126, Wiseman held that Yarimlim undertook, in solemn oath (*nīš* ᵈIM [*Adad*] *u* ᵈIŠDAR [*Išḫara* ?]), to deliver specified sacrifices upon "his installation as king of Alalakh (p. 63)." This still remains the most reasonable explanation of the text.

nessing gods to punish. Thus, for example, the gods moved against the Arab Uate' and his troops:

ina arrāti mala ina adēšunu šaṭra ina pitti išīmūšunūti[14]
As many curses as were written in their loyalty oaths, they (i.e., the gods) suddenly visited upon them.

The Assyrians regarded the acceptance by their subjects of the terms of *adū* oaths as tantamount to submission to Ashur. Ashurbanipal twice refers to the oaths of allegiance he imposed on Abiate, another Arab king. In a letter to the god Ashur,[15] he says:

Abiate mār [m]*Teri ana Ninua illikamma unaššiq šēpēya adē epēš ilūtīka rabīti ittīšu aškun*[16]
Abiate, son of Teri, came to Nineveh and kissed my feet. I had him take an oath in reverence of your great divinity.

While in the annal literature we read:

ana Ninua illikamma unaššiq šēpēya adē epēš ardūtīya ittīšu aškun[17]
He came to Nineveh and kissed my feet. I had him take an oath in obeisance to me.

In an address to the gods, one expects phraseology which glorifies them; in the royal annals, the power and might of the king are streessed. The interchangeability of terms points to functional equivalence. Swearing to serve the king was at the same time acknowledging the rule of the Assyrian god.

In like manner Esarhaddon describes the plea of the recalictrant king of Shupria, who, hoping to save his life, admits to improprieties toward the Assyrian monarch. Here are the Shuprian's words as related in Esarhaddon's letter to the gods:

ana napšāti mušširannima tanitti
[d]*Aššur lušāpā ladlula qurdīka ša ana*
[d]*Aššur šar ilāni ēgu amat Aššur-aḫu-idina*
šar kiššāti bēlīšu lā išemmu ḫalqu munnabtu
ša māt Aššur ana bēlīšu lā utarru ina
qātēya lēmur . . . ḫiṭṭu dannu ana [d]*Aššur*
aḫṭīma amat šarri bēlīya ul ašme.[18]

Spare my life so that I may proclaim the praise of Ashur and glorify your valor. He who is neglectful toward Ashur, king of the gods, does not obey the order of Esarhaddon, king of the universe; he who does not return Assyrian runaway slaves and refugees to their owners, should learn by my example . . . . I have committed a great wrong against Ashur, when I did not obey the order of the king, my lord.

[14] Asb. Rm.IX.60.

[15] Text K.2802 (=Streck, VAB 7, pp. 197ff.) has been restored and reconstructed according to Bauer, IWA, p. 66, 4b, and Borger, *Or* 26 (1957), 1. Therefore, Streck's referral of this text to Ishtar, p. 197 n. 3, needs correction. [d]*Aššur* is addressed throughout.

[16] Streck VAB 7, 202, 5. 6ff. *Adē epēš* is written *a-di e-peš*; cf. Streck's comment, *ibid.*, 202 n. *f*.

[17] Asb. B.VIII.33f. Cf. Bauer, IWA, p. 18, X.31 (broken!) for C prism.

[18] Borger, *Asarhaddon*, § 68, I, 17-21.

In this instance, according to Esarhaddon, the subject recognized his obligation to obey the royal word out of reverence for Ashur.

One wonders, however, whether this statement, reported in a letter to the gods, was in fact spoken by the Shuprian king. His words might be only the reverent musing of an Assyrian court scribe; and upon close reading of another Esarhaddon text, the *adû* with his eastern subjects, they turn out to be just that. That section of the *adû* document specifying the terms of support for Ashurbanipal's succession to the throne of Assyria speaks of *Aššur ilīkunu*, "Ashur, your god," and *Aššur-bāni-apli mār šarri rabû ša bīt rēdûti bēlkunu*, "Ashurbanipal, the crown prince, your lord," often in juxtaposition.[19] The use of such locutions, which present the recognition of the king and his god in a single breath, supports our view that by upholding the rule of the Assyrian king one automatically manifested acceptance of his god, Ashur. But, significantly, at the conclusion of this same *adû* document, in that section which purportedly contains a transcript of the oath ceremonies, the subjects themselves do not voice their submission to Ashur. Their first-person declaration makes no mention of Ashur or any Assyrian god.[20] Only a summary of the *adû* demands are sworn to.

Turning from questions of political loyalty, we note that three recent studies have examined the choice of deities called upon by Assyria to sanction *adû* oaths. Matitiahu Tsevat suggests that a dual policy was in effect; the oaths of eastern territories were enforced exclusively by Assyrian gods, while western territories were bound both by their native gods and those of Assyria.[21] This distinction, according to Tsevat, was determined by the extent of the Hittite rule, some five hundred years earlier. Since the Hittites recognized national deities other than their own in their treaty relations, Assyrian imperialism, in deference to this practice, followed the by-then standard procedure in western, one-time Hittite territories. Elsewhere, only Assyro-Babylonian gods were invoked.

McCarthy, on the other hand, hesitates to draw conclusions from the small amount of Assyrian material, where the evidence of one item, in a total body of three or four items, represents a deceptively significant percentage.[22] He notes in addition that even within its own cultural and chronological sphere, a single Hittite treaty pattern "did not impose itself rigidly,"[23] and omissions and variations are much in evidence. The general restriction of the god lists in the Assyrian *adû* is not the result "of simply arrogance or confidence in the universal sway of Ashur," but the belief that the gods of the enemy had abandoned their clients to join the Assyrian side.[24]

[19] Wiseman, VTE, 393-394, cf. 409.

[20] Wiseman, VTE, 494-512.

[21] Tsevat, "The Neo-Assyrian and Neo-Babylonian Vassal Oaths and the Prophet Ezekiel," *JBL* 78 (1959), 199ff., especially n. 7.

[22] Dennis McCarthy, *Treaty and Covenant* (AnBib 21, 1963), p. 79 n. 36.

[23] *Ibid.*, p. 29.

[24] *Ibid.*, p. 93 n. 50.

Frankena follows this line of reasoning and thinks that "in all likelihood, also the vassal treaties [of Esarhaddon] list native gods in their curse section."[25] Furthermore, he feels that "Assyrian scribes must have been often at a loss when they had to attribute curses to unknown gods of vassals," and so substituted familar gods in suitable sections of the treaty.[26]

What has been overlooked is the distinction which might be made between provinces administered directly by Assyria and independent vassal states. As will become evident[27] provinces were considered to be Assyrian in all matters, and it may not have been in place for their national deities to be accorded an official position. It has long been recognized that the inclusion of gods in individual lists was directly dependent upon the relative strength of the contracting parties; hence, e.g., the prominence given to the Babylonian Marduk to the seeming degradation of Ashur in the treaty of Shamshi-adad V with Marduk-zakir-shumi of Babylon.[28] In the Esarhaddon *adū*, of the seven extant names of territories with whom oaths were taken, three were provinces, one had recently surrendered to Esarhaddon, and the remaining three are otherwise unknown.[29] We suggest that these *adū* be viewed as having been concluded with provincial areas, and so no foreign gods need be mentioned. Those *adū* which include invocation of local gods, i.e., the Ashurnirari V and Esarhaddon-Ba'al oaths, were all executed with vassal states still maintaining a degree of independence.[30] So, too, the recently published, but very fragmentary, *adū* between Ashurbanipal and Uate', king of the Arabs, seems to include mention of the gods of Assyria and Qedar.[31]

[25] R. Frankena, "The Vassal Treaties of Esarhaddon and the Dating of Deuteronomy," *OTS* 14 (1965), 130, pointing to the broken lines in Wiseman, VTE, 466-471.

[26] Frankena, *op. cit.*, p. 131.

[27] See below, pp. 50ff.

[28] Rm.2427 originally published by Peiser, MVAG 3/6 (1898), 240-43; re-edited by Weidner, "Der Staatsvertrag Aššurnirâris VI. von Assyrien mit Matiʾilu von Bît-Agusi," *AfO* 8 (1932), 27ff. All scholars remark the prime place given to Marduk in the curse section, but fail to mention that the extant portion of the text does not include ^{d}*Aššur* at all. Weidner's speculation, that this *adū* text was a Babylonian copy of the treaty which made changes to accommodate Babylonian feelings, remains just that; for we have no evidence of two versions of a single *adū* ever being issued. Brinkman, in AnOr 43, pp. 204-205, treats the historical circumstances behind this treaty through which Marduk-zakir-shumi extended aid to the tottering Assyrian king.

[29] On identifications, see VTE, p. 82. Zamua, Elpa, and Sikrisu were all provinces. Urakazabana is noted among other tribute-bearing areas in Media in Borger, *Asarhaddon*, § 27, ep. 15, 32ff.

[30] Bīt-Agusi, with whom Ashurnirari concluded his *adū*, was not incorporated until after the eastern campaigns of Tiglath-pileser III (cf. Forrer, *Provinzeinteilung*, 56f.). The Esarhaddon treaty with Ba'al probably reflects the mutually beneficial relations established between Tyre and Assyria, after Assyria's victory over Abdimilkutti of Sidon (cf. Borger, *Asarhaddon*, § 27, ep. 5, 15-19) in *ca.* 677 B.C.E. See discussion in Weidner, AfO 8 (1932-33), 33f. Ba'al later joined Egypt in revolt and was conquered in 671 B.C.E.

[31] Deller and Parpola, "Ein Vertrag Assurbanipals mit dem arabischen Stamm Qedar," *Or* 37 (1968), 464-66, obv. 2'-3'.

Support for the suggestion of wide Assyrian use of local gods in *adû* comes from the letter of one Kabtia to Ashurbanipal. Kabtia, reporting from the Babylonian front, explains his failure to take the oath of loyalty to the king at the designated time; others, in the meanwhile, were to proceed according to schedule:

ṣābē mārēšunu u aššātīšunu adi ilānīšunu ana libbi adē ša šarri bēlīya lirbū[32]	The men, their sons and their wives, along with their gods, should take the oaths of loyalty of the king, my lord.

Who exactly these people are—whether families of Nippur and Uruk,[33] from the district of Rashu,[34] or soldiers within the Assyrian army[35]—is unclear. At any rate, the expression "their gods" suggests non-Assyrian personal deities.[36] Are we to suppose that they were witnesses to the oaths, whose names were actually inscribed in the documents presented to both parties? Or was their mere presence sufficient to add their sanction to the solemnizing of the *adû*? We are not told whether their participation was freely accepted or imposed by Assyrian authorities. But one thing emerges clearly: foreign gods have a role in the *adû* in all areas of Assyrian domination, irrespective of geographic considerations,[37] and in vassal states the vassal's gods were formally invoked.

This Assyrian resort to a vassal's native gods is unambiguously set forth in the following episode from Sargon's eighth campaign. After a victorious march through eastern Urartu, Sargon rewards his vassal Ullusunu for handsomely receiving the Assyrian host.

ša Ullusunu šarri bēlīšunu paššur takbitti maḫaršu arkussuma eli ša Iranzi abi ālidīšu ušaqqi kussāšu	As for King Ullusunu, their lord, I set a rich table before him. I elevated his throne higher than that of Iranzi, his father and

[32] ABL 202, rev. 10-13.

[33] So A. J. Delattre, PSBA 23 (1901), 335.

[34] Note that Kabtia had just returned from Rashu (cf. Streck, VAB 7, p. 804). If so, the men may have been Elamites, still independent; for the Elamites of Rashu were not subdued until the first Elamite war, when they and their gods were captured (Asb. Rm. V.59ff.).

[35] Pfeiffer, in *State Letters of Assyria* (AOS 6, 1935), 212, translated "soldiers with their . . . ." Induction of skilled units from conquered territories into the Assyrian army is well attested (cf. Lie, *Sargon*, 75; Asb. Rm.VII.5; Borger, *Asarhaddon*, § 68, III, 15). This would account for a possible foreign element spoken of in our text. See above, p. 29.

[36] Note the contrast in rev. 5-7 of the foreign gods with *ilānīka*, "your (i.e., the king's) gods."

[37] In passing, we note that in diplomatic correspondence, as well as in contractual agreements, national deities were not slighted. In a letter sent by Esarhaddon to the Elamite king Urtaku, the Elamite god Manzinir is mentioned at the end of a listing of Assyrian gods, all credited with rendering an oracular (?) decision (ABL 918, 9-11; on ^{d}*Manzinir*, cf. Streck, VAB 7, p. clxviii n. 1). Similarly, Tammaritu, a later Elamite king, greeted the Assyrian Ashurbanipal in the name of the gods of both countries (ABL 1400, obv. 4-5).

šašunu itti nišē māt Aššur ina paššur ḫidāti ušēšibšunūti maḫar Aššur u ilāni mātīšunu ikrubū šarrūtī[38]	begetter. They, together with the soldiers of Assyria, I seated at a festive table, and before Ashur and the gods of their country, they blessed my rule.

Present at the state banquet, confirming the solemnity of the occasion and witnessing the reaffirmation of Sargon's rule — herein suggestive of *adû* oath ceremonies — were the Urartian gods, who had been accorded a place of honor beside the imperial Ashur.

Cultic Dues and Services

Though no trace of religious obligation can be found in the *adû* oaths of allegiance, it could be argued that such obligation may have never been formally committed to writing. Assyrian imperial administrators may have, as a matter of course, demanded compliance with Assyrian religious patterns. After all, NA historical inscriptions do refer to the payment of "the tribute of the god Ashur," and the dedication of "Ashur's weapon" in conquered cities. Olmstead, once again, saw these items as evidence of Assyrian religious coercion.

> It is Ashur who commands that the boundary of his land should be extended, the tax and tribute are of the lord Ashur, when the heavy yoke of the king's lordship is placed on newly conquered peoples, it is in reality to the lord Ashur they are made subject, to him they were not submissive, and when subdued they are numbered with those subject before the lord Ashur.[39]

But a re-examination of the available evidence shows that the facts ought to be otherwise construed. Only the populations of those lands permanently annexed to Assyria as provinces experienced partial religious dictation; residents of vassal states were free of any religious obligations toward their Assyrian master.

Provincial Territories.—The treatment of Samaria illustrates the administrative policies in provincial territories. The defeat of Israel in 722 B.C.E. by Shalmaneser V was followed, two years later, by Sargon's reconquest of its rebellious capital, Samaria.[40] It was Sargon who annexed Samaria to Assyria and made it the capital of a newly created province. Sargon's policies in Samaria can be wholly reconstructed from several inscriptions, each of which contains excerpts from a larger account no longer extant.[41]

[38] TCL 3, 63-64.

[39] *Assyria*, p. 614.

[40] On this dating and other details of Samaria's fall, See Tadmor, JCS 12 (1958), 37-38; and our discussion below, pp. 99f.

[41] The following is based upon Lie, *Sargon*, 15-17; Gadd, *Iraq* 16 (1954), 179, col. IV 35-36; and Winckler, *Sargon*, 100.24 (cf. the partial text reconstructed by Tadmor, JCS 12 [1958], 33-35). The words *sittatīšunu* to *Samerina* are represented in full only in the Gadd Prism. This same prism records variant statistics: 27,280 captives; 200

27,290 nišē āšib libbīšu ašlula 50 narkabāti kiṣir šarrūtīya ina libbīšunu akṣurma / sittatīšunu ina qereb māt Aššur ušaṣbit āl Samerina / utīrma eli ša pāna ušēme nišē mātāti kišitti qātēya ina libbi ušērib LÚ *šūt rēšīya* LÚ *šaknu elīšun aškunma biltu maddattu kī ša Aššurī ēmidsunūti[ma u] / inūšunu ušaḫiz /*

27,290 inhabitants, who live there, I took captive. From among them, I organized 50 chariots as a royal unit, and the rest of them I resettled within Assyria. The city of Samaria, I rebuilt and made it larger than before; and brought people there from the lands which I had conquered. I placed my functionary as *šaknu*[42] over them, and imposed tax and tribute upon them, just as if they were Assyrian. I also had them trained in proper conduct.[43]

This text records the standard procedure for reorganizing a territory into a province. The native population was deported to distant cities and replaced with captives from other areas of the empire.[44] The new residents of Samaria were regarded in every way as Assyrian; the phrase used to describe this status is in no way unique to this account:

kī ša Aššurī . . . ēmidsunūti[45]
I imposed upon them . . . just as if they were Assyrian.

In other inscriptions a parallel expression interchanges with this one with no change in meaning:

itti nišē māt Aššur amnušunūti[46]
I counted them with the people of Assyria.

Considering the diverse backgrounds of the new provincials, governmental concern was directed toward training them in "proper conduct." The particulars

chariots impressed into royal service (IV 31-33). The final two words are represented only in the Winckler Prunkinschrift.

[42] The term *šaknu* has been left untranslated, due to difficulty in determining the exact function of this official within the Assyrian hierarchy. The most recent treatment is by R. A. Henshaw, "The Office of *Šaknu* in Neo-Assyrian Times," JAOS 87 (1967), 517-24; JAOS 88 (1968), 461-82.

[43] *Inu* is translated by CAD I, 152 as "knowledge, technical lore," and AHw 383 as "Berufsarbeit." But such translations would involve the supposition of an Assyrian program of job-retraining of deportees, not at all the intent of Sargon's order. We learn from the Dūr-Sharruken text (cf. n. 49) that the masters of *inu* instruct in matters of behavior becoming to Assyrian citizens. Cf. renditions of Landsberger, *City Invincible*, ed. by Kraeling and Adams (Chicago: University of Chicago Press, 1960), p. 177, "culture, erudition," and Oppenheim in ANET, p. 285 (and n. 1), "(social) positions."

[44] Saggs (*Iraq* 18 [1956], 55) calls attention to the concern evidenced by the Assyrian bureaucracy for the needs of relocated populations, so as to forestall the confusion of dislodgement. Cf. texts ND.2449, 2643, and 2725 published by Saggs, *ibid.*, pp. 40-43; and *Greatness*, pp. 245f. 2 Kgs 17.6, 24 preserves record of Samaria transfers. See below, p. 101 n. 23.

[45] E.g., Lie, *Sargon*, 329-330.

[46] Citations in AHw 604, *s.v. manū*.

of such behavior are specified more fully in a similar account relating the settlement of Dūr-Sharruken.

mārē Aššur mūdūte ini kalama ana šūḫuz ṣibitte palāḫ ili u šarri aklī u šāpirī uma''iršunūti[49]	I commissioned natives of Assyria, as overseers and supervisors,[47] versed in all lore, to teach them correct behavior[48] — to revere god and king.

For the citizens of Assyria, to revere god and king meant bearing the burden of taxation for both royal and temple needs. Foreign provincial residents were no different. Hence, Sargon claims, e.g.,

nīr ᵈAššur bēlīya ēmidsunūti[50]
I imposed the yoke of Ashur, my lord, upon them.

nīr bēlūtīya ēmidsunūti[51]
I imposed my royal yoke upon them.

The obligations incumbent upon the bearers of the yokes of Ashur and the king are sometimes specified:

ilku tupšikku kī ša Aššurī ēmidsunūti[52]
I imposed feudal duties[53] and corvée upon them as if they were Assyrian.

But corvée, even if termed "Ashur's yoke" and used to construct Assyrian temples and shrines,[54] is hardly equivalent to coercion of provincials to adopt Assyrian cults.

[47] The translation of this passage follows CAD A 1, 278, rather than the earlier CAD I, 152.

[48] On *ṣibittu*, see CAD Ṣ, 157. J. J. Finklestein *apud* Shalom Paul (JBL 88 [1969], 73 n. 3) derives *ṣ.* from *ṣabātu*, "to teach" (CAD Ṣ, 34 *s.v. ussu*) and compares its semantic parallel *iḫzu-aḫāzu* (CAD A 1, 180f.; I, 47).

[49] Lyon, *Keilschrifttexte Sargon's* (Leipzig: J. C. Hinrichs, 1883), 12.74.

[50] AHw, 794a, *s.v. nīru*; CAD A 1, 65, *s.v. abšanu.*

[51] *Ibid.* Since the usual expression is "I imposed my royal yoke upon them," Oppenheim (ANET, p. 285 n. 9) takes the "yoke of Ashur" to refer to a "special status of Assyrian" granted by Sargon to the settlers of Carchemish. But the phrase "yoke of Ashur" is only one of several interchangeable phrases used to describe the strength, valor and armies of the god and the king alike. E.g., *ummānāt ᵈAššur*, "the troops of Ashur" (Lie, *Sargon*, 62; 200) and *mundaḫṣīya*, "my warriors" (Lie, *Sargon*, p. 54, 8; 408); *kakki ᵈAššur*, "weapon of Ashur" (Lie, *Sargon*, 122) and *kakkēya dannūti*, "my mighty weapons" (Lie, *Sargon*, 280, p. 50, 13; 52, 6; 380). Moreover, the "yoke of Ashur" is imposed on cities other than Carchemish, without apparent distinction (cf. Lie, *Sargon*, 20; 189; p. 73, V 4, 13). We conclude that all colonists were treated alike, regardless of where they originated. K. Tallqvist, *Der Assyrische Gott* (StOr 4/3, 1932), p. 96, shows how the king and the god are equated in war contexts.

[52] E.g., TCL 3, 410; Lie, *Sargon*, 204; 205. See CAD E, 142f.

[53] Cf. CAD I, 73ff.; AHw, 371f.

[54] E.g., Lie, *Sargon*, p. 74, 8-11.

Out of the entire corpus of NA historical inscriptions, only three texts explicitly tell of cultic imposts:

(1) After capturing Ḫirimmu, on the Assyro-Babylonian border, Sennacherib specifies:

nagû šuātu ana eššūti aṣbat ištēn alpa 10 *immerē* 10 *imēr karāna* 20 *imēr suluppī rēšētēšu ana ginē ilāni māt Aššur bēlēya ukīn dārišam*[55]	I reorganized that distirct, and established one ox, ten sheep, ten homers of wine, twenty homers of its choicest dates as regular offerings for the gods of Assyria, my lords, for all times.

(2) Having subdued the Shamash-shum-ukin–led rebellion, Ashurbanipal reimposed upon Babylon

sattukkī ginē rēšūti ᵈ*Aššur u* ᵈ*Ninlil u ilāni māt Aššur*[56]	the finest regular sacrificial offerings for Ashur, Ninlil, and the gods of Assyria.

(3) Esarhaddon's reorganization and annexation of Egypt concludes with the statement:

sattukkī ginū ana Aššur u ilāni rabûti bēlēya ukīn dāri(-šam)[57]	I established regular sacrificial offerings for Ashur and the great gods, my lords, for all times.

Payments probably varied from area to area; the Ḫirimmu schedule may have been a daily due,[58] while in Egypt there is reason to believe that demands were more elaborate.[59] The central authorities in Nineveh are known to have kept watch over these provincial incomes; administrative documents in the Harper collection, dated to Esarhaddon, report no less than sixteen district governors, including two from provinces on the north Syrian coast, as being in arrears in remittance of sacrificial dues.[60]

The paucity of the sources, however, leaves several key questions unanswerable. We cannot tell whether all or part of the cultic dues were transferred to es-

[55] *OIP* 2, 55.59.

[56] Asb. Rm.IV.106-107.

[57] Borger, *Asarhaddon*, § 65, rev. 48-49. This same phraseology is used in the summary, Borger, *Asarhaddon*, § 57, obv. 15-16, without an identifiable referent.

[58] Cf. H. Tadmor, "Temple City and Royal City in Babylonia and Assyria" [Hebrew], in *City and Community* (Jerusalem: Historical Society of Israel, 1968), p. 185.

[59] See ANET, pp. 293-294 for suggested list of dues imposed on Egypt; cf. Borger, *Asarhaddon*, § 80.

[60] I.e., *ginē ša Aššur*, ABL 43, obv. 5, 24-25. (Collated text is now available in AOAT 5/1, no. 309.) Cf. ABL 724, 5-8. ABL 532 notes the non-delivery of the *ḫamussu*-tax from Barḫalza, occasioning interruption in the Ashur temple ritual.

Van Driel is of the opinion that these payments were contributions expected of Assyrian high officialdom, whether "on account of the offices that these persons were holding, or on account of the fact that they were possessors of vast estates in their own right." See his *Cult of Assur* (Assen: Van Gorcum, 1969), pp. 189f.

tablished Assyrian sanctuaries or if they were rendered at new cult places founded in the provinces.[61] Were payments made directly to cult installations, earmarked as their perquisites, or disbursed from general revenues as a permanent draft on local treasuries?[62] In all, the actual role required of provincial residents in Assyrian cults is unspecified, save perhaps what is inferable from the suggestive presence of "Ashur's weapon" in the province center.

To concretize the induction of new populations into Assyrian citizenship, the *kakki* ^d*Aššur*, "the weapon of Ashur," was erected in the province center. There seems little question that the weapon was the official military emblem of Assyria. The palace reliefs show it to have been present in the army camp during campaigns.[63] It was located beside the altar table upon which sacrificial meals were laid out.[64] Its form was that of a pointed lance topped by the symbolic representation of Ashur,[65] and is styled a *mulmullu parzilli*, "iron(-tipped) arrow,"[66] or perhaps even a *patar parzilli*, "iron dagger."[66a]

As the symbol of Ashur, the weapon is known to have been set up only in territories reorganized into Assyrian provinces by Tiglath-pileser III,[67] Sargon,[68] and Sennacherib.[69] During the reigns of Esarhaddon and Ashurbanipal, on the other hand, scribes limited mention of the weapon to its portrayal as the effective agent in battle, leading both monarchs to victory,[70] thus neglecting, for example, to tell whether the weapon was deposited in Egypt after the final conquest of that country by Esarhaddon.

[61] The opening lines of Esarhaddon's Samal text (Borger, *Asarhaddon*, § 65, obv. 18-27), which seem to bear on this problem, are too fragmentary to be of help.

[62] Sargon appears to have levied direct payments upon the subdued Aramaean tribes in the Gambulu region of Babylonia for the upkeep of Marduk and Nabu: *ṣibit alpēšunu ṣēnīšunu ana* ^d*Bēl* (*u*) *mār* ^d*Bēl ukīn šattišam* (Lie, *Sargon*, 331-332), "I established a tax on their cattle and flocks for Bel (and) the son of Bel annually." But in this instance, the levy was for local Babylonian, not Assyrian, cult needs. (Some time later, an Assyrian governor in Babylonia is known to have exacted a *ṣibtu*-tax on flocks consecrated to Marduk. See ABL 464, rev. 1ff.)

[63] See Barnett and Falkner, *Sculptures of Tiglath-Pileser III*, plate LX; Paterson, *Palace of Sinacherib*, plates 38, 76, 85, 95; Botta, *Monument de Ninive* 2 (Paris: Imprimerie nationale, 1849), plate 146. See figure 1. Inscription reads: *ušmanu ša* ^mLUGAL. [GI.NA] "Camp of Sargon."

[64] ANEP, 625.

[65] See fig. 2 and other materials in F. Sarre, *Klio* 3 (1903), 333ff.; E. D. VanBuren, *Symbols of the Gods in Ancient Mesopotamian Art* (AnOr 23, 1945), 162-65. On the winged disk occasionally associated with Ashur, cf. H. Frankfort, *The Art and Architecture of the Ancient Orient* (Baltimore: Penguin Books, 1963), pp. 66f.

[66] Compare Rost, *Tigl. III*, 160-61 and Thontafel, obv. 36.

[66a] Cf. ABL 292, 6; 350, rev. 6. E. Salonen, StOr 33 (1965), pp. 49-55, cites several passages in which *patru* might be better rendered "a dagger-shaped knife/sword;" see now, AHw 848, *s.v. patru*.

[67] Rost, *Tigl. III*, 10, 22 [180]; Thontafel, obv. 36, 44.

[68] Lie, *Sargon*, 94, 99.

[69] *OIP* 2, 62:89-91.

[70] Borger, *Asarhaddon*, § 68, I, 32; Asb. Rm.II.20-21; VI.53ff; VII.119ff.; IX.90ff.

Ashur's weapon may have been more than an "outward sign of political dominion."[71] The iron arrow erected in the Median district of Bahiannu was inscribed, noted Tiglath-pileser III, with the tale of *lītat* [d]*Aššur bēlīya* "the victories of Ashur, my lord."[71a] Sparse statements in Sargon's annals allude indeed to the weapon's religious significance, but only in general terms.

ilāni alikūt maḫrīya ina qerbīšu ušēšibma[72]
The gods, who march in front of me, I settled in it (i.e., Kishesim).

kakke [d]*Aššur bēlīya ana ilūtīšun ašk[un]*[73]
The weapon of Ashur, my lord, I established as their god (i.e., in Ḫarḫar).

More information is available from older texts. As a divine emblem, the *patrum ša Aššur*, "the dagger of Ashur," is known to have been used in legal contexts in the Old Assyrian period. Assyrian colonists in Anatolia gave testimony, undertook obligations, dispensed judgments, and sealed documents in the presence of this weapon.[74] A *kakki ša Aššur*, also mentioned in the OA texts, was resorted to in ordeals. The defendant seems to have been required to "lift" or "draw out" the weapon of the god from its sheath — the culprit being unable to do so because of divine refusal to cooperate.[75] In these ordeal contexts the *kakki ša Aššur* is mentioned along with other divine symbols, the *patrum ša Aššur*, and the *šugarrium ša Aššur*, "the spear (?) of Ashur."[76]

The use of weapons in OA ordeals is suggestive for the NA period. Oppenheim has identified several ordeals in the Harper correspondence involving the "lifting of the *kalappu*-weapon."[77] Furthermore, a deified *kalappu* ([d]*kalappu*) and a deified *kakku* ([d]*kakku*) were among twelve other gods who would accompany the NA king to the Dagan temple during sacrificial rituals.[78]

Since these weapons played a part in the legal and cultic life of the NA period,

[71] So, Meissner, BuA 1, p. 141.

[71a] His MA predecessor, Tiglath-pileser I, had made use of an engraved bronze bolt (*birqi siparri*) to warn against rebuilding and resettling a site consigned to permanent desolation. See AKA, 79, 6.15-21.

[72] Lie, *Sargon*, 94. The variant in Sargon's Iranian stele reads:
[ ] [d]*Ištar bēlīya alikūt pānīya u*[ ] *ina qerbīšu ušarme*
[ ] Ishtar, my lords who march before me, [ ] I deposited within it.
See Levine, *Two Neo-Assyrian Stelae from Iran*, p. 38, line 39.

[73] Lie, *Sargon*, 99.

[74] See H. Hirsch, *Altassyrische Religion*, AfO Beiheft 13/14 (1961) 64-65. Use of divine weapons in legal proceedings during the Old Babylonian period can be compared in Walther, LSS 6/4-6, 192ff.; and R. Harris, "The Journey of the Divine Weapon," AS 16, 217-224.

[75] Oppenheim, "Lexikalische Untersuchungen zu den 'Kappadokischen' Briefen," AfO 12 (1937-39), 342-46.

[76] *Ibid.*

[77] Oppenheim, "Deux notes de lexicographie accadienne," Or 9 (1940), 219-21; Deller, Or 32 (1963), 474.

[78] Cf. Ebeling, "Kultische Texte aus Assur," Or 21 (1952), 139, 24; AHw 424a.

their display in new provinces probably served as more than just a reminder of reverence due Assyrian gods; a cult in their honor was likely instituted.[79] Once again, however, the role demanded of provincials in such a cult remains unknown.

At the same time, this installation of Assyrian cults within the provinces did not preclude the continued practice of local, native cults. Although outright statements to this effect are unavailible in the extant NA corpus, we may infer that such a policy was in force by juxtaposing two Sargonid texts discussed earlier. Sargon's postconquest dealings in the Ḫarḫar region of Media (*ca.* 716 B.C.E.) are described both in his annals and on the newly recovered Iranian stele. The annals report the establishment "of the weapon of Ashur, my lord, as their god" (see above, n. 73). The stele, at this point, omits all mention of Ashur's weapon, substituting instead a report of Assyria's rebuilding of temples and the return of Ḫarḫarite gods to their shrines (see above, p. 38, n. 101). While the reason for these disparate historical entries is unclear, their juxaposition warrants the conclusion that the introduction of imperial cults into the provinces in no way supplanted local cults. Indeed, Sargon's action abetted their continued observance.

Vassal States. — Assyrian treatment of independent vassal states was markedly different from that of the provinces. Such states were able to maintain a certain autonomy, although usually a pro-Assyrian force was in control. The circumspect ruler prevented the destruction and take-over of his homeland by appearing at the Assyrian court, along with other tribute-bearers, to proclaim his allegiance publicly. Tribute payments included fixed sums (*biltu u maddattu*),[80] occasion-

[79] K. Galling, *Der Altar in den Kulturen des alten Orient: Eine archäologische Studie* (Berlin: Curtius, 1925), p. 41, finds a cult honoring these weapons "easy to understand," but presents no evidence for one. He seems to follow H. Schäfer, "Assyrische und ägyptische Feldzeichen," *Klio* 6 (1906), 396ff., who paralleled Assyrian pictoral material to late Roman practice. On Roman standard worship, see, C. H. Kraeling, "The Episode of the Roman Standards at Jerusalem," *HTR* 35 (1942), 263-90.

I have left out of consideration the fragmentary passage in the Tiglath-pileser III Prism III R 10, no. 2, 10-11, because the references are insufficiently clear. The text, partially restored by ND. 4301 + 4305 (=*Iraq* 18 [1956], pl. 23, rev. 14′) and ND. 400 (=*Iraq* 13 [1951], pl. 11, 16), reads:

[ṣalam ilāni rabûti bēlī]ya u ṣalam šarrūtīya [ša ḫurāṣi . . . ēp]uš ina qereb ekal ša āl ḫa[zutu . . .] x ilānīšunu amnūma	[the image of the great gods,] my [lords] and my royal image [of gold . . . I ma]de, and in the palace of Ga[za . . .] x their gods, I appointed.

A divine symbol of some sort appointed as/with the gods of Gaza would not be out of place, since there is some suggestion that provincial status (?) may have been granted the city. Note that ND. 400, 18 reads: *[itti nišē māt] Aššur amnu.* Cf. the remarks of Wiseman, *Iraq* 13 (1951), 22.

[80] A full treatment of tribute collection and distribution procedures is found in Wm. J. Martin, *Tribut und Tributleistungen bei den Assyren*, (StOr 8/1, 1936). A convenient review of all taxes payable to Assyria is given by Tadmor in "Temple City," pp. 185-88 (see above, n. 58).

ally enhanced by special gifts in honor of state events (*tāmartu/nāmurtu, igisē*).[81] At times, vassal states had to supply a quota of men for the Assyrian army during campaigns in their region. In sum, wholly political demands were their lot.

NA sources tell of no religious impositions made upon vassals—neither of sacrificial dues nor of religious symbols erected in their territories. It is conceivable, however, that in the interest of good relations with the Assyrian suzerain, a vassal's occasional gifts might have included donations to the suzerain's gods. An interesting glimpse into the importance attached to religious gifts is found in ABL 268, a report by an official of Ashurbanipal. He has intercepted

3 sīsē piṣūti . . . u tillīšunu ša kaspi [ina] muḫḫi siparri munē'e [ša] tilli šaṭir [ištu ? Ta]mmariti [x]-il teppir šar māt Elamti [a]na ᵈIštar Uruk[85]	three white horses . . . and their silver trappings.[82] On the bronze "turner"[83] of the trappings was written: [From] Tammaritu [. . .] the *teppir*-official[84] of the king of Elam to Ishtar of Uruk.

Delivery of the horses sent by enemy Elamites to the goddess of Uruk was delayed, pending further instructions from Nineveh. Gifts to a god other than one's own apparently carried political overtones, and so the careful border guard intercepted the offensive horses and their trappings. Gifts to Assyria's gods, on the other hand, must have been warmly welcomed. But no specific demands for such gifts are known to have been made.

Vassal states were not without their symbolic reminders of Assyrian rule. In every land through which the Assyrian army marched, steles were set up to mark the limits of Assyrian domination.[86] The ubiquitous stele was not an innovation of Assyria, but was widely used by her to boast of victories and conquests.

It has been claimed that in the NA empire the stele belonged to the cult of a deified king.[87] In the palaces and temples of defeated states steles were erected, and the residents "commanded to worship the royal image . . . Ashur had ordered . . . set up 'as a sign of victory and might.' "[88]

[81] On *tāmartu/nāmurtu*, special gifts sent to curry favor with the overlord, see Martin, *Tribut* p. 24; and cf. AHw 730.

[82] On *tillu*, see Borger, *Asarhaddon*, p. 59 n. 43, and the works cited.

[83] Cf. AHw 673a. Our translation follows that of Oppenheim in *Letters from Mesopotamia* (Chicago: University of Chicago Press, 1967), p. 157.

[84] Oppenheim reads: "[Property (?) of] Tammariti, [a gift] of the *teppir*-official." On the Elamite *teppir*, see the remarks of Sollberger, *JCS* 22 (1968), 32, and the references cited there. Older translations parsed *ilteppir* as a I/3 of *šapāru*, "to send." But *šapāru* does not otherwise exhibit this tendency towards vowel harmony. Cf. Ylvisaker, *Zur Babylonischen und Assyrischen Grammatik*, LSS 5/6 (1912), p. 33, for examples, and GAG, 9f.

[85] ABL 268, obv. 13-rev. 1.

[86] Meissner, BuA 1, p. 141, spoke of both "Ashur's weapon" and the stele "as outward signs of dominion." He was followed by Lie, *Sargon*, p. 17 n. 8, and Schrade, *Verborgene Gott*, p. 76. But since the weapon did convey religious significance (cf. above, pp. 53-55), such broad statements must be qualified.

[87] See Olmstead, American Political Science Review 12 (1918), 67-72.

[88] Olmstead, *Assyria*, p. 177.

At first glance, the evidence supporting this view seems incontrovertible. Olmstead comments at some length on the activity depicted upon the engraved bronze gates of Balawat (reproduced in ANEP 364):

> A sculptor works in the water, mallet on chisel, at a representation of the king which is complete save that the surrounding cartouche is still to be incised. So perfect is the royal figure that an official already has taken his position on a platform erected among the rocks and adores his master's effigy. Other Assyrians lead up a ram for the sacrifices and drag on his back a reluctant bull destined to meet the same end.[89]

Furthermore, when excavations at Nimrud recovered the now famous stele of Ashurnasirpal, before it stood a "low triangular altar resting on lions feet and with a circular hollowed top. We are in the presence of the central fact of the empire, the worship of the deified ruler."[90]

Additional data to support this view were supplied by mid-seventh century B.C.E. documents from the province of Guzana (Tell-Halaf), which show that private oaths were sometimes taken before the gods and the [d]*ṣalam šarri*, "the statue of the king," to which divine honor was due.[91] Ungnad noted that personal names of the type *Ṣalam-šarri-iqbi* "can only be translated 'the king's image has ordered,'" obviously crediting the statue with oracular powers.[92]

Hayim Tadmor has sought to circumscribe the extent to which worship of steles was practiced. In his discussion of Tiglath-pileser III's Philistine campaigns, he wrote:

> The clearest sign of enslavement was the royal Assyrian cult which was introduced there, i.e., the service of the stele of the king of Assyria in the central shrine of Gaza. Only those vassal states which were not annexed to Assyria were forced to practice this cult, whereas the people of Assyria proper and residents of Assyrian provinces were absolved from it.[93]

But these commonly held views have not met with universal acceptance, and with good reason. Kurt Galling raised several objections. His typological study of the altars found in proximity to steles — both those found *in situ* and those represented on palace reliefs — differentiated at least two distinct architectural styles: (1) peaked incense (?) altars, and (2) round table altars.[94] Peaked altars are usually shown stationed at temple gateways and entrances; their location

[89] Olmstead, *Assyria*, p. 116.

[90] *Ibid.*, pp. 103-104; cf. also p. 87. See figure 3 for Layard's record of the original find-site of the stele and altar. Cf. also Layard, *A Second Series of the Monuments of Nineveh* (London, 1853), pl. 4.

[91] A. Ungnad, AfO Beiheft 6 (1940) 63 n. 5.

[92] *Ibid.*, p. 58 n. 21.

[93] H. Tadmor, "The Assyrian Campaigns to Philistia" *in Military History of the Land of Israel in Biblical Times* [Hebrew], ed. by J. Liver (Jerusalem: Maarachoth, 1964), p. 264.

[94] Galling, *Altar*, p. 45.

at some distance from the steles militates against a direct cultic connection between the two.[95] Galling further reasoned that since the round altar standing in front of the Ashurnasirpal stele bears a dedicatory inscription to Bel, "the offerings were directed to the gods, and would bring, coincidently, benefit to the king."[96] It might also be pointed out that this stele of Ashurnasirpal, from the portal of the Ninurta temple at Nimrud, is the only NA stele excavated to date which was found with an altar positioned at its base.[97]

Gadd commented upon the pictoral representations engraved on the steles:

> It cannot, however, be inferred from this that the Assyrian kings exacted worship of themselves as gods, either from their own citizens or from conquered foreigners. On the stelae it is noteworthy that the king himself is always depicted in an act of worship. He holds out his right arm, making a peculiar gesture which the Greeks, as mentioned before, thought to be a snapping of the fingers. The king would certainly not be so represented if the stela itself was to be the object of worship. The fact seems rather to be that such monuments were at once a visible symbol of sovereignty and, when placed in temples (as they sometimes were, both at home and abroad), were intended to associate the king in every act of worship there performed, both as earthly representative of the gods, and as participant in every favour they might vouchsafe to grant.[98]

There is more to be said for this view. Steles bearing the likeness of the king and divine symbols were set up not only in settled areas; at times they were founded by sea shores or engraved in rock on far-off mountain passes. Olmstead himself thought that the choice of inaccessible sites may have been prompted by a desire "to avoid mutilation at the hands of enemies."[99] The Assyrian term *ṣalmu* does not distinguish between upright steles and carved reliefs.[100] It is

[95] Unger, in RLA, 1, 73f., *s.v.* "Altar," listed examples of peaked "Strassenaltäre" brought to light in Babylon. Cf. *ibid.*, plate 11c. The excavation reports, however, were more modest in their interpretation of these "enigmatic" brick structures. A few were best taken as "pedestals;" others were reconstructed after altar patterns depicted on Assyrian wall reliefs. All lacked cultic contexts. See O. Reuther, *Die Innenstadt von Babylon,* WVDOG 47 (1926) 70ff.

[96] Galling, *Altar*, p. 44. Recent excavation at Khorsabad uncovered fourteen "round-topped altars," similar to the Ashurnasirpal altar which, according to their inscriptions, were dedicated by Sargon II to the Sibitti gods. See Fuad Safar, "The Temple of Sibitti at Khorsabad," *Sumer* 13 (1957), 219-221. On the function of these altars, see our remarks below, p. 76 n. 53.

[97] Cf. the remarks of S. Page, *Iraq* 30 (1968), 139 n. 1, and D. Oates, p. 125.

[98] C. J. Gadd, *The Assyrian Sculptures* (London: British Museum, 1934), p. 16; quoted in full by Frankfort, *Cylinder Seals* (reprint London: Gregg Press, 1965), p. 196. See n. 104 below.

[99] Olmstead, *Assyria*, p. 314, following L. W. King, PSBA 35 (1913), 66ff.

[100] Landsberger, *Bischof*, p. 52 n. 92, questions whether the *ṣalmu* of the king set up in temples were all relief in form. Some, he considers, to have been statues (life-size and/or miniature), but notes that a full investigation is still needed. See, provisionally, the classification of *ṣalmu* by E. D. Van Buren, "The *ṣalmê* in Mesopotamian Art and Religion," Or 10 (1941), 65-92; and CAD Ṣ, *s.v. ṣalmu.*

this latter type of *ṣalmu* which is being fashioned in the Balawat door engraving (ANEP 364). The upper register portrays a sacrifice to the gods being prepared to celebrate a victory, while in the lower register a relief of the king is being carved on the hillside at the headwaters of the Tigris.[101] Or, consider the transmaritime Cyprus stele commissioned by Sargon to mark the recognition of Assyrian suzerainty by the island's seven kings.[102] Active worship of such distant monuments and reliefs would have been a near impossibility. At most, only an occasional passerby or caravan would chance upon them, with no one in authority present to demand homage to them.

To be sure, the presence of a stele in the temple of a conquered city might have endowed it in time with heightened significance. A procedure by which steles were sanctified has been suggested by Ungnad:

> The priesthood ascribed to the image of the king, placed on the same stage as the gods or divine images, the ability to give "orders." In agreement with this is the custom, evidenced in our documents (i.e., from Guzana), that contracts were concluded in front of the image of the king.[103]

This conception was no doubt fostered by the presence on the stele of divine symbols, before which the king was shown making obeisance.[104] Finally, this

[101] Note the verbal description recorded by Shalmaneser: *ina rēš ēni ša Idiglat (u) Purattu allik ṣalam šarrūtīya ina kāpīšina ulziz* (Layard, *Inscriptions in the Cuneiform Character from Assyrian Monuments* [London, 1851], 92.92), "I marched to the sources of the Tigris and the Euphrates, and set my royal relief on their cliffs" (following AHw 445, *kāpu*; CAD Ṣ 83 renders *kappu* "banks").

[102] The latest publication of the cuneiform text is VAS 1, 71. A partial translation is given in ANET, p. 284. The discovery of the stele at Larnaka, in the rubble of a late building, points to its having been moved from the original location. See, Eb. Schrader, *AAWB* 1881, VI, pp. 4-7.

[103] Ungnad, AfO Beiheft 6, p. 58 n. 21.

[104] Cf. Streck, VAB 7, p. 270, IV, 1-3 — an Ashurbanipal text:

ina ūmēšuma ušēpišma narā šiṭir šumīya ṣalam ilāni rabûti bēlēya ēsiqa ṣīruššu šarrūtīya musappû ilūtīšun maḫaršun ulziz	At that time, I had a stele made, with an inscription bearing my name. I engraved the image of the great gods, my lords, upon it and my royal image standing in front of them, imploring their divinity.

Cf. OIP 2, 84.55; Borger, *Asarhaddon*, § 57, rev. 3-4.

An alternate suggestion should also be considered. If the *ṣalmu* in question is a statue of the king, rather than a royal stele (cf. above, n. 100), then the sanctification of the *ṣalmu* would be no different from the sanctification of other "power-charged objects" hallowed in Mesopotamian religion. According to Henri Frankfort, royal statues "placed before the god, perpetually recalled the donor to him. Hence, being effective, it had power. Since it did not decay, it was immortal. In both respects it partook of divinity. Power, however, means life; and life requires sustenance. Hence the statue received regular offerings of food and drink so that it would maintain its friendly service." But in no way do these circumstances prove that the kings were worshipped as gods. See

documentary evidence cited by Ungnad from the Guzana province is enough to undermine Tadmor's suggestion that only nonannexed vassal territories were forced to practice the royal cult.

In sum, we note that steles were placed throughout the Assyrian realm, as well as exported to vassal territories. They served to mark the farthest reaches of Assyrian influence and reminded all onlookers of the political loyalties expected of them. No textual statements are available which tell of demands for their worship or describe ritual instituted upon their erection. Within Assyria and its provinces the steles did take on a quasi-religious significance. But, again, this is far from deification or imposition of a cult of the king. The concluding lines of Sargon's Cyprus stele favor this interpretation. The words of this formulaic text, directing future rededication of the stele, are not wholly unique; they do, however, set forth the stele's unmistakable purpose—glorification of the gods, to whom all honor was due:

[*ina ar*]*kat ūmi rubu arkū*	In the future, when a later prince comes
[*musarā*]*ya līmurma liltasi*	upon my [inscription], let him read it.
[. . .] *ilāni rabūti litta''idma*	Let him praise the [. . .] of the great gods.
[*šamni*] *lipšuš niqā liqqi*[105]	Let him anoint it, and offer a sacrifice.

Conclusions

Our re-examination of Assyrian imperial organization finds that we must reject conventional statements which view "the whole organization centered around the worship of Ashur, the deified state and the reigning king[106] fanatically imposing active worship of Assyrian gods upon defeated populations.[107] Assyria distinguished between territories annexed as provinces directly under her control and vassal lands under native rule. The latter were free of any cultic obligations toward their master. Only within annexed provinces was the cult of Ashur and the great gods seemingly required, inasmuch as their residents were counted as Assyrian citizens. But considering the inconclusiveness of Assyrian historical sources, we hesitate to specify those rituals imposed upon provincials beyond the rendering of taxes to palace and temple; the only sure sign of an

Frankfort's full discussion in *Kingship and the Gods* (Chicago: University of Chicago Press, 1948), pp. 295-312.

[105] VAS 1, rev. 59-61. At the end, CAD Ṣ, 83 reads "(to it)." But even if the sacrifices were offered "to the stele" (an unexampled notion), they seem clearly directed to the gods whose valor is praised, not to the king. Note that on the Sargon stele from Asharné (RA 30 [1933], 55), the concluding formula, similar to the one we have quoted, continues: [*ni*]*qā liqqi* ᵈ*Aššur*. . . Thureau-Dangin's suggested rendition was: "qu'il offre un sa[crifice]: Assur [exancera sa prière.]" Cf. the Sennacherib inscriptions, OIP 2, 147.35 and 148.26, which read: ᵈ*Aššur* (*u* ᵈ*Ištar*) *ikribīšu išemmi.*

[106] A. T. Olmstead, "Oriental Imperialism," American Historical Review 23 (1917-18), 758.

[107] So, Sidney Smith, CAH 3, p. 91.

Assyrian cult in the provinces is the oft-mentioned installation of "Ashur's weapon."

In the final analysis, Landsberger's suspicion may prove correct: Assyria "never forced conquered peoples to revere Ashur," but remained content to show Ashur's superiority to their own gods.[108]

[108] Landsberger, *City Invincible*, p. 177.

FIG. 1 Assyrian Military Camp

(See page 53)

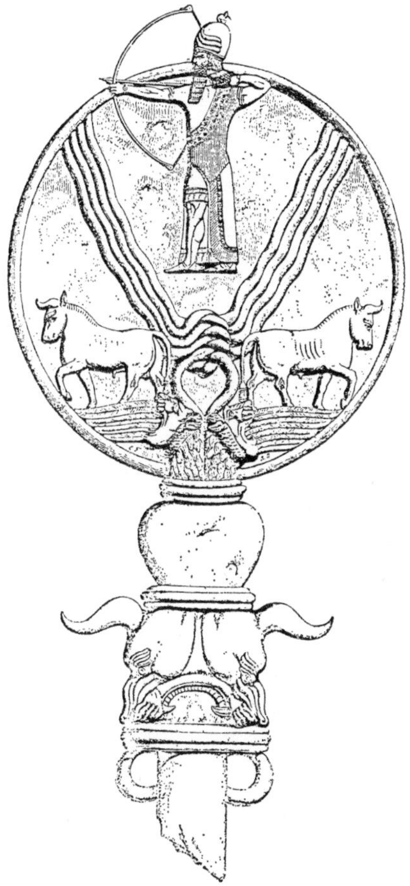

FIG. 2 "Ashur's weapon"

(See page 53)

FIG. 3 Stele of Ashurnasirpal and altar at Calaḫ

(See page 57)

4. JUDAH IN THE ORBIT OF ASSYRIA

HAVING established that Assyrian administrative policies distinguished between provincial and vassal territories, we are now prepared to re-examine the nature and source of those religious innovations within Judah and Israel often seen as impositions of Assyrian imperialism. Inasmuch as political status within the empire determined the degree of subserviance to the Assyrian master, we begin by tracing Judah's political history as currently reconstructable from biblical and Assyrian sources.

Judah — an Autonomous Vassal State

Throughout the entire century of Assyrian domination of Syria-Palestine (*ca.* 740-640 B.C.E.), Judah succeeded in retaining its nominal independence by consistently submitting to the political will of Assyria. It was never annexed to the empire, and so was spared the disastrous fate of northern Israel.

As early as 738, following his defeat at the head of the twelve-state Syrian coalition, Azaryahu of Judah recognized Assyrian suzerainty.[1] His grandson, Ahaz, later undertook tribute payments as vassal of Tiglath-pileser III, frightened, it seems, by the immediate presence of Assyrian forces engaged in their first Philistian campaign (734).[2] Despite direct military pressure to join the "Syro-

[1] Tadmor, "Azriyau of Yaudi," SH 8 (1961), 270f., suspects that the rout of Judah's armies probably ended with the payment of a separate war indemnity, thus explaining the absence of Judah from the list of tributary states in the Tiglath-pileser III annals.

[2] See M. Noth, *History*, pp. 258-59; Cf. Tadmor, "Azriyau," p. 265, and E. R. Thiele, *The Mysterious Numbers of the Hebrew Kings* (2nd ed.; Grand Rapids: Eerdmans, 1964), p. 130. Judah's weak military position, as evidenced by the attacks of Philistines and Edomites (cf. 2 Chr 28.16-18; 2 Kgs 16.6 [read according to the text as emended by Montgomery, *Kings*, pp. 458 and 462]), accounts for the ready acceptance by Ahaz of Assyrian authority. Cf. Tadmor, "Campaigns," pp. 263f. The letter ND. 2773 (=Saggs, *Iraq* 17 [1955], 131-33 and 151f.) may describe this period of disturbance in Trans-Jordan (?) prior to the Assyrian arrival. See the discussion of Hallo, Bib Arch *Reader* 2, p. 172; and B. Mazar, IEJ 7 (1957), 237f.

Just how close to Judah Assyria moved is shown by the Nimrud relief depicting the capture of Gezer, taken by Tiglath-pileser "to secure his flank while he moved south into Philistia." See H. D. Lance, BibArch 30 (1967), 44; cf. Hallo, BibArch *Reader* 2, p. 172; Kallai, VT 8 (1958), 153 n. 3; and the objections of W. F. Albright, BASOR 92 (1943), 17 n. 6. Tadmor, BibArch 29 (1966), 89, would date this event to the close of the 733/32 B.C.E. campaigns. The most recent publication of the Gezer relief is in Barnett and Falkner, *Sculptures of Tiglath-Pileser III*, pl. LXII, and p. 24.

Ephramite" League in rebellion,[3] Ahaz remained loyal to Assyria.[4] In 732 he personally greeted the victorious Tiglath-pileser III after the Assyrian conquest of Damascus.[5]

This posture of submissiveness continued into the reign of the succeeding king, Hezekiah; the results of the summary treatment of Samaria at the hands of Sargon (720 B.C.E.) were apparently not lost on Jerusalem.[6] But by 712 Hezekiah became involved in rebellion against Sargon at the side of Ashdod. After the loss of the border fortress, Azekah, "Judah averted by some means the central Assyrian attack,"[7] resuming its vassal status.[8] A letter recently recovered at Nimrud notes the receipt of horses as part of the tribute from the subdued principals in this rebellion.[9]

Upon the death of Sargon, Hezekiah organized the southern Palestinian states in further revolt, occasioning a most serious threat to Judah's territorial integrity. In a single campaign (701 B.C.E.) Sennacherib stripped Judah of "46 walled cities and countless small towns in their environs"[10] to force its complete surrender. Apparently willing to accede to the continued autonomy of vassal Judah, Assyria withdrew.[11] The lost cities were annexed to Philistia,[12] and

[3] See 2 Kgs 16.5; Isa 7.1, 5-6. On the basis of ND. 4301 + 4305 (=*Iraq* 18 [1956], pl. XXII), rev. 5′, it seems that Hiram of Tyre joined with Rezin and Pekah in this anti-Assyrian alliance. Cf. Tadmor, "Azriyau," pp. 264f. n. *g*.

[4] See 2 Kgs 16.7-9. The Ahaz declaration: "I am your vassal, your son" disassociated Judah from the rebel cause, and reminded Assyria of its obligation to protect loyal vassals (cf. above, p. 44). On the formula of submission, see Loewenstamm, *Lĕšonénu* 34 (1969), 148.

[5] 2 Kgs 16:10. The mention of Ahaz (*Iauḫazi*) among Assyria's vassals in the building inscription II R 67 (= Rost, *Tigl. III*, pp. 54ff.; ANET 282) is associated by Noth (*History*, p. 261) with the events of 732 B.C.E., by Tadmor ("Campaigns," p. 264) with those of 734 B.C.E. Tadmor's dating is to be preferred. The absence of Samaria, along with the continued reference to Mitinti of Ashkelon, would indeed be peculiar in a list prepared after the 732 B.C.E. victories.

[6] See Nimrud Inscription (= Winckler, *Sargon*, 168.8, ***mušakniš māt Iaudi ša ašaršu rūqu***, "(He, Sargon,) who subjugates far-off Judah." This inscription is dated *ca.* 720 B.C.E. Cf. comment by Tadmor, *JCS* 12 (1958), 38 n. 146.

[7] Tadmor, JCS 12, 83. See his full discussion of the Azekah battle, pp. 80-84. B. Oded holds that Azekah belonged to Ashdod (not Judah) in 712 B.C.E., since it had been occupied during the Philistine penetration reported in 2 Chr 28.18. See *Sefer Breslavi* (Jerusalem: Kiryat Sefer, 1970), 84 n. 19. Resolution of this geographical issue was earlier offered by Kallai, *The Tribes of Israel* [Hebrew] (Jerusalem: Mosad Bialik, 1967), 314-16.

[8] See Nineveh Prism A (= Winckler, *Sargon*, 188) 29-30 and comments by Tadmor, JCS 12, pp. 79ff.

[9] Text ND. 2765 is presented in full in Appendix II.

[10] Cf. 2 Kgs 18.7-8, 13; OIP 2, 32.18ff.

[11] Brevard Childs' monograph, *Isaiah and the Assyrian Crisis* (SBT 3, 1967), reviews the vast literature which has engulfed historical study of Sennacherib's 701 B.C.E. campaign to Judah (cf. pp. 11-19 and bibliographic citations) and presents a fresh form-critical analysis of the several biblical witnesses.

[12] The recent suggestion by M. Eilat ("On the Political Status of Judah after Sen-

Jerusalem alone was left to pay the oppressive war indemnity and the increased annual tribute.[13] A tax record from Nineveh reflects the impoverished conditions which must have prevailed for the next decades: Moab and Ammon delivered sums greater than the "ten minas of silver from the inhabitants of Judah."[14]

Manasseh, son of Hezekiah, ruled over the diminutive Judahite state for a lengthy fifty-five years. Throughout, he remained a loyal subject of Assyria, except for the short and questionable interval of his incarceration. 2 Chr 33.11-13 tells of the capture of Manasseh and his forced appearance before an Assyrian monarch in Babylon.[15] Had the incident been reported in Assyrian annals, it

nacherib's Conquest of Lachish" [Hebrew], *Yᵉdiot* 31 [1967], 140-56) that "an Assyrian governor and garrison" were stationed at Lachish to keep watch over affairs in southern Palestine is untenable. As proof, Eilat cites ABL 218, which mentions a Philistine regiment located at URU *lu-qa-še*. This otherwise unknown town cannot be identified with biblical Lachish, which appears in Assyrian transcription as *la-ki-su* (OIP 2, 156.XXV, 3; cf. Amarna *la-ki-si/ši/ša* - VAB 2, 287, 288, 328, 329 and 335). Besides, the Sennacherib annals clearly state that captured Judahite territory was parcelled out between Ashod, Eqron, Gaza, and Ashkelon (OIP 2, 33.33-34; 70.29). A recollection of this expropriation was found in Ezek 16.26-27, by O. Eissfeldt. See "Ezechiel als Zeuge für Sanheribs Eingriff in Palästina," PJB 27 (1931), 58-66.

Likewise, the presence at Lachish of a large public building patterned on Assyrian blueprints in and of itself proves little concerning the political organization of the city (Aharoni, *Yᵉdiot* 31 [1967], 80-91; quoted by Eilat, *Yᵉdiot* 31, p. 145). Cf. A. Alt, "Die Territorialgeschichtliche Bedeutung von Sanheribs Eingriff in Palästina, in *Kleine Schriften* [= KS] *zur Geschichte des Volkes Israel* 2 (München: C. H. Beck, 1953), pp. 245-58. On incorporation of native regiments into the Assyrian army, specifically with reference to Lachish, see R. D. Barnett, "The Siege of Lachish," *IEJ* 8 (1958), 161-64.

[13] Cf. 2 Kgs 18.14-16; OIP 2, 33.35-49.

[14] ABL 624. Translation of the text is given in ANET, p. 301. See discussions by R. H. Pfeiffer, JBL 47 (1928), 185-86, and Wm. Martin, *Tribut*, pp. 49-50.

[15] The original skepticism concerning the historicity of the Chronicles' account of Manasseh's imprisonment has now all but been forgotten. Wellhausen considered the verses an invention of the Chronicler, so that Manasseh "does not escape punishment, while on the other hand the length of his reign (55 years) is nevertheless explained" (*Prolegomena*, p. 207). The selfsame evaluation had been advanced earlier by K. H. Graf, "Die Gefangenschaft und Bekehrung Manasse's, 2 Chr. 33," ThStKr 32 (1859), 467-94. Later commentators were less harsh in their judgment: they regarded only the framework story of Manasseh's repentance as fictional; the capture, historical (e.g., Curtis, *Chronicles* [ICC, 1910], p. 498; Myers, *Chronicles* [AB, 1965], p. 199).

What has been left unexplained by these later writers is the absence from Kings of the historical "fact" of Manasseh's revolt and capture. We assume that the editor of Kings omitted from his work any event which might be interpreted as punishment, if only in some small way, of that king blamed for the loss of the kingdom (see 2 Kgs 23.26). Note that mention of Manasseh's building activities at Jerusalem was similarly overlooked (cf. 2 Chr 33.14). For the Chronicler, however, the story of Manasseh's capture confirmed a basic theological premise: each individual was adjudged during his own lifetime. Besides, the Chronicler did not make Manasseh out to be the sole cause of Judah's downfall, as had the editor of Kings before him (cf. 2 Kgs 24.3; 2 Chr 33.17, 23; 36.14-15). Cf. observations of E. L. Ehrlich, "Der Aufenthalt des Königs Manasse in Babylon," TZ 21 (1965), 285f.

would have indicated that he had been suspected of active rebellion. But the annals only mention Manasseh as a loyal vassal. He, "Manasseh, king of the city of Judah" (*Menasī šar āl Iaudi*), was among the twenty-two western kings summoned to the court of Esarhaddon to deliver materials for the reconstruction of the royal storehouse at Nineveh.[16] With minor variations in their ranks, these same rulers presented gifts to Ashurbanipal, who then proceeded with their help to conquer Egypt.[17] Neither Assyrian report can be connected with the Chronicles passage, lacking, as they do, any indication of arrest.[18]

Ever since E. Schrader's original suggestion,[19] most writers have found the appropriate occasion for Manasseh's revolt to be the civil war led by Shamash-shum-ukin against Ashurbanipal. The uprising in Babylon reportedly stirred revolt in other territories. With the main insurrection in hand by 648 B.C.E., Ashurbanipal moved to make reprisals as far west as Edom and Moab,[20] at which time he may have brought Manasseh into line "for possible involvement on the side of Babylon."[21]

[16] Borger, *Asarhaddon*, § 27, ep. 21, 55. Esarhaddon's Nineveh inscriptions do not specify the year of Manasseh's tribute. Olmstead (*Assyria*, p. 368) supposed that the building projects were undertaken by Esarhaddon "at the beginning of his reign;" while Tadmor (En. Miq. 4, cols. 259. n. 9) associates the incident with the events of 677 B.C.E.; *viz.*, the defeat of Sidon and the building of Kar-Esarhaddon. See Borger, *Asarhaddon* § 27, ep. 5, 80-81. Cf. also, Tadmor, BibArch 29 (1966), 98.

[17] Asb. C.I.24-47. Only the "C" edition of the Ashurbanipal annals, compiled in *ca.* 647 B.C.E., saw fit to include by name the full list of 22 kings in its description of the events of 668/67 B.C.E.; while the contemporaneous accounts of the Egyptian campaign simply state that kings from "Trans-Euphrates" countries (*šarrāni eber nāri*; on *eber nāri*, see CAD E, 8; AHw 181) came to Assyria's aid (cf. K. 228 + [= Streck, VAB 7, pp. 158ff.], obv. 25; Asb. E.II.10). The "C" listing would be of little historical value were we to assume that it was compiled by the "C" editors, reflecting conditions in their own days; for it is unlikely that 20 out of 22 kings, who ruled in the days of Esarhaddon (*ca.* 676 B.C.E.), still ruled in 647 B.C.E. Nor would it be of value if the list was indiscriminately borrowed from the Esarhaddon inscriptions. A source, no longer extant, which listed western monarchs in 668/67 B.C.E., must have been available to the "C" editors, for in two cases the Esarhaddon list shows evidence of having been up-dated. Cf. Borger, *Asarhaddon*, § 27, ep. 21, 60-62; Asb. C.I.32-34 — under kings of Arwad and Bīt-Ammon.

[18] Cf. the contrary view of John Gray, *Kings*², pp. 709f. According to his novel interpretation, the western kings "were either in command of units of their own nationals" in service to the Assyrian overlord "or were hostages for the loyalty of their subjects in the Assyrian rear." Neither suggestion, however, finds support in any Assyrian text. Kurt Galling (*Chronik* [ATD, 1954], p. 168) is able to synchronize 2 Chr 33 with the Esarhaddon reference only by assuming the present biblical account has been "re-written" by the Chronicler.

[19] Schrader, *Die Keilinschriften und das Alte Testament* [=KAT²] (2nd ed; Giessen: J. Ricker, 1883), pp. 366-72.

[20] Asb. Rm.VII.108-116.

[21] W. F. Albright, *The Biblical Period from Abraham to Ezra* (New York: Harper Torchbooks, 1963), p. 79; Bright, *History*, p. 292; Hallo, BibArch *Reader* 2, p. 185 n. 153; MacLean, IDB 3, 254-55; Myers, *Chronicles*, pp. 189f.; Landersdorfer, *Könige* (HS, 1927), p. 224. Cf. also, early bibliography in Streck, VAB 7, pp. ccxcivf., and ccclxiii.

Serious objection to this reconstruction must be raised. Ashurbanipal's campaign to the west was concerned with maintaining control over the major Arabian trade routes. Action was, therefore, limited to territories east of the Jordan River. Moreover, the list of defeated towns and districts in the Ashurbanipal cylinder Rm.VII.108-116 shows neither geographical nor chronological order, suggesting that it is a late compilation of sporadic local army reports.[22] Judah was in no way implicated, being situated as she was, outside the area of concern.

Consequently, the alternate suggestion put forward by Hans Hirschberg, basing himself upon G. Smith, merits closer attention.[23] He noted that Esarhaddon's campaign to Egypt in 671 included punitive actions against cities along the Phoenician coast that had allied themselves with the Egyptian rebel, Tarqu. Tyre and Ashkelon are known to have come under serious attack. In addition, one very fragmentary inscription, in summary fashion, seems to record the pacification of all twenty-two western monarchs on this same occasion.[24] These circumstances account well not only for the "capture" of Manasseh, who had presumably sided with the anti-Assyrian coalition, but provide the background for the additional settlement of refugees in the Samaria province reported in Ezra 4.2.[25]

We can only imagine the terms under which Esarhaddon reinstalled Manasseh on the throne; but if similar reports from the annals are any indication, a renewed pledge of loyalty and increased tribute headed the list.[26] Not even at this junc-

[22] One of the clearest indications of the false historical impression created by the Asb. Rassam annal account — which is itself the result of intense editorial reworking — is its inclusion of Moab among the punished. The earlier "B" edition preserves another report of the initial battles, in which Kamashalta, king of Moab (read: *māt Ma-'a-bi* [!] with *Iraq* 7 [1940], 99, 37) subdued the marauding Qedar tribes, sending prisoners to Nineveh (Asb. B.VIII.43ff.). An early attempt to date the several Arabian campaigns is given by Streck, VAB 7, pp. cclxxxiiiff. See now, Eph'al, *Nomads*, pp. 103-19.

[23] Hirschberg, *Studien zur Geschichte Esarhaddons*, pp. 62-66; George Smith, *The Assyrian Eponym Canon* (London, [1875], p. 169.) Cf. also, Olmstead, *Assyria*, pp. 380-84; and *idem, Palestine-Syria*, p. 486.

[24] See Borger, *Asarhaddon*, § 67, 30-35, and Weidner, OLZ 27 (1924), 647f.

[25] That Samaria received new settlers need not necessarily mean that it had participated in revolt nor even suffered deportation itself. The very act of re-settlement must have had a disciplinary effect upon the residents of the reception center. E.g., Ashurbanipal's removal of Kirbitians to Egypt was not followed by transfers from the South (Asb. E.IV.1-10; now restored by *Iraq* 30 [1968], BM 134481 iii; 128305 ii). Cf. discussions of Samaria resettlements cited below, p. 101 n. 23. On the suggested co-ordination of Ezra 4.2 with the gloss in Isa 7.8, see G. B. Gray, *Isaiah* (ICC, 1912), pp. 119f.

[26] Cf. Asb. Rm.II.8-19, cited regularly in the commentaries ever since Schrader's original work (see n. 19). Note, as well, Sargon's pardon of Ullusunu (Lie, *Sargon*, 87-89) and the fear expressed by Babylon's residents during their revolt against Ashurbanipal: *enna aššа nittekiruš ana biltini itarra*, "Now because we have rebelled against him, it will be charged against us (lit. "returned/added to our burdens")," (ABL 301, rev. 1-5).

ture is there any ground for supposing a change in Judah's autonomous vassal status.[27]

Manasseh remained constrained for the next quarter century. But by the close of his reign Assyria seems to have permitted the building of Jerusalem's outer defenses and the restationing of Judahite forces in the countryside, perhaps to counter the increasingly hostile position of Pssametichus I in Egypt.[28]

Manasseh's son, Amon, ruled for but two short years (642-640 B.C.E.), assassinated by a court plot of unknown motivation. The "people of the land" promptly executed the conspirators and installed the minor Josiah, thus upholding the Davidic line of succession (2 Kgs 21.19-26).[29]

Current opinion favors viewing this episode as an attempt at revolt against Ashurbanipal by anti-Assyrian elements, with the "people of the land" representing "those forces in Judah who wished to prevent a military encounter with Assyria."[30] But the facts might be construed otherwise. The last record of Assyrian intervention in the affairs of southern Palestine dates to 643 B.C.E.[31]

[27] Y. Aharoni presumes that following the Manasseh revolt the royal store-cities, organized by Hezekiah to co-ordinate administrative efforts within Judah (cf. 2 Chr 32.27-29), were "finally disbanded by the Assyrian authorities who may have considered it a dangerous source of power" (*The Land of the Bible: A Historical Geography* [Philadelphia: Westminster Press, 1967], p. 346). This suggestion is based upon Aharoni's analysis of the royal (*lmlk*) stamp seals from seventh century B.C.E. Judahite sites. But his view would have us suppose the survival of Hezekiah's districting after the dismemberment of Judah which followed the 701 B.C.E. defeat (see above, p. 66). Further epigraphical and archaeological criticism of Aharoni's *lmlk* thesis can be found in P. W. Lapp. "Late Royal Seals from Judah," BASOR 158 (1960), 11-22; F. M. Cross, "Judean Stamps," EI 9 (1969), 20-23; and H. D. Lance, "The Royal Stamps and the Kingdom of Josiah," HTR 64 (1971), 315-22.

[28] 2 Chr 33.14. Cf. Sellin, *Geschichte des israelitisch-jüdische Volkes* 1 (Leipzig: Quelle and Meyer, 1924), p. 281; followed by W. Rudolph, *Chronikbücher* (HAT, 1955), p. 317; and Myers, *Chronicles*, p. 199. DeVaux noted that the "defense work undertaken at Jerusalem by Ezechia (2 Chr 32.5; cf. Isa 22.9-11) was continued by Manasseh" (*Ancient Israel* [New York: McGraw-Hill, 1961], p. 230). See the archaeological evidence now collected by E. Vogt, "Das Wachstum des alten Stadtgebietes von Jerusalem," *Biblica* 48 (1967), 338-43. Cf. below, n. 152.

[29] The "people of the land" as "a fairly loosely constituted power group . . . championing . . . the house of David" is discussed by S. Talmon, "The Judaean 'Am Ha'aretz in Historical Perspective," *Proceedings of the Fourth World Congress of Jewish Studies* 1 (Jerusalem, 1967), pp. 71-76. See also, H. Tadmor, JWH 11 (1968), 65-68.

[30] So, A. Malamat, "The Historical Background of the Assassination of Amon, King of Judah," IEJ 3 (1953), 27 (= *Tarbiz* 21 [1951], 126); followed by Bright, *History*, pp. 294f.; Myers, *Chronicles*, p. 200; cf. Noth, *History*, p. 272 (independent of Malamat ?).

[31] Malamat reconstructed a Palestine-wide revolt against Assyria in 640 B.C. by synchronizing Amon's assassination with the revolts of Tyre and Acre reported in Asb Rm. IX. 115-128, assuming "these events took place during the great revolt of Elam between the years 641-639 B.C.E." ("Assassination," 27 n. 3; following Streck's dating, VAB 7, p. ccclxi). But the Rassam cylinder edition of the annals must now be dated to 643 B.C.E. (cf. Tadmor, *The Proceedings of the Twenty-fifth International Convention of Orientalists* 1 [Moscow, 1962], p. 240), thus upsetting any possible coincidence.

Nomadic invasions, perhaps Scythian, kept Assyrian military forces occupied on the northern reaches of the empire, it now seems, as early as 640.[32] Consequently, at the time of Amon's assassination, fear of Assyrian reprisal would have been a minimal factor in Judahite politics.

Moreover, the political assertiveness of the "people of the land" had anything but restraining effects. As representatives of traditional Judahite values,[33] the "people of the land" must have planned and nurtured Josiah's regency, which ended in the overthrow of Judah's foreign alignments and far-reaching cultic reforms. Assyrian non-intervention in this nationalistic activity suggests that Judah, as early as 640, had begun to free itself of vassal restraints, long before the final disintegration of the empire which set in with the death of Ashurbanipal in 627.[34]

Beginning in his twelfth year, little more than a century after the first appearance of Tiglath-pileser III in Palestine, Josiah extended Judah's jurisdictional authority into northern Israel — i.e., the Assyrian province of Samaria — a move which earlier would have signaled open rebellion against Assyria.[35] That he was able to proceed unhindered implies that Nineveh had lost all effective control over its Palestinian provinces.[36]

[32] New details on the "Scythian" troubles which developed for Assyria in the four years between 643-639 B.C.E. are now available in additional fragments of the "H" prism, dated 639 B.C.E., published by Millard, *Iraq* 29 (1967), 106-10. H. Cazelles, "Sophonie, Jérémie, et les Scythes en Palestine," RB 74 (1967), 24-44, would remove the earliest battles with the northerners to 655 B.C.E. See especially, p. 32 n. 31 (contra Tadmor, above, n. 31).

[33] Cf. Talmon, "Am Ha'aretz," p. 76.

[34] Joan Oates' study, "Assyrian Chronology, 631-612 B.C.," *Iraq* 27 (1965), 135-59, contains the latest review of the chronological uncertainties of the close of the NA era. Cf. Borger's differing solutions in WZKM 55 (1959), 63-76; *JCS* 19 (1965), 59-78.

[35] Cf. 2 Kgs 23.15-20; 2 Chr 34.1-7. J. Liver, En. Miq. 3, col. 420, found the inclusion in the Ezra census lists of returnees from north Israel evidence of Josianic expansion. But, cf. Aharoni, *The Land of the Bible*, pp. 356 and 362ff., and on Josiah, pp. 349ff. A new challenge to the theorists of a Josianic "empire" is now offered by H. D. Lance, *HTR* 64 (1971), 331f.: "If the [*lmlk*] stamps are Josianic in date, then the total absence of the stamps in the north can only mean that in the time of Josiah *not even trade was carried on with the territory of the former northern kingdom*" (italics *sic*). Lance correctly notes that the Biblical account lays claim to activity within north Israel only of a religious nature.

[36] It has become a commonplace among scholars to connect Josiah's cultic reforms with the wave of rebellion which swept the Assyrian empire after the death of Ashurbanipal (cf., e.g., Cross and Freedman, JNES 12 [1953], 57). But while Kings knows of revolts against Assyria and Babylonia by Hezekiah (2 Kgs 18.7 — among other pious acts !), Jehoiakim (2 Kgs 24.1), and Zedekiah (2 Kgs 24.20), no such act is credited Josiah. This absence may be due, not to an oversight on the part of the Kings editor, but to his accurate reflection of the by-then non-existent Assyrian control in Palestine. Cf. T. H. Robinson, *History*, p. 417.

According to W. F. Albright (*The Biblical Period*, p. 80), Josiah may have remained

The course of Assyria's century-long domination emerges clearly: Judah was permitted to retain its national sovereignty in return for loyal submission to Assyrian political will. One is impressed by Assyria's apparent reluctance and/or inability to expend efforts on incorporation of Jerusalem — implying, thereby, the city's insignificance for imperial goals. Accordingly, as an independent vassal state Judah suffered none of the religious impositions known to Assyrian provinces. The genesis of foreign innovations in the Judahite cult during the NA era, often seen as impositions of the Assyrian empire, must now be sought in other areas.

Foreign Cults in Judah

Modern historians may still find occasion to debate the sources of Judahite idolatries during the Neo-Assyrian age, but for the biblical author the source was quite clear. Ahaz "followed the ways of Israel's kings" (2 Kgs 16.3), and Manasseh "erected altars for Baal and made an Asherah, as Ahab king of Israel had done" (2 Kgs 21.3).

This sin of "following the ways of Israel's kings" is not the usual Judahite royal sin reported in Kings, viz., continued worship at rural sanctuaries after the completion of the Jerusalem temple.[37] It cannot be identified with "the sin of Jeroboam, son of Nebat," Israel's first king, who broke away from the Jerusalem temple and the Davidic house. Ahaz and Manasseh were guilty of reverting to those pagan practices against which the Israelites had been forewarned prior to their entry into Canaan. Note that Manasseh paganized Judah by imitating the nations round about, in flagrant disregard for Mosaic law (cf. 2 Kgs 21.6, somewhat abbreviated from Deut 18.10-11).

This description of late Judahite idolatry as a reversion to Canaanite practice is not to be judged mere schematic and non-historical rhetoric, the product of Deuteronomistic historiography.[38] Only twice in Judah's early history, during the reigns of Solomon-Rehoboam (1 Kgs 11.2ff.; 14.24) and Jehoram (2 Kgs 8.18) are Canaanite cults reported to have flourished. Moreover, certain of the pagan cults embraced by Ahaz and Manasseh were decidedly new. Ahaz was the first to "pass his son through fire" (2 Kgs 16.3). Manasseh, in addition to restoring Baal and Asherah, introduced the worship of the "heavenly host" into the Jerusalem temple (2 Kgs 21.3; cf. 23.12). Even if we assume that the

a "nominal vassal of the Assyrians," assuming the obligations of caretaker of north-Palestinian provinces during this period of upheaval (cf. Myers, *Chronicles*, p. 205).

Still to be considered by historians is the extent of Egyptian interest in Syrian affairs at this juncture. Might the Egyptian military assistance to Assyria in 616 B.C.E. have been proceeded by a ceding of Assyrian rights in Syria-Palestine? See provisionally, S. Smirin, *Josiah and His Age*, 21-22; Freedy and Redford, JAOS 90 (1970) 477f.; and J. Milgrom, Beth Mikra 44 (1971) 25, esp. n. 13.

[37] E.g. 1 Kgs 15.14; 22.44; 2 Kgs 12.4; 14.4; 15.4, 35.

[38] Such is the assessment which emerges from M. Noth's discussion in *Überlieferungsgeschichtliche Studien* (Tübingen: Max Niemeyer, 1967), pp. 85f.

description of events from the reigns of Hezekiah through Josiah was "a matter of personal reminiscence and interest within the Deuteronomic circle"[39] — thus the ready availability of detailed items — no schema is discernible which will explain the sporadic reference to early monarchic idolatry.

It may be supposed, therefore, that the Kings historiographer did record historically accurate information as to the period of public inauguration of certain cults,[40] even though he viewed all foreign cults under the general rubic *Canaanite idolatry*. Properly, only those foreign cults which can be isolated as late intrusions are of significance in assessing the Assyrian influence upon Judahite religion during the eighth and seventh centuries B.C.E. Thus, the following inquiry focuses on three select pagan innovations: the altar reform of Ahaz, the cult of Molech, and the astral cults.

Altar Reform of Ahaz. — During a visit to Damascus to greet Tiglath-pileser III after the Assyrian conquest of that city (732 B.C.E.), Ahaz observed an altar whose design he sent back to Jerusalem. The priest Uriah had an altar built according to the imported model, ready for use by the time the king returned. The new altar replaced the old Solomonic bronze altar, which was set aside for use by the king in his own private worship.[41]

Opinion is divided as to the ground for this innovation. The statement of Martin Noth may be cited as typical of a majority of scholars.

> When king Ahaz of Judah surrendered to Tiglath-Pileser, he had to make room for the Assyrian religion in the official sanctuary in Jerusalem. An altar, . . . modelled no doubt on an Assyrian altar which stood in the new provincial capital of Damascus,

[39] J. Gray, *Kings*², p. 34.

[40] We cannot positively rule out the presence of popular, unofficial pagan cults throughout the monarchic period simply on the basis of the Kings report alone (as would Kaufmann, *Tolᵉdot* 3, pp. 220-23; 233-36). Kings, rarely, if ever, tells of popular practice, in its focus upon monarchic guilt. (On 1 Kgs 14.22-24; 2 Kgs 17.19, cf. commentaries *ad loc.*) The possibility must be considered that certain idolatries were known from an early date, but only later became a matter of concern to official YHWHism. See further comments below, p. 89 n. 133. On the historicity of the cultic notices in Kings in general, see A. Jepsen, *Die Quellen des Königsbuches* (Halle: Max Niemeyer Verlag, 1956), pp. 72-76.

[41] 2 Kgs 16.10-18. John Bright (*History*, p. 259, following W. F. Albright, ARI⁵, pp. 161f.) contends that the "time-honored" bronze altar "continued in ritual use as before (v. 15)." Bright's construing the text in this manner disregards the explicit statement in v. 15 that Ahaz ordered the regular offerings transferred to the new "large altar," leaving the old altar solely for his visitations (*lᵉbaqqēr* — cf. Ps 27.4).

According to some, the service at the bronze altar henceforth included "examination of the sacrifice for omens . . . the intrusion of the vast Babylonian system of omen-sacrifices" (Montgomery, *Kings*, p. 461; cf. also Gray, *Kings*², p. 637; Snaith, *Kings* [IB, 1954], p. 277; DeVaux, *Ancient Israel*, p. 410; and Ehrlich, *Mikrâ ki-Pheschutô* 2 [Berlin: M. Poppelauer, 1900], p. 368.) But this view can only be sustained through importing a meaning for the verb *lᵉbaqqēr* (v. 15) and a method of divination otherwise unattested for the reign of Ahaz or any other king.

> . . . [and] the official Assyrian religion had a place alongside the traditional worship of Yahweh in the state sanctuary in Jerusalem.[42]

According to Olmstead, the impositions included "a throne for the new divine king, . . . set up in the house where once Yahweh had reigned in power, and the royal entry . . . turned about by Ahaz from before the face of the statue of the Assyrian king".[43]

Other commentators suppose that the model for the altar was Syrian, its importation prompted by "aesthetic reasons, intending to enrich the ritual of the Jerusalem temple."[44] Šanda noted that the account as related in 2 Kings contains no criticism of Ahaz,[44a] apparently having found nothing wrong with

[42] Noth, *History*, p. 266. Cf. Bright, *History*, p. 259; Montgomery, *Kings*, pp. 459ff.; Gray, *Kings*², p. 635; IDB 1, 64-66, *s.v.* "Ahaz;" and the previous studies quoted by them.

[43] *Assyria*, p. 198. Cf. Olmstead's later comment, *Palestine-Syria*, p. 452, in which he was somewhat less decided: "A throne for the divine king was built in the temple and the outer royal entry was turned to the house of Yahweh from before the face of the king of Assyria, presumably represented in stele form."

Olmstead's suggestion seems to be based, in part, on the Septuagint reading of the obscure wording in 2 Kgs 16.17-18. There, Ahaz stripped the temple of certain furnishings and altered two of its architectural features: the *msk hšbt* — the "Sabbath canopy" (cf. Montgomery, *Kings*, p. 464; otherwise Gray, *Kings*², p. 635, n.ᵃ) or "dais" (*Jerusalem Bible*, cf. LXX) and the king's entranceway. All this was done *mippnē melek* ʾ*Aššūr*, i.e., "because of" (KHAT, ICC) /"at the instance of" (OTL)/"in deference to" (*Jerusalem Bible*) /or "before" (Olmstead) the king of Assyria.

There is no indication whatsoever that any further innovations beyond the new altar were made at this juncture. Had a royal stele of Tiglath-pileser been erected, as Olmstead thought, we should expect a notice of it. Moreover, there is no reason to think that the Assyrian king would have taken offense at the continued display of royal prerogatives in Judah (i.e., a special entranceway for Ahaz symbolizing his sovereignty, cf. Gray, *Kings*², p. 638). Often loyal vassal kings were treated with honor — evidently no offense to Assyria's rule. See TCL 3, 62-63, for Sargon's treatment of Ullusunu.

Only Hugo Winckler's observation does justice to the sense and structure of this entire section. Comparing 2 Kgs 16.7-9 + 17-18 with 2 Kgs 18.13-15 + 16, he noted the same editing, with concluding verses that tell of removing precious metals to pay a heavy Assyrian tribute (*Alttestamentliche Untersuchungen* [Leipzig: Pfeiffer, 1892], pp. 48f). Cf. the earlier remarks of O. Thenius, *Die Bücher der Könige* (*Kurzgefasstes exegetisches Handbuch zum Alten Testament*; Leipzig: Weidemann, 1849), p. 362.

The rich adornment of the Sabbath covering and the king's private entranceway were apparently removed (*hēsēb* = 2 Kgs 16.18; cf. 2 Sam 20.12), and, along with the bronze oxen (16.17), sent as gifts to the king of Assyria. Cf. A. Šanda *Die Bücher der Könige* (Münster in West.: Aschendorffsche Verlag, 1911), *ad loc.* Bull figurines were received as tribute by Ashurnasirpal, cf. AKA, p. 366, 66.

[44] Snaith, *Kings*, p. 275; DeVaux, *Ancient Israel*, pp. 410f.; and Landersdorfer, *Könige*, pp. 198f. Similarly, Thenius, *Könige*.

[44a] Šanda, *Könige* 2, p. 207. The neutrality of 2 Kgs 16.10-18 with respect to the Temple alterations is especially patent when we consider that Ahaz' encroachment upon the priestly prerogatives at the altar (2 Kgs 16.12) is noted without comment. Contrast the fate of Uzziah in 2 Chr 26.16-21. On the term *qārab* (ʿ*al*/ʾ*el*), "to encroach," see

the new altar.[45] The priest Uriah, a loyal Yahwist according to Isaiah's testimony (cf. Isa 8.2), is not said to have resisted the installation order.[46]

This second view finds support in the altar's subsequent history. 2 Kgs 16.15 is careful to note that the new altar served only a legitimate YHWH cult, unlike other idolatries practiced by Ahaz.[47] Accordingly, it survived the cultic reforms of both Hezekiah and Josiah, which purged Judah of foreign practices.[48] The Ahaz altar must have still been in place during Jerusalem's last days, for the prophet Ezekiel reports seeing the original bronze altar by the temple's northern gate, where it had been moved by Ahaz in making room for his Damascene import (cf. Ezek 9.2).[49]

That the altar was of Syrian, not Assyrian, provenance emerges most clearly from Kurt Galling's comparative typological study of Near Eastern altars. Holocaust altars were wholly unknown in Mesopotamia; table altars, set with the prepared rations of the divine repast (not unlike royal banquets),[50] were in regular use.[51] As Oppenheim explains; ancient Israelite concepts of "burning of the offered food" and the accompanying "blood consciousness" are not paralleled in Mesopotamia:

the exhaustive treatment by Jacob Milgrom, *Studies in Levitical Terminology* 1 (*Near Eastern Studies* 14; Berkeley: University of California Press, 1970), pp. 5-56.

Montgomery, *Kings*, pp. 459f., thought that the "objective non-moralizing narrative" was due to "the grandeur of the new altar (which) made greater popular impression than its contradiction to the native cult." Gray's suggestion, *Kings*², p. 631, to see in the "Deuteronomic introduction (vv. 3ff.)" condemning Ahaz sufficient reason for "the absence or supression of criticism of the king in vv. 10-18," is inadequate. For, at best, the editor's utilization of a non-critical account of the altar reform leaves the reader with mixed impressions of the king: Ahaz, the outright idolator, yet attends to the needs of the YHWH cult.

[45] Not so the editor of Kings. He must have quoted — verbatim? — this temple report to example Ahaz' apostasy, i.e., Ahaz dared modify traditional temple patterns.

[46] Snaith, *Kings*, p. 275.

[47] See the balanced remarks of R. J. Thompson, *Penitence and Sacrifice in Early Israel Outside the Levitical Law* (Leiden: Brill, 1963), pp. 132-34, on the ritual enjoined by the king.

Note the contrasting verbal forms of *qṭr* in 2 Kgs 16.4, 13. Non-Israelite censing is generally represented by *qiṭṭēr*, Israelite censing by *hiqṭīr* (cf. BDB, 882-83). On the use of *hiqṭīr* in Chronicles, see S. Japhet, VT 18 (1968), 350f.; and on the anamolous form in 1 Sam 2.16, see S. R. Driver, *Notes on the Hebrew Text and the Topography of the Books of Samuel* (Oxford: Clarendon Press, 1913), p. 31.

[48] 2 Kgs 18.4; 23.6, 11f. Kaufmann, *Tolᵉdot* 2, p. 234 n. 4, refers to 2 Kgs 23.12 as evidence of private pagan altars introduced by Ahaz after 732 B.C.E. Y. Yadin, as well, would connect this verse and the evidence of sun worship in vs. 11 with the "Dial of Ahaz" (2 Kgs 20.11), part of a "special structure with cultic character." See Yadin, EI 5 (1958), 92f. The altars destroyed by Josiah were located "on the roof of the upper-chamber of Ahaz," but there is no indication that Ahaz built them.

[49] See Cooke, *Ezekiel* (ICC, 1936), p. 105; and Fohrer, *Ezechiel* (HAT, 1955), p. 51.

[50] Cf. ANEP 451 with 624, 625, and 626.

[51] Galling, *Altar*, pp. 43, 44, and 54ff.

> Deep-seated differences between the West — represented best by the Old Testament — and Mesopotamia with regard to the concept of sacrifice . . . separates the two sacrificial rituals in the two cultures.[52]

These considerations alone should have been enough to discourage any suggestion that Assyria influenced Ahaz to introduce a new altar for Israelite worship.[53]

Most recently, Saggs took note of the sacrificial dissimilarities which existed between Israel and Assyria and argued that the new altar is to be traced to Phoenicia. It was introduced by Ahaz in an "attempt to strengthen links with Tyre, the chief port of Phoenicia," thus breaking through the ring of enemies which had landlocked Judah.[54] But this reconstruction of events is patently erroneous. It goes against the textual evidence which sets the altar in Damascus. Moreover, Judah's enemies in 733-732 B.C.E. included Tyre, a participant, along with Aram and Israel, in the revolt against Tiglath-pileser.[55]

Finally, Judah's political status in 732 speaks against the liklihood of Assyrian cult impositions. The trip of Ahaz to Damascus was not Judah's first act of submission as a vassal kingdom to Assyria. Azaryahu, the king's grandfather, had paid an indemnity to Tiglath-pileser III in 738, and Ahaz himself had delivered tribute to Tiglath-pileser in 734.[56] As noted above, vassalage did not

[52] Oppenheim, *Ancient Mesopotamia*, p. 192; cf. pp. 186-92 for fuller description of temple ritual. Also, BibArch *Reader* 1, pp. 161-65. The absence of bloody sacrifice in Mesopotamia is noted by Meissner, BuA 2, p. 84; Blome, *Die Opfermaterie in Babylonian und Israel* (Rome: Pontifical Biblical Institute, 1934), p. 172; and Oppenheim, *Ancient Mesopotamia*, p. 365 n. 18, who observes: "The references to blood collected in CAD sub *damu* show clearly that blood was of no importance in Mesopotamian cult or magic." See further D. J. McCarthy, "The Symbolism of Blood and Sacrifice," JBL 88 (1969) 166-76, and *idem*, JBL 92 (1973) 205-10.

[53] Attempts at relating Ezekiel's visionary altar projected for the rebuilt sanctuary (Ezek 43.13-17) to the Ahaz "Assyrian" altar should be likewise abandoned. The Assyrian altar mentioned in Cooke's *Ezekiel*, p. 468 (cf. Haran, En. Miq. 4, cols. 774f.; reproduced in ANEP, 576, 577) is in reality not an altar at all, but a *nēmedu*, "support," as the inscription it bears indicates. Upon such "sockets" or "pedestals" cult objects were often displayed (cf. Opitz, AfO 7 [1931], 83-90). The style and dimensions of the pedestals resemble those of more mundane "footstools," also termed *nēmedu*. A. Salonen, *Die Möbel des Alten Mesopotamien* (AASF B 127, 1963), pp. 144ff., generally renders "divan;" cf. AHw, 776.

"Round-topped altars" of the type represented in ANEP 580 may also have served *nēmedu*-functions. The antecella of Khorsabad's Sibitti temple was lined with no less than fourteen such "altars" (cf. above, p. 58), suggesting their use as cult socles (that is, if this site was not the temple storeroom). See Safar, *Sumer* 13 (1957), fig. 3 (Arabic section).

[54] H. W. F. Saggs, *Assyriology and the Study of the Old Testament* (Cardiff: University of Wales Press, 1969), pp. 19-22. Saggs did not deny the Assyrian practice of enforcing a vassal's recognition of the overlord's gods (p. 21 n. 2); rather in this instance, he was led to seek political motives outside the Assyrian sphere.

[55] See above, p. 66 n. 3.

[56] These chronological facts expose yet another incongruency in the usual reconstruction (cf. n. 42 above); no one bothers to explain why cult impositions began only in 732 B.C.E. and not at the start of Judah's vassalage some years earlier.

entail the introduction of Assyrian cults in place of or alongside native cults. The Ahaz altar, fashioned after Syrian models and located in the Jerusalem temple — itself styled after Phoenician prototypes[57] — must have been a voluntary adoption, part of a general pattern of cultural accommodation, the full dimensions of which will emerge below.

Cult of Molech. — One of the most vexing problems of late Judahite religion is the notorious cult of Molech. Due to the inconsistent biblical accounts of the cult, opinion is divided as to its nature and extent. It is well to begin, therefore, with an analysis of the separate legal, historical, and prophetic texts.

Legal texts are unequivocal in their descriptions of the prohibited cult. The priestly "Holiness Code" outlaws "dedicating" (*nātan*) and "transferring" (*he^{ce}bīr*)[58] offspring to the god Molech, without indications of the procedure (Lev 18.21; 20.1-5). The context implies that the Molech rite was sexually and/or magically offensive. Deuteronomic law, too, employing analogous terms, prohibits the "transfer by fire/passing through fire"[59] of sons or daughters (no god is mentioned) — this in a list of traditional Canaanite divinatory practices (Deut 18.10).[60]

The terms of Deut 12.31, enjoining Israel from "burning (*śārap*) their sons and their daughters in fire" in service of YHWH as do the Canaanite nations in service of their gods, are entirely different. Not only is Molech absent, but the usage of *śārap* contrasts with priestly technical terminology, which never uses that verb in sacrificial contexts. In priestly texts, *śārap* is always extra-ritual; it refers to disposal of refuse and invariably takes place outside the camp.[61] These verbal distinctions, coupled with contextual considerations, point to two separate rituals identifiable within legal literature: (1) a divinatory fire cult of Molech that did not involve child sacrifice, and (2) a common Canaanite cult of child sacrifice.

Historical accounts record similar distinctions. Of both kings Ahaz and Manasseh it is said: "He passed his son through fire" (2 Kgs 16.3; 21.6). An end to this royal observance of Molech ritual came with the Josianic reforms; according to 2 Kgs 23.10, the Molech cult site — Tophet[62] — in the ben-Hinnom

[57] See G. E. Wright, *Biblical Archaeology* (Phila.: Westminster Press, 1957), pp. 136-42, and the bibliography cited there, p. 145.

[58] The verb *l^{e}ha^{ca}bīr* in Exod 13.12 is used as a semantic parallel to *qaddēš*, "consecrate," in 13.2. See Driver, *Exodus* (Camb. B., 1953), *ad* 13.12; BDB, 718. The priestly term for "sacrifice" of dedicated creatures, *zābaḥ* (cf. Exod 13.15), is conspicuously absent from Lev 18 and 20.

[59] Cf. usage in Num 31.23.

[60] Note that soothsaying (*ʾōb, yiddᶜonī*) as described in Deut 18.11, also adjoins the Molech text in Lev 20.1-5, i.e., 20.6.

[61] Citations are gathered in BDB, 977.

[62] According to W. R. Smith, *The Religion of the Semites* (repr. New York: Meridian Books, 1956), p. 377 n. 2 (adopted in BDB, 1075), Tophet "is properly an Aramaic name for fireplace, or for the framework set on the fire to support the victim." Cf. the reservations of Gray, *Kings*², pp. 735-36.

Older rabbinic etymologies connect Tophet with the Hebrew ***pātah***, "entice," see

valley was defiled at that time. On the other hand, child sacrifice is reported among the foreign Sepharvites, settled in Samaria after the Assyrian annexation: "They burned (*śārap*) their children in fire to Adrammelek and Anammelek, gods of Sepharvaim" (2 Kgs 17.31).

It is in the denunciations of Jeremiah and Ezekiel that the terminological distinctions are lost. The verbs "transfer/pass through fire" and "burn" are freely interchanged, and new vocables—"sacrifice" (*zābaḥ*) and "slaughter" (*šāḥaṭ*)—are introduced (cf. Ezek 16.20-21; 23.29).[63] Jeremiah accuses the Jerusalemites of child sacrifice to Baal and Molech, which the people seem to regard as legitimate dedications to Israel's YHWH (e.g., Jer 7.31; 19.5; 32.35). These broad denunciations clearly do not discriminate between the burning of children as "offerings to Baal" (19.5) and the "transfer to Molech" of sons and daughters at "Baal cult sites in the ben-Hinnom valley" (32.35).[64]

The thrust of prophetic polemics resulted in a literary fusing of the two separate rituals distinguished in legal contexts.[65] At the same time, items common to both the divinatory Molech and the child sacrifice cults advanced this prophetic amalgam. Both cults ritually employed fire, and both were at some time associated with the Tophet site.[66] Defiled by Josiah, the Tophet may have been rededicated after his death to serve a popular sacrificial cult in which royalty no longer had a part.[67] Finally, both cults addressed deities who

T. B. Erubin 19a; and *tāpap*, "drum, play the timbrel," see Abarbanel at Lev 20.1ff.: "The children, as they expired, cried out loudly due to the intensity of the fire. In order not to arouse the compassion of father and mother at the wailing and crying of their sons, the pagan priests sounded the 'tophet,' to confuse the listeners and prevent the screams of the children from being heard." Cf. also Rashi at Jer 7.31, and Radak at 2 Kgs 23.10.

(On the attestation of 2 Kgs 17.17, and late Israelite cult in Samaria in general, see below, pp. 105ff.)

[63] Are these terms part of the prophetic rhetoric or was the victim "first slain and then burnt?" So, Cooke, *Ezekiel*, p. 169; Šanda, *Könige* 2, p. 195. Note the singular reading in 2 Chr 28.3, with reference to Ahaz: "He burnt (*hibᶜîr*) his sons." If the verb in question is the Chronicler's own explication, and not a late scribal product, then it may have originated with the prophetic remarks on Molech. Cf. Rudolph, *Chronik, ad loc.*

[64] Cf. now the analysis by M. Weinfeld, independent of the one presented here, also touching upon the literary distinctiveness of the several Molech traditions, in "The Cult of Molech and Its Background" [Hebrew], *Fifth World Congress of Jewish Studies* (Jerusalem, 1972) 45-47.

[65] Further examples of Jeremiah's tendency to generalize in his judgment of Judahite morality are discussed by Kaufmann, *Tolᵉdot* 3, pp. 448f.

[66] The expansive note of the Chronicler at 2 Chr 28.3, "He [i.e., Ahaz] censed in the ben-Hinnom valley," must certainly mean that the Chronicler visualized the Tophet as the site of rituals other than just child sacrifice.

[67] Consider that the threat leveled at the Tophet site (Jer 7.32f.; 19.11f.) can only have had substance if the prophet's audience still held the Tophet sacred. The Jeremiah passages on child sacrifice are here understood to include eye-witness accounts of late unofficial cults. Kaufmann, on the other hand, argued (*Tolᵉdot* 3, pp. 388f.) that their context suggests description of "past sin" from Manasseh's age. But inasmuch as the passages in question are undated, our interpreting them as evidence of aberrant post-

shared the common epithet *melek*, "king" — all in all, circumstances noxious to prophetic teachings.[68]

The inaccuracies of the prophetic picture have been maintained in nearly all subsequent scholarly studies. The one difference which separates investigators is the question, Which of the two rituals, the divinatory or the sacrificial, is to be read into all texts?[69]

John Gray argues the case of a sacrificial Molech ritual. The god name Molech derived from the divine title *melek*, "king," and was associated throughout the entire Canaanite cultural sphere with various manifestations of the astral god of desert origin *Aṯtr.[70] From early times, Molech was worshiped in Judah; note the presence of a cult to the Ammonite god Milcom in Solomon's Jerusalem (1 Kgs 11.7).[71] Samaritan children were sacrificed to gods whose names exhibit the same *melek* element (2 Kgs 17.31).[72] Still open to question, notes Gray, is the possibility that certain biblical passages which mention Molech in reality describe a "votive offering," just as late Punic inscriptions studied by Otto

Josianic revivals is also tenable. Note that Kaufmann did admit to Ezekiel's witnessing "decadent wild roots" in Jerusalem during this same period (see pp. 502, and 447f.).

[68] If the Jeremiah texts in question prove to be the product of Deuteronomistic annotators, then our construction might be re-worded: The literary fusing in prophetic texts of the two separate Molech rites derives from Exilic conditions, when specific points of ritual were no longer remembered or considered important.

[69] Nachmanides at Lev 18.21 does mention an anonymous attempt at separating "sorcery" (i.e., passing through fire) from "sacrifice of little ones" to Molech.

[70] J. Gray, "The Desert God 'Aṯtr in the Literature and Religion of Canaan," JNES 8 (1949), 72-83; *idem*, IDB 3, *s.v.* "Molech."

[71] Gray (JNES 8 [1949], 79) identifies the Ammonite Milcom with the Moabite god Kemosh-Ishtar (cf. Mesha Inscription 17 in KAI 181) on the basis of Judg 11.24, where the god of Ammon is named Kemosh. Ibn Ezra and Nachmanides anticipated Gray's identification, cf. *ad* Lev 18.21. But the collocation of 2 Kgs 23.10 and 13 militates against this identification; the author of this narrative evidently considered Molech and Milcom as two separate deities.

[72] The identification of Adrammelek and Anammelek with gods known in Syrian and/or Assyro-Babylonian pantheons remains disputed. The Hebrew text, unemended, takes the element *ʾdr* as a divine epithet meaning "mighty." For examples, cf. Harris, *A Grammar of the Phoenician Language* (*AOS* 8, 1936), p. 75; KAI 258, 2 (?); and Montgomery, *Kings*, p. 476. Ungnad's original suggestion (AfO Beiheft 6, p. 58), emending *ʾdr* to *ʾdd* (Adad) on the basis of Assyrian personal names (e.g., *Adad-milki-ilaya*) attested in the Tell-Halaf archive, is widely accepted. See A. Pohl's popularization in *Biblica* 22 (1941), 35; and W. F. Albright, ARI^5, pp. 157f. Cf. the earlier remarks, Eb. Schrader, KAT^3, p. 84 nn. 2 and 3.

Deller's involuted recovery of Assyrian names types which translate Hebrew *DN-*mlk* as *DN-*šarru* (*Or* 34 [1965], 382-83) is wholly gratuitous. The writing **Adad-mlk* shows that the Hebrew is not a translation but a transliteration of an Assyrian name; for the Hebrew form of ^{d}*Adad* would have appeared as Hadad. Consequently, we do not have, nor do we expect lexical evidence supporting Deller's equation MAN/*šarru* = UMUN = *milki*. See Mazar, En. Miq. 1, cols. 117f. On Anammelek, see Montgomery, *Kings*, p. 476.

Eissfeldt use *mlk* as a sacrificial term.[73] Albright agreed: *Malik*, "king," or its derivative *Muluk*, "kingship," ought to be regarded "as the patron of vows and solemn promises and children might be sacrificed to him as the harshest and most binding pledge of the sanctity of a promise."[74]

Pedersen affirms that the Israelites adopted the Canaanite custom of "sanctification of the first-born" by sacrifice to God (cf. Exod 22.28).[75] But at the same time, biblical religion "shrank from fully accepting" this demand for holiness by restricting human sacrifice to times of disaster; normally, consecrated children could be redeemed through animal substitution (Exod 34.20). Without regular staff or site, says Kaufmann, the child sacrifice remained primarily a private devotion.[76] Not until the days of Manasseh, in an hour of national distress, did people publicly sacrifice children to appease an angered YHWH (cf. Mic 6.7).[77] But such gruesomeness was soon discouraged by Judah's prophets, who denounced this practice as an idolatrous abomination (cf. Jer 7.30; Ezek 20.25).[78]

The several non-sacrificial conceptions of the Molech cult must also be surveyed. According to an account recorded in the Babylonian Talmud, the term "transfer to Molech" refers to a ceremony of induction during which youthful initiates were delivered by their parents to pagan priests, who, in turn, passed them between two large bonfires.[79] S. R. Driver was convinced that the

[73] Originally published by Otto Eissfeldt, *Molk als Opferbegriff im Punischen und Hebräischen und das Ende des Gottes Moloch* (Halle: Max Neimeyer Varlag, 1935). Subsequent Punic studies are summarized in Albright, *Yahweh and the Gods of Canaan* (Garden City: Doubleday Anchor, 1969), pp. 226-44. The somewhat cavalier approach to biblical evidence exhibited by the proponents of Eissfeldt's view was recently exemplified by M. Noth's note on Lev 20.5: "We should see in *mlk*, even in the Old Testament passages, a sacrificial term, and translate *lmlk* "as a *mlk*-sacrifice." Admittedly, Lev 20.5 would be against this, for . . . *ham-molek* must be understood as the name of a god. Now vv. 2b-5 certainly contain secondary detailed additions . . . (which) rest on a thorough misunderstanding of the expression *lmlk*" (*Leviticus* [OTL, 1965], p. 148.) Criticism is fully mustered by W. Kornfeld, "Der Moloch, eine Untersuchung zur Theorie O. Eissfeldts'," WZKM 51 (1948-1952), 287-313.

[74] Albright, *ARI*^{5}, p. 157; DeVaux, *Ancient Israel*, pp. 444-46.

[75] Pedersen, *Israel: Its Life and Culture* 3-4 (London: H. Milford, 1926), pp. 318-22.

[76] Kaufmann, *Tol*^{e}*dot* 2, pp. 267f. Lev 20.5 threatens punishment for only the violator and his family.

[77] Cf. the desperate sacrifice by the king of Moab of his first-born son during the enemy siege of his capital (2 Kgs 3.27). A novel attempt to interpret this sacrifice as a "magical act" designed to put a curse upon Israel is offered by Kaufmann, *Collected Works* [Hebrew] (Tel-Aviv: Dvir, 1966), pp. 205-207.

[78] Kaufmann, *Tol*^{e}*dot, loc. cit.* Cf. Bright, *Jeremiah* (*AB*; 1965), p. 57. M. Greenberg, *ᶜOz L*^{e}*David: Studies Presented to David Ben-Gurion*, (Jerusalem: Kiryat Sefer, 1964) p. 437 n. 3, notes that the juxaposition of the Deut 12.31 prohibition of child sacrifice to the command in 13.1: "neither to add to nor to take away from" the Mosaic law suggests the currency of a view in certain circles that YHWH demanded such sacrifices of Israel. (The Massoretic division of the text after 13.1 was apparently based on this interpretation.)

[79] T.B. Sanhedrin 64a. This account and other Midrashic expansions were traced by

"peculiar and characteristic expression 'to cause to pass through the fire'" meant

> that the rite in question was a kind of *ordeal*, in which for instance, an omen was derived from observing whether the victim passed through the flames unscathed or not, or which was resorted to for the purpose of securing good fortune.[80]

Basing himself on classical examples, T. H. Gaster wrote:

> It is possible also that the Israelite writers have confused with human sacrifice a more innocuous practice, widely attested, of passing children rapidly through a flame as a means of absorbing immortality or giving them extra strength.[81]

Finally, N. H. Snaith, in a recent note reviving the Talmudic account,[82] argued that since Lev 18.21 is embedded in a list of illicit sex relationships, the law must have forbidden cultic prostitution in the name of Molech.[83]

These two opposing scholarly views of the Molech cult need not necessarily be considered mutually exclusive. For, as we have demonstrated, a distinction does in fact exist between the legal-historical and prophetic traditions. Priestly law prohibiting Molech divination in no way discredits Jeremiah's eye-witness report of child sacrifice. But neither can the prophet's sweeping denunciation invalidate the legal evidence of Molech divination, unfortunately only paralleled in extra-biblical observations.

One question remains: If Israelite religion frowned upon the adoption of Canaanite cults, especially immolation, how is the public revival of diverse Molech cults in eighth century B.C.E. Judah to be explained? Other critical moments had passed without stimulating interest in child sacrifice.[84]

Albright's widely accepted explanation is this:

> A new Aramaic culture, composed of Canaanite and Neo-Assyrian elements with the latter dominant, was spreading rapidly over the West, strongly supported by Assyrian military power.[85]

While child sacrifice seems to have been discontinued in Phoenicia by the seventh century B.C.E. at the latest,[86] in Aramaic-speaking areas it lingered on.

G. F. Moore to classical reports of Carthaginian ritual ("The Image of Moloch," JBL 16 [1897], 161-65).

[80] *Deuteronomy* (ICC, 1902), p. 222.

[81] Gaster, IDB 4, p. 154; cf. Barnett, EI 9 (1969), 8.

[82] Snaith, "The Cult of Molech," VT 16 (1966), 123-24.

[83] Contrast M. Noth, *Leviticus*, pp. 136 and 146, for whom the verses in question are "very loosely fitted in with the list of sexual transgressions;" cf. Eissfeldt, *The Old Testament: An Introduction* (New York: Harper & Row, 1965), p. 234.

[84] Alternately, the absence of an attested Molech cult before Ahaz may mean that early biblical writers regarded such practice, where present, as insignificant, and so, left it unreported.

[85] Albright, *ARI*^{5}, p. 156.

[86] *Ibid.*, p. 158; see O. Eissfeldt, *Ras Schamra und Sanchunjaton* (Halle: Max Neimeyer Verlag, 1939), pp. 69-71.

> Human sacrifice to the god Adad is attested among the Aramaeans of Gozan at the source of the Khabur in northern Mesopotamia (late tenth century), in Late-Assyrian economic texts under Aramaean influence, and in the North-Syrian cult of Sepharvaim . . ., where children were sacrificed (II Kings 17:31) to the god Adrammelech.[87]

This broad attribution of Molech-type sacrifices to Aramaic culture must be modified, for the extra-biblical documentation is at best inconclusive regarding the actual or intended performance of sacrifice. In a tenth century B.C.E. dedicatory text from Gozan, the Aramaean prince Kapara warns the violator of his stele:

7 mārēšu maḫar Adad liširupu[88] *7 mārātēšu ana ᵈIštar ḫarimātu luramme*[89]
May he burn seven of his sons before Adad. May he release seven of his daughters to be cult prostitutes for Ishtar.

The schematic formulation of this imprecation suggests that old traditional terms of divine sanction have been preserved.

Likewise, a small number of late NA economic texts specify sacrifice of children as a penalty for initiating future litigation of contracts.

māršu rabū ina ⁽ᵈ⁾*ḫamri ša ᵈAdad išarrap*[90]
He will burn his eldest son in the sacred precinct of Adad.

māršu ana ᵈSin išarrap mārassu rabīte itti 2 sūtu dam erēni ana ᵈBēlet-ṣēri išarrap[91]
He will burn his son to Sin.[92] He will burn his eldest daughter with 20 silas of cedar balsam to Bēlet-ṣēri.

lū māršu rabū lū mārassu rabītu itti 2 imēr riqqē ṭābūte ana Bēlatu-ṣēri iš[arrap][93]
He will b[urn] either his eldest son or his eldest daughter with 2 homers of sweet-smelling spices to Bēlet-ṣēri.

In addition to human sacrifice, some of these same contracts specify the

[87] Albright, *Yahweh and the Gods of Canaan*, pp. 240-41.

[88] I.e., *li₈-ši-ru-pu* = *lišrupu* (cf. CAD Ḫ, 101). Albright (AnSt 6 [1956], 81f.) suggested reading *lit-taš!-ru-pu* (a IV/2 verbal form—cf. *GAG* 81e) so as to eliminate the unique *li₈* reading. But another Gozan text reads the verb *li-ši-ru-pu* (AfO Beiheft 1, p. 75, 5).

[89] AfO Beiheft 1, p. 72, II.4-7.

[90] ARU 41.18; cf. *ibid.* 161.2, 160.8. On *ḫamru*, see CAD Ḫ, 70. On the reading *māru* for DUMU.UŠ, rather than *aplu*, see CAD A 2, 176.

[91] ARU 163.20-22; cf. *ibid.* 96a.17-18 (which contains only the second clause of this unit). Our reading, where different from ARU, is based on CAD E, 278.

[92] ND. 496, 25 (=*Iraq* 13 [1951], pl. 16) reads: *māršu rabū ina pan ᵈSin*, "his eldest son before Sin." In this Nimrud text, GIBÍL = *šarāpu* is written ÁŠ; which must be a scribal or copyist's error. Deller, Or 34 (1965), 383f., maintains this unusual ÁŠ reading, though it gives no verbal equivalent. Deller also suggests that GIBÍL-*u* be read *iqallu*, synonymous with *išarrap*.

[93] ARU 158.27-30 (cf. CAD I, 114). On the lacuna, see below, n. 98.

presentation of gifts (e.g., white horses,[94] large bow, hierodules) to sundry gods and/or strange ordeals[95] as further penalties. In the vast majority of cases, however, monetary fines replace ritualistic punishments.[96]

Because NA contracts unrealistically heap up penalty clauses, together with stiff fines well beyond the means of the average citizen, most Assyriologists concur with Meissner's assertion that these penalties could never have been actualized. They were intended as solemn formulae—"a kind of oath . . . that the contracting party fulfilled in fear of the gods as avengers of contract violations."[97] Nevertheless, the very utilization of these clauses is evidence of Neo-Assyrian esteem for ancient ceremonial, and suggests that under certain circumstances a defendant might legally claim literal reprisal, even of sometimes harsh penalties.[98]

At best, therefore, the evidence tells of vestigial human sacrifice amidst eighth century B.C.E. Assyro-Aramaean cultural traditions. Increased contact with Aramaeans during the Neo-Assyrian age may have awakened dormant superstitions among Judahites, though child sacrifice need have been no more prevalent in Judah than it seems to have been in Assyria proper. For loyal YHWHists, however, even this sporadic cult was a sign of unwelcome acculturation to pagan norms,[99] whose impetus we must yet investigate.

[94] Cf. below, pp. 86f.

[95] The descriptions of these ordeals remain shrouded in linguistic difficulties, only one being relatively clear. The accused is forced to eat one mina of "plucked wool" followed by a "quick gulp" of water or beer, apparently intended to cause painful expansion of his stomach. Cf. von Soden, Or 26 (1957), 135-36; CAD A 1, 143.

[96] Did these sums represent equivalent values, as at Nuzi where ceremonial fines were payable in kind? See E. A. Speiser, "Nuzi Marginalia," Or 25 (1956), 9-15.

[97] Meissner, BuA 1, p. 182. A summary of early discussion is found in Fr. Blome, *Opfermaterie*, pp. 407-10.

[98] In the original publication of these contracts, ADD 3, pp. 345-56, Johns was "inclined to suppose" that *šarāpu* merely meant "to dedicate" a child to the service of a god. He based himself on a reading of ARU 158.30 = *i-rak-*[*kas*], for the more frequent *išarrap*. The lacuna was subsequently read in ARU, *i-š*[*ar-rap*]; by Deller, Or 34 (1965), 383, *i*-SAL-[ ]. Overlooked by Johns were the terms of dedication of persons to temple service: *šarāku*, "present" (ARU 44.9); *šûlû*, "devote" (ARU 45.6). In these texts *rakāsu* is used solely for the "binding" of horses. (ND. 496.32 now provides another dedication term, *nadānu*.)

No less speculative is Deller's suggestion (*op. cit.*, pp. 385f.) that children were spared sacrifice by becoming cult personnel, and only the burning of spices was actually performed. His entire argument rests on the collocation of child sacrifice and cult prostitution penalties in several contracts; e.g., the Gozan text quoted above (cf. n. 89). No textual evidence is available for either the figurative interpretation of the verb *šarāpu* or the substitution of punishments.

[99] The vehemence with which Jeremiah and Ezekiel attack "Molech" does not necessarily testify to the frequency of child sacrifice. Both prophets would have seized upon this "abhorrent act" (cf. Deut 12.31), however infrequent, in bolstering their claim to the justness of YHWH's decision to destroy Judah. See Kaufmann, *Tolᵉdot* 3, pp. 383ff.; 446ff., for a discussion of prophetic theodicy from the days of Judah's fall.

Astral Cults. — Among Manasseh's cultic innovations in the Jerusalem sanctuary was worship of *ṣᵉbāʾ haššāmayim*, "the heavenly host" (2 Kgs 21.3), i.e., the sun, moon, stars, and planets (cf. 23.5; Deut 4.19). At open-air altars in the two temple courts (2 Kgs 21.5) and the roof of the royal residence (23.12), the heavenly host was served by "bowing," "censing," and "libation." The sun, in particular, enjoyed the dedications of horses and chariots, delivered to the temple at the office of one Netanmelek (23.11). The "host" was apparently an imageless cult,[100] and although occasionally cited in company with Baal and Asherah, no specific deity was ever invoked by name in its service (cf. 17.16; 21.3).[101]

Beyond official Jerusalem, Manasseh sponsored the personnel of the heavenly host in the rural towns of Judah (23.5). Even after Josiah's cultic reforms, the private worship of the "Queen of Heaven" could still be witnessed by Jeremiah. Children gathered wood and men kindled the fire, while the women kneaded the dough to prepare cake offerings[102] in family service of the "Queen" (Jer 7.18).[103]

As with other pagan cults, commentators generally agree that "this developed astral worship . . . came in with the Assyrian domination as part of the obligation of subject states to the empire.[104] So, for the most part, the "Queen of Heaven" is identified with the Mesopotamian goddess Ishtar, who appears as *šarrat šamē*, "the queen of heaven."[105] The sun (Hebrew *šemeš*), as the god Shamash,

[100] In Ezek 8.16 twenty-five men bow in the direction of the rising sun. On the number "25," cf. Cooke, *Ezekiel*, p. 99; and N. Sarna, *Proceedings of the Fourth World Congress of Jewish Studies* 1 (Jerusalem, 1967), p. 175 n. 87.

[101] Jeremiah's reference in 32.29 to the service of Baal at roof-top altars may be no more than a verbal lapse, in as much as only astral cults usually required visual sighting of the objects of veneration. Cf., for example, Jer 19.13; Deut 4.19. But, cf. Montgomery, *Kings*, p. 533.

[102] According to some, the opaque *lhᶜṣbh* in Jer 44.19 refers to the crescent shape of the cakes baked. Cf. Rashi; Bright, *Jeremiah, ad loc.*; BDB, 781. Ruth Amiran, interpreting this verb as referring to the plastic arts, would see the sun goddess clasping the solar disk in many of the excavated Palestinian figurines. See Amiran, "A Note on Figurines with 'Disks' " [Hebrew], EI 8 (1967), 99-100.

[103] Bright, among others, thinks the cult "especially popular among the women" (*Jeremiah*, p. 265). But we are twice told that the women proceeded with the complicity of their husbands, who acknowledged: ". . . we, ourselves, our forefathers, our kings and our princes" all worshiped the "Queen" (cf. 44.17, 19). Besides, the women appear to have been cult ministrants, preparing and presenting food and libations, appropriately to a female deity. The strong defense of the cult by the women in Jer 44 (see below) reflects the generally-held biblical view of a female proclivity for idolatry. Foreign queens were often the source of Israel's pagan diversions. Cf. 1 Kgs 11.4-5; 16.31; 2 Kgs 8.18.

[104] Montgomery, *Kings*, pp. 519f.; Gray, *Kings*², p. 648.

[105] The original presentation was by Eb. Schrader, "Die *mlkt hšmym* und ihr aramäisch-assyriches Aequivalent," SPAW 1886/1, pp. 477-91; *idem*, ZA 3 (1888), 353-64; cf. Zimmern, KAT³, pp. 440-42. A new, but tenuous identification of the "Queen" with the Sun god ŠPŠ, styled "Dame ŠPŠ" in Ugaritic text UM 52.54, is presented by M. Dahood

received a gift of horses, befitting a god known by "the Akkadian title . . . *rākib narkabti* — 'chariot-rider.' "[106]

We have already investigated this supposition in general and found it baseless; Assyria imposed no religious obligations upon its vassals. Furthermore, astral cults were not the exclusive patent of Assyrian religion. Šanda[107] and Montgomery[108] already noted that the biblical "listing of Baal, sun and moon is typically Syrian,"[109] i.e., Aramaean. The reverance of celestial bodies can, in fact, be traced back to the second millennium B.C.E. in Syria-Palestine as part of common Semitic tradition.[110]

Biblical writers share this point of view. According to the Deuteronomist, astral worship was practiced by Israel's neighbors prior to their arrival (Deut 4.19), and although forewarned, the Israelites eventually succumbed to the "host's" enticement (2 Kgs 17.16). The popular "Queen of Heaven" cult in the seventh century B.C.E. has all the appearances of being more than just a "poor, feeble" superstition,[111] of recent adoption. When confronted by Jeremiah, the Judahite exiles in Egypt defended their continuing worship of the "Queen." Their argument: "But ever since we left off censing to the Queen of Heaven and pouring out libations to her, we have lacked everything and have been consumed by sword and famine" (Jer 44.18). At least a century later, the "Queen," i.e., Anath, according to Porten's identification,[112] was still being worshiped at Elephantine, perhaps even in association with YHWH.[113] Such tenacity does not suggest

in "La Regina del Cielo in Geremia," *Rivista Biblica* 8 (1960), 166-68. Cf. also, Rudolph, *Jeremia* (HAT², 1958), p. 51.

[106] Montgomery, *Kings*, p. 533; cf. Gray, *Kings²*, p. 736. This erroneous ascription has made its way into many handbooks. The title *rākib narkabti* is to be translated "charioteer" and refers to the god Bunene, the trusted advisor of Shamash. Cf. VAB 4, 260, 33. See Tallqvist, *Götterepitheta*, p. 175; and RLA 2, 76. A second god ᵈUR̃.Á.ĹA is known as the *mukīl appāti*, "chariot driver" (lit. "holder of reins," cf. CAD A 2, p. 183) of Shamash; cf. CT 24, 32.108; and Tallqvist, p. 455.

[107] Šanda, *Könige* 2, p. 348.

[108] Montgomery, *Kings*, p. 530.

[109] *Ibid.* Aramaean inscriptions from the eighth and seventh centuries B.C.E. mention ŠMŠ and ŠHR, sun and moon gods respectively. See KAI 202 B, 24; 214, 2 and 3; 215, 22; 222 A, 9; 225, 9.

[110] A convenient summary of the literary evidence is given by M. Dahood, *Le Antiche Divinita' Semitiche*, ed. S. Moscati (Rome: Università di Roma, 1958), pp. 65-94. Cf. also, M. Plesner and J. Licht, En. Miq. 4, *s.v. "kōkāb,"* col. 47 and *idem,* En. Miq. 3, *s.v. "yārēaḥ,"* col. 838; and H. Gese, in *Die Religionen Altsyriens, Altarabiens und der Mandäer* (Stuttgart: Kohlhammer, 1970), pp. 166-69.

[111] So, Kaufmann, *Tolᵉdot* 3, p. 390.

[112] See B. Porten, *Archives from Elephantine*, pp. 164-65. At the Aramaean colony in Syene, a temple to the "Queen of Heaven" is known. The Egyptian term "Lady of Heaven" served as an epithet for the goddess Anath, as early as the fifteenth century B.C.E. (cf. Beth Shean stele, ANET, p. 249). So, already, U. Cassuto, *The Goddess Anath* [Hebrew] (Jerusalem: Mosad Bialik, 1958), pp. 49-50.

[113] Porten, *Archives from Elephantine*, pp. 176-79.

that astral cults were new Assyrian importations, first introduced by Manasseh, but rather outgrowths of local traditions, popularly rooted.[114]

Fixing astral worship within the matrix of Canaanite civilization does not account, however, for its special prevalence during Assyria's century. That the sun and the "Queen" were worshiped "in an Assyrian form" may be a reasonable assumption,[115] yet wholly unconfirmed, due to the generality of biblical descriptions. We are able to trace, and this only in the broadest outline, but one astral cult to Assyrian sources,[116] viz., the presentation of horses to the sun.

Ernst Weidner has shown that in Assyria, in contrast to Babylonia, the horse served important ritual functions.[117] Because of the long Mitannian rule in northern Mesopotamia, the Indo-Aryan conception of white, shining steeds as the intimates of the gods took hold in Assyria. Shalameser II, for example, allocated cedar balsam to the white horses listed among the gods who had private chapels in the Ashur temple complex. An allowance issued by Adad-nirari III also provided food rations for horses.[118] Late NA economic texts specify among other penalties:

2 *sīsē piṣūte ina šēpā* *ᵈAššur irakkas*[119]
He shall bind 2 white horses at the feet of Ashur.

4 *sīsē piṣūte ina šēpā* *ᵈSin āl Ḫarran irakkas*[120]
He shall bind 4 white horses at the feet of Sin, who dwells in Harran.

The popularity of Sin of Harran was wide-spread among the Aramaeans of northern Syria; e.g., Bar-rakib of Sam'al identifies the moon god Sin with his own god Baal Harran.[121] The symbol of Baal Harran, a lunar crescent on a post

[114] Cf. I. Eph'al, En. Miq. 4, col. 1159. That the "heavenly host" was a standard part of Israelite conceptions of the divine realm is also clear from 1 Kgs 22.19; popular veneration of such divine beings, alongside YHWH, can probably be illustrated by Job 31.26f.

[115] So, Cooke, *Ezekiel*, p. 99; Rudolph, *Jeremia, loc. cit.*; based solely upon the name correspondence noted above, n. 105.

[116] Gaster would connect the sun worship in Ezek 8.16 with the seasonal weeping rite for Tammuz in 8.14, disregarding the disjointed, catalogue quality of the idolatries witnessed by the prophet. See, Gaster, *Thespis* (New York: Harper Torchbooks, 1961), pp. 46f.

[117] E. Weidner, "Weise Pferde im Alten Orient," BiOr 9 (1952), 157-59.

[118] *Ibid.*, p. 159. See also, Ebeling, *Stiftungen und Vorschriften für assyrische Tempel* (*Deutsche Akademie der Wissenschaften zu Berlin* 23, 1954) text 6 (=KAV 78).

[119] To Weidner's citations, "Pferde," p. 158 n. 14, add: ARU 169.17; 171.21; 173.23; ND. 3426, obv. 17-18 (=*Iraq* 15 [1953], pl. 12); ND. 2305, 2306 (3 horses !), 2323, 2326 (=*Iraq* 16 [1954], 36-42).

[120] To Weidner, "Pferde," p. 158 n. 15, add: ARU 170.17-18 (2 horses!); 174.7. 553.13-15 reads: *iddan* for *irakkas*.

[121] On the Bar-rakib stele, reproduced in ANEP, 460, the king of Sam'al displays a lunar crescent beside the inscription *mrʾy bʿlḥrn*, "My lord, Baal Harran." Cf. KAI, 218 and commentary. Y. Yadin suggests viewing Baal Harran as a new introduction "into the pantheon of Samal under Assyrian influence," paralleling or even replacing the local mood god Baal Hamman. See Yadin, "Symbols of Deities at Zinjirli, Carthage and

decorated with fillets,[122] can be found a century later farther south at Gezer in Judah. To a deed of sale, dated 649 B.C.E., a certain Natanyahu (NA$_4$.KIŠIB ^{m}*Na-tan-ia-u*) affixed his stamp seal, whose prominent feature was the lunar crescent of Baal, i.e., Sin of Harran.[123]

Can we assume that in addition to adopting astral symbolism, Judahite moon cultists also appropriated the horse rituals of Sin of Harran? Were the horse dedications to the sun in Jerusalem (2 Kgs 23.11) of like source?[124] If proved affirmative, then the lines of penetration of Assyrian forms of astral worship are clear. Assyrian cults were accomodated within Aramaean circles in syncretistic form, and through Aramaean mediation ultimately made their way to seventh century B.C.E. Judah. In Judah, new forms dressed up old Canaanite ritual in a blatant assimilatory trend, whose impetus must concern us now.[125]

Hazor," *Near Eastern Archaeology in the Twentieth Century: Essays in Honor of Nelson Glueck* (Garden City: Doubleday, 1970), pp. 210f. In that case, one would have to posit two moon deities of related Aramaean derivation vying for position. Is it not simpler to follow Landsberger's suggestion (*Sam'al* [*Veröffentlichungen der Türkischen Historischen Gesellschaft* 16; Ankara, 1948], p. 46 n. 114) and view Bar-rakib's declaration as expressing his Assyrian affinities; hence his identification of the local moon god with the god honored by his overlord. This also explains the Assyrianized moon symbolism noted by Yadin, *loc. cit.*

[122] On moon emblem, see Van Buren, *Symbols of the Gods in Ancient Mesopotamian Art*, pp. 64 and 66 n. 10.

[123] A photograph of this tablet appears as frontispiece to R. A. S. Macalister, *The Excavation at Gezer* 1 (London: John Murray, 1912); the text is treated on pp. 27-30 of the same volume. The seal with astral signs published by N. Avigad, "A Seal of 'Manasseh Son of the King,'" IEJ 13 (1963), 133-36, was originally thought to be Hebrew, but is now considered to be of Moabite provenance. See Avigad, *Near Eastern Archaeology in the Twentieth Century: Essays in Honor of Nelson Glueck*, p. 294 n. 52 and the epigraphic remarks of J. Naveh in *ibid*, p. 283, n. 19.

[124] Shamash was certainly not the sole Mesopotamian deity to ride a chariot; that only his equestrian rites were appropriated by syncretistic circles within Judah may indicate the sun god's long-standing popularity in the Syro-Palestinian cultic sphere. By way of illustration, note: The gods Anu, Ninurta, Shamash and Adad rode to the New Year's festival house in horse-drawn chariots. See F. Thureau-Dangin, *Rituels Accadiens* (Paris: Geuthner, 1921), 82.2, 102.4-9; cf. Pallis, *The Babylonian Akîtu Festival* (Copenhagen: F. Høst and Son, 1926), pp. 154-56. Ashurbanipal repaired the *narkabtu ṣīrtu rukub* ^{d}*Marduk*, "the stately chariot, coach of Marduk" (Streck, VAB 7, 300.12, 148.32). At the behest of Sennacherib, the figure of the god Amurru, the charioteer of Ashur, was engraved on the gate of Ashur's country festival house. See OIP 2, 140.8.

[125] Weidner, "Pferde," p. 159, considers 2 Kgs 23.11 to be a "last echo" of adoration of horses mediated by Indo-Aryans, so weak that it consisted only of nondescript horse statues. Kings tells of no such long-standing tradition. The "kings of Judah" mentioned in 23.11 refer only to Manasseh and Amon. So, too, the ancestral idolatries which determined Judah's fate were ascribed to these same two archtypical apostates. Cf. 2 Kgs 21.20, 23.37.

Model horses, wheels and chariots discovered at numerous Palestinian sites are regularly spoken of as "votive objects" associated with sun worship. See, e.g., H. G. May, *Material Remains of the Megiddo Cult* (OIP 26), pp. 23-25; and K. Kenyon's recent find of "fertility figurines and horses with discs on their foreheads . . . a most vivid illustration

Summary.—Our review of Judahite cultic practices during the eighth and seventh centuries B.C.E. uncovered no evidence of Assyrian cults imposed upon Judah in any biblical source. Mesopotamian elements, where discernable—e.g., horse dedications to the sun god—seem to have gained entrance into Judah through Aramaean mediation, only after having merged with local Palestinian pagan traditions.[126]

This picture agrees with the one drawn earlier from Assyrian sources; viz., vassal states were free of any cultic obligations toward their Assyrian overlord and his gods, and did not suffer any interference in their native cults.

It follows that if we are to understand the motivations behind Judah's pagan innovations, we must fall back upon the Deuteronomistic report of Manasseh's reign, the one clear statement of origins: Manasseh misled the populace into wicked ways (2 Kgs 21.9).

Acculturation and Assimilation

If we exclude Assyrian coercion as the impetus behind the royally sponsored foreign cults of seventh century B.C.E. Judah, what is left? Some scholars feel that Manasseh sought to ingratiate himself with his Assyrian overlords by outwardly embracing the Assyrian cult, in order to preserve what he could of his small kingdom.[127] But 2 Kgs 21 does not describe Manasseh's paganism as being a superficial matter; a radical change in native Judahite religion had been undertaken. Besides, no Assyrian texts suggest that the Assyrian king expected his vassals to alter their national religions on his account. Ingratiation involved public recognition by a vassal of Assyria's political suzerainty, nothing more. So Bar-rakib of Sam'al erected a stele, upon which an Aramaic inscription proclaimed:

> I am Bar-rakib, son of Panammuwa, king of Sam'al, vassal of Tiglath-pileser, lord of the four quarters of the earth. Because of the loyalty of my father and my own

of the heathen practices with which Josiah had to deal," reported in "Israelite Jerusalem," *Near Eastern Archaeology in the Twentieth Century: Essays in Honor of Nelson Glueck*, pp. 244-46. But, as was admitted by May, these models want for clear cultic contexts. Besides, Josiah "burned" the sun chariots he found in the Jerusalem Temple (2 Kgs 23.11), a procedure ill-suited for clay models or bronze figurines. Cf. Šanda, *Könige* 2, p. 347.

[126] Only by interpreting the mention of the Canaanite Baal and Asherah (2 Kgs 21.3) as veiled allusions to "Ashur and Belit and the gods of Assyria" (so, Gressman, ZAW 1 [1924], 324ff.; cf. Montgomery, *Kings*, p. 529) can Assyrian deities be found mentioned in the biblical text (see the observations of Kaufmann, *Tol^{e}dot* 1, p. 95). This is not to say that the traditional Canaanite cults were untouched by prevailing fashion. The curious *semel* viewed by Ezekiel in the Temple's outer court (Ezek 8.3ff.) and identified by the Chronicler with Manasseh's Asherah image (cf. 2 Chr 33.7 and 2 Kgs 21.6) was, according to W. F. Albright, a "figured slab" (orthostat), "unmistakably" modeled after Syro-Assyrian practice (see *ARI*^{5}, pp. 159f. and n. 121; and En. Miq. 5, cols. 1055-56, *s.v.* "*semel*").

[127] See, e.g., the remarks of N. Snaith, *Kings*, p. 310; and Fohrer, *Geschichte*, pp. 126ff., cited above, p. 4 n. 19.

loyalty, my lord Rakib-el and my lord Tiglath-pileser placed me on the throne of my father.[128]

Bar-rakib saluted his Assyrian overlord by associating Tiglath-pileser III with Rakib-el, the patron deity of the Sam'al dynasty; Manasseh's pagan acts were of a different kind.

Others, following Wellhausen's original formulation,[129] find evidence of a violent reaction against the strict demands of prophetic monotheism in Manasseh's rebuilding of rural cult sites destroyed by his father Hezekiah (2 Kgs 21.3). The old popular syncretistic cults of Baal and Asherah were revived; Mesopotamian ritual was eagerly welcomed. Opposition, in the persons of loyal YHWH prophets, was ruthlessly eliminated (cf. 21.16).[130]

Kaufmann rejects this view by hewing closer to the biblical text.[131] The very fact that Manasseh had to institute bloody purges, like Jezebel in north Israel, apparently in order to put through his religious innovations, attests to the absence of any deep-seated popular paganism. He explains the enigma of a king "raised on the knees of YHWHistic belief . . . attracted to idolatry as certainly the result of an emotional crisis" brought on by "political subjugation" to Assyria.[132] A superficial paganism spread through the country only by virtue of its royal sponsorship; it was thoroughly uprooted in the subsequent Josianic reforms.

Both these scholarly positions base themselves upon the accounts given in 2 Kings, but fail to evaluate critically the viewpoint of the Kings histories. The focus of the Deuteronomistic historian is almost exclusively upon monarchic misconduct, which he considered the determinant of Israel's lot.[133] In order to justify YHWH's destruction of Judah, Manasseh is made out to be the idolator

[128] The full Aramaic text is published in KAI, 216.

[129] J. Wellhausen, *Israelitische und jüdische Geschichte*, p. 125.

[130] See, among others, R. Kittel, *Geschichte des Volkes Israel* 2, pp. 517ff.; E. Sellin, *Geschichte des israelitisch-jüdischen Volkes* 1, pp. 278-80; Robinson, *History*, pp. 402f; Bright, *History*, pp. 290-91.

[131] Kaufmann, *Tol^{e}dot* 2, p. 234.

[132] Kaufmann, *ibid.*

[133] This theme is most explicit in YHWH's response to Solomon's prayer at the Temple inauguration, 1 Kgs 9.6-7: "But if you turn from following Me, you and your children, and not keep My Instruction (and) My Law which I set before you, and turn to the service of other gods by bowing to them, then I will cut off Israel from the land which I gave them. . . ." This point is missed by M. Noth in his *Überlieferungsgeschichtliche Studien*; and by G. von Rad in "Die Deuteronomistische Geschichtstheologie in den Königsbüchern," *Gesammelte Studien* (München: Chr. Kaiser Verlag, 1961), pp. 189-204. Cf. above, p. 73 n. 40.

However, von Rad does deal with the Deuteronomist's unique view of the monarchy in his *Old Testament Theology* 1 (New York: Harper and Row, 1962), p. 344: "The Deuteronomistic history and the word (of God) which creates history . . . is all related in the most direct way to the kings. They are the real object of this operative word, it is they who are sustained by it and they who by it are destroyed. The people stands and falls with them."

par excellence, with little regard paid to historical circumstances.[134] Consequently, no substantive information on the state of popular religion, as viewed either by Wellhausen or by Kaufmann, is obtainable from 2 Kings.

Nor should Manasseh be considered the ruthless patron of paganism simply on the basis of the indictment in 2 Kgs 21.16, which reads: "Moreover, Manasseh shed so much innocent blood that he filled Jerusalem from end to end; besides his sin which led Judah to sin, by doing what displeased YHWH." Commentators, ancient and modern, agree with Josephus: "He killed all the righteous among the Hebrews, nor did he spare even the prophets, some of whom he slaughtered daily."[135] Post biblical tradition counts Isaiah among the loyal who perished during this reign of terror.[136]

This interpretation seems to derive from the context. The charge of murder in 2 Kgs 21.16 follows directly upon the prophetic threat of punishment for continued apostasy in vss. 10-15, as though implying that Manasseh not only disregarded these warnings but also slew his opponents.

However, the connection of 21.16 with the preceding prophecies is by no means necessary.[137] Persons other than prophets or opponents of the king's religious policy might well have been done to death. Killing the innocent is associated by Jeremiah with the violent oppression of the alien, orphan, and widow by king and subject alike (cf. Jer 22.3, 17; 7.6). Lamentations recalled the complicity on the part of Judah's priests and prophets in the innocent murder of the just (Lam 4.13). Ezekiel likewise accused Jerusalem's ruling classes of slander, bribery, and usury, thus turning Jerusalem into "the bloody city" (cf. Ezek 22.6 ff., 25 ff.).[138]

Just as the Israelite Ahab was censured for his zealous support of foreign paganism coupled with an abandonment of justice,[139] so, too, Manasseh. The

[134] Cf. von Rad, *OT Theology*, pp. 338f. See also, *idem, Gesammelte Studien*, pp. 190-91.

[135] Josephus, *Jewish Antiquities* 10.(3.1.)38 (Loeb edition).

[136] Cf. T.B. Sanhedrin 103b; T.B. Yebamot 49b; Louis Ginzberg, *Legends of the Jews* 4 (Philadelphia: Jewish Publication Society, 1913), pp. 278-79; 6 (1928), pp. 372-75; *The Lives of the Prophets, JBL Monograph Series,* 1, ed. by C. C. Torrey, p. 34. See Montgomery, *Kings*, p. 521; Snaith, *Kings*, p. 313 and Kaufmann, *Tol^{e}dot* 2, p. 268 for a similar viewpoint. The death of prophets told of in Jer 2.30, 34, may refer to affairs from a later period; cf. the death of Uriah, Jer 26.20-23.

The rise of prophetic martyr tales during the Hasmonean era, of which our Isaiah report is but one item, and its relations to the Qumran sect is treated by D. Flusser, "Martyrdom during the Second Commonwealth and Early Christianity" [Hebrew], in *Holy War and Martyrology* (Jerusalem: Historical Society of Israel, 1967), pp. 61-71.

[137] The particle *v^{e}gam*, "moreover," may be used non-consecutively, e.g., 1 Kgs 16.7; 2 Kgs 13.6, 23.24 and very often climactically, cf. C. J. Labuschagne, "The Emphasizing Particle *gam* and its Connotations," *Studia Biblica et Semitica: Studies Presented to T. C. Vriezen* (Wageningen: H. Veenman, 1967), pp. 193-203.

[138] Among the ruling classes indicted were princes (reading *n^{e}śīʾēhā* in 22.25; cf. Cooke, *Ezekiel, ad loc.*), priests, nobles, prophets, and "the people of the land" (see above, p. 70 n. 29).

[139] The parade example is the judicial murder of Naboth in 1 Kgs 21; cf. 2 Kgs 9.7.

charge of bloodshed in 2 Kgs 21.16 should be read as a charge of social wrong-doing, climaxing the parallel which the Deuteronomist drew between the corrupt houses of Ahab and Manasseh (cf. especially 2 Kgs 9.7; 21.3).[140]

It is this Deuteronomistic comparison, however tendentious, which suggests the motive of Manasseh's pagan importations. Ahab's idolatry was prompted by the Phoenician princess Jezebel;[141] it may not be insignificant that Meshul-lemeth from Yotbah, a town in north Israel long under Assyrian rule,[142] was the mother of Manasseh's son and successor.[143] Women are notorious throughout biblical history for their promotion of alien, often ancestral, cults,[144] and Manasseh's wife may have been one factor in the insinuation of foreign elements. Other analogous factors may be gleaned from a study of scattered evidence available in extrabiblical archaeological and literary remains.[144a]

The eighth and seventh centuries B.C.E. saw the rise of the first area-wide empire in the Near East under the leadership of Assyria. Through successive military campaigns and population exchanges, Assyrian domination upset local

[140] Note the two-fold blood-guilt of Ahab in 2 Kgs 9.7, idolatry and social wrong. The "prophetic" denunciation, 2 Kgs 21.12-15, expressly compares Ahab and Manasseh (21.13). Cf. Robinson, *History*, pp. 402f.; E. Nielsen, "Political Conditions and Cultural Developments in Israel and Judah During the Reign of Manasseh," *Proceedings of the Fourth World Congress of Jewish Studies* 1 (Jerusalem, 1967), p. 104.

[141] Cf. 1 Kgs 16.31. 2 Kgs 8.18 tells of the infectious spread into Judah of Baal worship after the marriage of Joram with a daughter of Jezebel.

[142] Yotbah was captured by Tiglath-pileser III in 733 B.C.E. Cf. Rost, *Tigl. III*, 232 (=ANET, p. 283). On the identification of the site, see Forrer, *Provinzeinteilung*, pp. 60-61 and En. Miq. 3, col. 672, *s.v.* "Yoṭbā." and the literature cited there; to which add, Albright, *Biblical Period*, n. 157.

[143] Cf. 2 Kgs 21.19. Aharoni believes that Manasseh's marriage to Meshullemet, and the later marriage of Josiah to Zebudah of Rumah in Galilee (also occupied by Tiglath-pileser III), 2 Kgs 23.26, were politically inspired. The Judahite monarchy substantiated its claim to rule "all Israel" by cementing ties with the vanquished northern state. See, Aharoni, *The Settlement of the Israelite Tribes in Upper Galilee* [Hebrew] (Jerusalem: Magnes Press, 1957), p. 132. Cf. the earlier remarks of S. Smirin, *Josiah and His Age*, p. 56.

H. L. Ginsberg objects, thinking that by marrying into an Israelite family, Manasseh would have degraded himself "from a vassal to a subject of Ashurbanipal" and would have aroused suspicions of plotting to seize Assyrian territories. See, Ginsberg, *Alexander Marx Jubilee Volume* (New York: Jewish Theological Seminary, 1950), p. 349 n. 12. But, as will immediately become clear, Assyrian administration encouraged open borders in furthering its goals. On additional contacts between Assyrian-occupied Israel and Judah, see below, pp. 107f.

[144] See above, p. 84 n. 103. S. D. Goitein reasons that "the removal of women from the (official) Temple service led to their being caught up in the popular beliefs and cults, wide-spread in the ancient East, more so than men." See his full remarks in "Women's Literature in the Bible," in *Bible Studies* [Hebrew] (Tel-Aviv: Yavneh, 1967), pp. 271ff.

[144a] Oppenheim's sketch of the "network of interstate contacts from court to court" in the mid-second millenium B.C.E. serves as an enlightening forward to the ensuing discussion; see JAOS 93 (1973), 264-65.

cultural patterns which had remained relatively stable for centuries. A boast of Sargon's after the victories of 716 B.C.E. discloses not only the imperial goals of economic control over Mediterranean commerce, but the means by which formerly distant peoples first met:

karri māt Muṣur kanku aptēma	I opened the sealed port of Egypt.
nišē māt Aššur u māt Muṣur itti	I let Assyrians and Egyptians mix freely
aḫāmeš ablulma ušēpiša maḫīru[145]	and engage in trade with each other.

Although spared provincial annexation because of its non-strategic geographic location,[146] Judah was not excluded from the benefits of this free-trade policy. Pottery finds at many seventh century B.C.E. sites testify to commercial contacts between Judah and Assyria.[147] "Imported Assyrian palace ware" has been identified by Aharoni among the ruins of Ramat Rahel.[148] Jerusalem's markets bustled with merchant activity (cf. Zeph 1.11),[149] and Judahites plied the trade routes of Mesopotamia. A sale of wheat, transacted in Nineveh in the spring of 660,[150] was measured *ina* GIŠ.BAR *ša māt Iaudi*—"according to the Judahite *sūtu*."[151]

Judah's economy recovered slowly from Sennacherib's destructive invasion, and by the mid-seventh century B.C.E. Jerusalem expanded into new suburbs in the north and west: the "Mishneh" and "Machtesh."[152] Official state visits to foreign capitals[153] may have prompted Jerusalemites to "up-date" local architecture voluntarily, as in the days of Ahaz.[154] In other parts of the country builders copied the "Assyrian open-court" design, first introduced in the provincial admin-

145 Lie, *Sargon*, 17-18; completed by Gadd, *Iraq* 16 (1954), 179, 46-49. On dating this episode, cf. Tadmor, *JCS* 12 (1958), 35, 77-78.

146 See above, p. 72.

147 Cf. Ruth Amiran, *The Ancient Pottery of the Land of Israel* [Hebrew] (Jerusalem: Mosad Bialik, 1963), p. 350.

148 Y. Aharoni, *Excavations at Ramat Rahel* (Rome: Università degli studi di Roma, 1964), p. 31.

149 G. Boström, *Proverbiastudien* (Lunds Universitets Årsskrift 30/3, 1935), pp. 91-97, advances the idea that separate foreign bazaars were authorized by the court to stimulate trade (e.g., 1 Kgs 20.34); but, very often, the customs of foreign traders led to antagonism from pious Israelite circles; e.g. Neh 10.32; 13.15f.

150 Cf. ARU 325.10, *araḫ Aiaru* ᵐ*Giriṣapūni*, "the month of Iyar, (in the eponymate of) Giriṣapūnu." See RLA 2, p. 448.

151 ARU 325.2.

152 Cf. Zeph 1.10; 2 Kgs 22.14; 2 Chr 33.14, and see above, p. 70. B. Mazar, En. Miq. 3, *s.v.* "Jerusalem," cols. 801, 811, 824, dated the expansion to the days of Uzziah. Cf. Gray, *Kings*², p. 610. Current archaeological exploration in Jerusalem has uncovered a massive fortification wall on the hill west of the Temple Mount, dateable to Iron Age II, i.e., the seventh century B.C.E. See N. Avigad, "Excavations in the Jewish Quarter of the Old City of Jerusalem, 1970," IEJ 20 (1970), 130-34 and IEJ 22 (1972), 193-200.

153 Cf. Borger, *Asarhaddon*, § 27, ep. 21, 55; § 67, 34.

154 See the discussion of the Ahaz altar reform above, pp. 73-77.

istrative centers of Megiddo and Hazor.[155] In art, as well as architecture, foreign forms attracted Judah's wealthy. Phoenician ivories, formally known to us only from Samaria's palaces, might now be traced to Jerusalem. Among the ivories recently recovered at Nimrud is a section from an ivory plaque inscribed with Hebrew characters with affinities to those typical of the late eighth–early seventh centuries B.C.E.[156]

Among the populace, acculturation proceeded apace. Judahite soldiers joined other Westerners levied for the Egyptian campaigns of Ashurbanipal.[157] Although organized into a separate national military unit,[158] these soldiers were certainly exposed to customs and languages other than their own.[159] In the countryside of Judah, the intermingling of populations went much further, with foreigners settled to the immediate west and north of Judah in Assyrian provinces.[160] In addition to Hebrew, Assyrian and eventually Aramaic[161] became

[155] Cf. R. Amiran and I. Dunayevsky, "The Assyrian Open-Court Building and its Palestinian Derivatives," BASOR 149 (1958), 25-32; and Y. Aharoni, "The 'Persian Fortress' at Lachish — An Assyrian Palace?" Y^adiot 31 (1967), 80-91. A further example of Assyrian construction is now being unearthed at Tell Jemme; see the preliminary report, G. W. Van Beek, "Assyrian Vaulted Buildings at Tell Jemme," Qadmoniot 6 (1973), 23-27.

[156] The inscription ND. 10150 was published by A. R. Millard, "Alphabetic Inscriptions on Ivories from Nimrud," Iraq 24 (1962), 45-49. See too, M. E. L. Mallowan, *Nimrud and Its Remains* 2 (London: Collins, 1966), p. 595; and J. Naveh, *Lĕšonēnu* 30 (1966), 67. If one may be permitted to speculate on the basis of this inscription, which falls well within the established canons of Hebrew epigraphy, it seems that our ivory — beyond attesting to luxurious living among Jerusalem's wealthy — bears witness to the presence in Judah of local craftsmen working in a foreign art medium. Up to now, it has generally been assumed that ivories of Phoenician manufacture adorned the palaces of the Near East. (A summary discussion on Phoenician ivories, their stylistic features, manufacture and distribution can be found in Frankfort's *The Art and Architecture of the Ancient Orient*, pp. 188-95.) But Judah's kings may have supported a native ivory industry, growing out of the earlier Solomonic ivory trade (cf. 1 Kgs 10.18 and 22).

[157] Cf. Asb. C.I.25. See 2 Kgs 24.2; Jer 35.11 for Babylonian use of local levy, there against Judah; and Saggs, *Iraq* 25 (1963), 146, 151.

[158] The levy may have been completed by natives who had been previously deported, e.g., by Sennacherib (cf. OIP 2, 32.18ff.), and were serving as palace guards in Nineveh. On the Lachish regiment, see R. D. Barnett, IEJ 8 (1958), 163-64; and on impression into royal service in general, see W. Manitius, "Das stehende Heer des Assyrerkönige und seine Organisation," ZA 23 (1910), 114f., 220ff. J. E. Reade now discusses identification of foreign recruits as depicted on palace reliefs in Iraq 34 (1972), 105, 106f.

[159] This was certainly true if these soldiers became part of the first Judahite settlers in Egypt, as argued by B. Porten, *Archives from Elephantine*, pp. 8-13.

[160] Philistia was resettled by Sargon after 712 B.C.E. (cf. Lie, *Sargon*, 261), and Samaria, beginning in 720 B.C.E., continuously served as a reception center for foreign captives (cf. below, p. 101 n. 23).

[161] Although dockets in Aramaic are known as early as the reign of Tiglath-pileser III (cf. Bowman, JNES 7 [1948], 73ff.), at the time of Rabshakeh's mission to Hezekiah, Aramaic could still be used for private diplomatic correspondence (2 Kgs 18.26). On realia of the scene before the walls of Jerusalem, see Childs, *Isaiah and The Assyrian*

the languages of daily discourse. At Gezer, business transactions were recorded in standard Neo-Assyrian legal formulae.[162] As noted above, the stamp seal of the Judahite landowner Natanyahu, on one of the Gezer tablets, features pagan lunar symbolism.[163]

A striking eye-witness account of the cosmopolitan atmosphere in Jerusalem prior to the Josianic reforms,[164] complementing the picture derived from extra-biblical finds, survives in the prophecies of Zephaniah. The scene he describes is not one of violent religious reactionism nor of enforced paganism. Quiet, complacent assimilation prevails. Courtiers ape "foreign dress" and "skip over the threshold" in Philistine fashion,[165] while filling the temple with the gain of their lawlessness and treachery (Zeph 1.8-9). Zephaniah warns of the impend-

Crisis, pp. 80-83. Among the Aramaeans of the empire as well, bi-lingualism has been shown to have existed by S. Schiffer, *Die Aramäer* (Leipzig: J. C. Hinrichs, 1911), pp. 41-42.

[162] Macalister, *Gezer*, pp. 23-29; tablet I is dated 652 B.C.E., tablet II, 649 B.C.E.

[163] Cf. above, p. 87. Macalister's astonishment (*ibid.*, p. 29) over the use by a Hebrew of a lunar emblem is no longer remarkable.

Kurt Galling treats the population make-up and organization of Gezer in "Assyrische und persische Präfekten in Gezer," PJB 31 (1935), 75-93. The presence at Gezer of a person bearing an Egyptian name and title *ḫazānu*, "magistrate" (cf. CAD Ḫ, 163ff.) — a witness to the Natanyahu sale — is explained by Galling as indicating Assyrian confirmation of the "old indigenous" population in their administrative posts, as they were not Israelite (pp. 85f.). But that non-Israelites ruled in Israelite Gezer seems unlikely after the city's two-hundred-year annexation to Judah and Israel. Cf. 1 Kgs 9.16-17 and Z. Kallai, *The Tribes of Israel* [Hebrew] (Jerusalem: Mosad Bialik, 1967), pp. 70f., 81. It is more reasonable to assume that the Egyptian *ḫazānu* was a deportee, settled at Gezer by either Esarhaddon or Ashurbanipal. Borger, *Asarhaddon*, § 80, I, contains a partial list of skilled Egyptians impressed into Assyrian service. Cf. also, ABL 1009. See the further remarks on land tenure under Assyria by B. Mazar, "The Tobiads," IEJ 7 (1957), 232f.; and, dissimilarly, M. Noth, *History*, p. 263.

[164] On the dating of Zephaniah, see the summary remarks of Eissfeldt, *Introduction*, pp. 423ff., and Kaufmann, *Tolᵉdot* 3, pp. 348-55. Recent attempts to lower the date of the prophet's ministry, e.g., D. L. Williams, "The Date of Zephaniah," JBL 82 (1963), 77-88, are unconvincing. Williams renders the Hebrew *šᵉʾar habbaʿal* as "the remnant of Baal" (1.4) — allegedly the uncompleted work of Deuteronomic reform. But the expression means "the last vestige of Baal," i.e. Baal worship eradicated and left without heir (//*šēm*); cf. Schwally, ZAW 10 (1890), 169; BDB, p. 984. He also interprets "thickening upon their lees" (1.12) as disappointment with failure of reform, rather than expressing self-satisfied contentment as shown by the parallel in Jer 48.11 (//*šaʾᵃnan, šoqēt*).

Other items in Zephaniah are better suited to the Assyrian period, e.g., the imagery of destruction so frequent in NA inscriptions. On the "salting and seeding" of a conquered city, Zeph 2.9, see A. Honeyman, "The Salting of Shechem," VT 3 (1953), 192-95; S. Gevirtz, "Jericho and Shechem, A Religio-Literary Aspect of City Destruction," VT 13 (1963), 52-62. On the thorough dismantling of Nineveh and its becoming a roost for wild animals, Zeph 2.13-15, cf. OIP 2, 84.51-54; Borger, *Asarhaddon,* § 27, ep. 5, 69-70.

[165] This seems to be the most reasonable explanation of the practice; cf. Targum and Radak *ad loc.* and 1 Sam 5.5.

ing doom of YHWH which will overtake all those who "bow on roof-tops to the heavenly host" and "swear by YHWH" and "their king"[166] at one and the same time (1.5). But these arrogant Jerusalemites believe: "YHWH will neither benefit nor harm" (1.12).[167]

In a word, the diminutive Judahite state was buffeted on all sides by the cultural patterns dominant in the Assyrian empire. Although Assyria made no formal demands for cultural uniformity among its subjects, one of the by-products of political and economic subjugation was a tendency toward cultural homogeneity. Involved as it was in imperial affairs, Judah was faced with the problem of assimilation of foreign norms, on a national scale, for the first time in its history. Abetting this natural process of assimilation were Judah's leading circles, who, according to Zephaniah, had become disenchanted with Israel's God.

A feeling of disillusionment in YHWH's ability to change the fortunes of his people was abroad. Isaiah's promises of ultimate victory over the Assyrian enemy notwithstanding (e.g., Isa 10.12-19), Judah's observable situation for close to a century was subservience to the will of Assyria. Owing to this political decline, Judahites succumbed to the lure of new gods. The Chronicler editorially mocked Ahaz, but caught the current mood: "He [i.e., Ahaz] sacrificed to the gods of Damascus who strike at him, thinking: Since the gods of the Aramaean kings aid them, let me sacrifice to them so they will aid me (too)."[168]

Manasseh's restoration of the rural cult sites and their pagan accouterments, rejected by the reforms of his father, Hezekiah (cf. 2 Kgs 21.3), becomes intelligible as well, once we recognize the religious exigencies of the late Neo-Assyrian era. T. H. Robinson had supposed:

> He may have felt, as many in Judah certainly did feel, that these shrines were legitimate centres of the worship of Yahweh, and that even Hezekiah had no right to overthrow them. Not a few must have traced the calamities which befell the land during Sennacherib's invasion to Hezekiah's sacrilege, and have welcomed the restoration of the old ways.[169]

[166] The consonantal *mlkm* is almost universally vocalized by commentators *milkom*, i.e., the god of the Ammonites (cf. 1 Kgs 11.5). There is little question that the prophet's intent was to contrast worship of Israel's YHWH with that of a foreign deity. But as Schwally noted (ZAW 10 [1890], 214), at least two intrusive cults simultaneously utilized the title *melek*, "king," cf. 2 Kgs 23.10, 13. Lacking decisive information, the ambiguity of the consonantal text is to be retained. Cf. Ehrlich, *Mikrâ* 3, p. 456.

[167] A later generation, living in the shadow of imminent destruction, believed themselves abandoned by YHWH; in Ezek 8.12, idolatrous elders think: "YHWH does not see us; YHWH has left the country." (Such a remark may preclude advancing this section of Ezekiel's temple vision to the days of Manasseh [cf. Kaufmann's remarks, *Tol^edot* 3, pp. 499-502], considering the absence of despair in the report of Zephaniah.)

[168] 2 Chr 28.23. Heaton's recent ascription of "superstitous impetuosity" to Ahaz seems ill-suited within the context here described. See *The Hebrew Kingdoms* (*New Clarendon Bible* 2, Oxford: Clarendon Press, 1968), pp. 102f.

[169] Robinson, *History*, p. 403. Cf. A. Lods, *The Prophets and the Rise of Judaism* (London: Routledge & Kegan Paul, 1937), pp. 123ff.

That such feelings were indeed known in Judah can be shown. 2 Kgs 18.22 preserves a negative evaluation of Hezekiah's reform as delivered by the Assyrian Rabshakeh, in his challenge to Jerusalem's defenders: "But if you say to me, 'We trust in YHWH our God,' is it not he whose cult sites and altars Hezekiah removed, ordering Judah and Jerusalem, 'Before this altar in Jerusalem you shall worship'?" It would seem that the Kings historian utilized the Rabshakeh's remarks — reflective of a "blatant pagan point of view"[170] — to broadcast his evaluation of Manasseh's restoration of rural cult sites: a willful rejection of YHWHistic tradition as interpreted by the Deuteronomists.[171]

This unprecedented demoralization threatened Judah's unique cultural and religious identity; only with the return of national self-confidence, which was to follow upon the decline of Assyria, could the assimilation of Manasseh's age be halted.

[170] So, B. Childs in *Isaiah and the Assyrian Crisis*, p. 82: "Only someone completely removed from the Hebrew religion could have interpreted Hezekiah's reform as an insult to Israel's deity." M. Weinfeld, *JNES* 23 (1963), 208ff., connects the Rabshakeh passage with the prophetic school of Isaiah, who, in this "veiled protest" expressed its disapproval of Hezekiah's reform. But it is hard to conceive of Isaiah supporting the rural sanctuaries, laced as they were with vestigal pagan accouterments (cf. 2 Kgs 18.4); albeit accommodated by some within YHWHism (on which, see, Kaufmann, *Tol^{e}dot* 2, pp. 126f., 262, and 266). Rabshakeh's remarks, if not "genuinely historical" (so, Childs, *loc cit.*), are then likely the veiled Deuteronomic polemic against those who would reinstate the rural sanctuaries in the name of YHWHism.

[171] Spearheading the opposition to the Hezekian reforms may well have been the personnel of the rural sanctuaries, displaced by the centralization of worship within Jerusalem. It has been argued that Manasseh early came under the influence of the Judahite "people of the land" and the rural priesthood, who had allied against the economic and religious monopoly of the Jerusalem sanctuary. (Note that 2 Chr 31.19 records the dependent status of the "Aaronide priests [who lived] on the pasture lands of their cities.") This speculation is contained in the discussion on the rise of Jerusalem as a "cosmopolitan and hieropolitan" center in M. H. Ben-Shalosh [pseud.], "History in the Times of the First Temple" [Hebrew], *Sepher Yerushalayim*, ed. by M. Avi-Yonah (Jerusalem and Tel-Aviv: Mosad Bialik and Dvir, 1956), pp. 120-31.

5. ISRAEL UNDER ASSYRIAN RULE

From Vassal State to Province

NORTH Israel's political history contrasts markedly with Judah's successful avoidance of Assyrian annexation. The main routes to Egypt and Arabia, connecting with the port cities on the Philistian coast, traversed Israelite territory, so that Assyria's ambitions at economic hegemony over Mediterranean commerce inevitably encroached upon the Israelite territories. Contact with the revitalized Neo-Assyrian empire of Tiglath-pileser III proved fatal almost from the start, and within just twelve years of the first outbreak of hostilities, Israel lost its independence.

The brief period of anarchy which followed the lengthy and successful rule of Jeroboam II (789-748 B.C.E.) ended with the emergence of Menahem the Gadite as king in Samaria (2 Kgs 15.8-15).[1] He did not join the ill-fated Azaryahu rebellion of 738,[2] but chose to secure his throne by paying a heavy tribute to Pul, i.e., Tiglath-pileser III.[3] Payment was met by a levy upon "all *gibbōrē haḥayil*[4] — 50 silver shekels per man."[5]

[1] According to Thiele, "a rival reign of Pekah in Gilead which began the same year that Menahem slew Shallum" explains the lengthy 20 years of Pekah noted in 2 Kgs 15:27 (*Mysterious Numbers*, pp. 124ff.). This difficult chronology notwithstanding, M. Haran considers Menahem's early years (*ca.* 748-738 B.C.E.) to have been free of internal strife and Assyrian interference, evidence the Israelite attack on distant Tipsah on the Euphrates — 2 Kgs 15:16 (see VT 17 [1967], 284-90; and J. Liver, En. Miq. 5 cols. 31-32). Tadmor (see "Azriyau," p. 249) observed that Assyrian sources uniquely refer to Menahem as ^{m}*Meniḫimme āl Samerināya*, "Menahem, the Samaritan" (Rost, *Tigl. III*, 150), rather than the "Omride," reflecting perhaps the weakening internal conditions after the appearance of Tiglath-pileser III in the West (post-743 B.C.E.). But the term "Samerina" may be no more than a variant designation for Israel, as is now evident from the Adad-nirari III stele from Tell-Rimah, wherein Joash is named ^{m}*Ia'asu māt Samerināya*. See *Iraq* 30 (1968), 142, 8.

[2] Probably a sign of continued weakness, rather than political astuteness. So, Tadmor, "Azriyau," pp. 248ff.

[3] Rost, *Tigl. III*, 150; 2 Kgs 15:19. The widely accepted view that Pul was Tiglath-pileser's Babylonian throne name is newly disputed by J. A. Brinkman on the basis of a source distribution study, which produced "no evidence that 'Pulu' was ever used as a contemporary name for the king in Babylonia or anywhere else." See his full treatment in AnOr 43, pp. 61-62 and n. 1544. As Brinkman conjectures, perhaps Pul "was his name in Assyria before he came to the throne or . . . it was employed as a quasi-hypocoristic for the second element of the name Tiglath-pileser" (n. 317).

[4] Best interpreted as a technical term indicating Israelite freeholders, owing military service to the crown. Cf. S. E. Loewenstamm, En. Miq. 2, cols. 387f.; Tadmor, JWH 11 (1968), 63 n. 33. Montgomery, *Kings*, p. 451, considered this "ancient military expression

Anti-Assyrian forces in Israel, led by Pekah, soon renewed the confrontation with Assyria by assassinating Menahem's son, Pekahya, in order to align Samaria with Damascus in revolt.[6] Tiglath-pileser retaliated with two campaigns to Damascus in 733 and 732 B.C.E., at the same time wresting extensive territories from Israel.[7] From these, he carved out three Assyrian provinces, following traditional geopolitical lines:[8] Du'ru, on the Mediterranean coast;[9] Magidu, in

— lit. 'men of valour' — had changed its meaning to one of economic significance," and rendered it "magnates of wealth."

[5] 2 Kgs 15:20. Wiseman, *Iraq* 15 (1953), 135 n. 1, conjectures that the 50 shekel levy corresponded to the worth of each man "as a slave at current Assyrian values." On the basis of a new study of the numerical symbols, the paleography and archaeological data, Y. Yadin dates the Samaria ostraca to Menahem's ninth and tenth years, suggesting that the Assyrian tax was payable in naturalia, assessed at silver value. See "Ancient Judaean Weights and the Date of the Samaria Ostraca," SH 8 (Jerusalem, 1960), pp. 17-25; cf. the concurring remarks of F. M. Cross, BASOR 165 (1962), 35, and the alternate proposal of Y. Aharoni, BASOR 184 (1966), 16-19; and *idem, The Land of the Bible*, pp. 315ff.

[6] Cf. 2 Kgs 15:23-26. On the participants in the "Syro-Ephramite League," see above, p. 66 n. 3. An interpretation of these hostilities as an attempt "to dislodge Judah from Transjordania" is now set out by B. Oded in "The Historical Background of the Syro-Ephraimite War Reconsidered," CBQ 34 (1972), 153-65.

[7] See 2 Kgs 15:29; 1 Chr 5:6, 25-26. The most recent treatments of the Assyrian march through "the land of Naphtali" are by Y. Aharoni, *The Settlement of the Israelite Tribes in Upper Galilee*, pp. 129-32, and H. Tadmor, "The Conquest of the Galilee by Tiglath-pileser III, King of Assyria" [Hebrew] *Proceedings of the Twenty-Fourth Convention of the Israel Exploration Society* (Jerusalem, 1967), pp. 62-67.

Israelite holdings in northern Trans-Jordan had already been greatly reduced as a result of Aramaean incursions prior to 733 B.C.E., according to Tadmor's reconstruction of Assyrian border lists; see "The Southern Border of Aram," IEJ 12 (1962), 114-22.

[8] This point is stressed by A. Alt in "Das System der Assyrischen Provinzen auf dem Boden des Reiches Israel," KS 2, pp. 188-205. Cf. Forrer, *Provinzeinteilung*, pp. 60ff., and 64.

[9] A. Alt claims that Tiglath-pileser had already annexed part of Israel's coastal plain during the 734 B.C.E. Philistine campaign ("Tiglath-pileser III. Erster Feldzug nach Palästina," KS 2, pp. 150-62; adopted by Noth, *History*, p. 258). He argues from the scant information related on the recently recovered Nimrud annal ND. 400, 10-13 (=*Iraq* 13 [1951], 23), which reads:

[kīma ur]qīti pagrē mun[daḫ]ṣēšunu umalla [ṣēri . . .] [ma]ršītīšunu alpēšunu ṣēnīšunu immerīšunu [. . . .] *ina qereb ekallīšu* [ ]x-*dīšunu amḫuršunūtima mātsunu u*[x]	I filled the [steppe like gr]ass with the corpses of his warriors . . . [I carried off] his flocks: cattle, goats, and sheep. Inside his palace [I erected . . .] I received their [ ]. Their land I [ ].

This victory over an unknown territory is sandwiched in between battles in northern Phoenicia, by the city of Ṣi[mirra] and the Philistian Gaza. If Alt is correct and this broken section does refer to Israel (cf. already Wiseman, *Iraq* 13 [1951], 22), then we must assume an Assyrian invasion of Israelite hinterland in order to accomplish some action (the erection of a stele ?) in the palace of Samaria. Such a detour is highly unlikely in view of the goals of the 734 B.C.E. campaign — the control of Philistian maritime

the Galilee and Jezreel valley; and Gal'aza, in Gilead.[10]

This first Assyrian annexation did not include widespread population exchanges, typical of imperial incorporation. Prisoners taken from Galilean towns were not replaced by foreign settlers, thus leaving many areas substantially Israelite.[11] It seems that Assyria was ready to accede to the continued existence of a vassal Israelite state, confined to the Ephramite hills around its capital, Samaria, as long as that state would not become burdensome to the empire. So, the rebel king Pekah having already been ousted, Tiglath-pileser III confirmed the pro-Assyrian Hoshea as Israel's last king.[12]

Sometime after 725,[13] Hoshea broke faith with his Assyrian overlord, Shalmaneser V, by concluding a rebellious alliance with the Egyptian court.[14] Despite

centers. Tadmor, "Campaigns," p. 264, reasons that these lines relate a further attack in the vicinity of Ṣimirra. If so, then in 734 B.C.E., Tiglath-pileser marched unmolestingly through Israel's coastal holdings, directly to Gaza. (A new conjecture on the involvement of Hiram of Tyre in these battles was put forward by this writer in JCS 25 [1973], 97 n. 11.)

[10] A new study by B. Oded, "Observations on Methods of Assyrian Rule in Transjordania after the Palestine Campaign of Tiglath-pileser III," JNES 29 (1970), 177-86, posits the division of Gilead into "four Assyrian administrative units:" Gal'aza, Ṭab'el, Gidir, and Hamat (pp. 179ff.). This idea, an elaboration of Forrer's suggestion in *Provinzeinteilung*, pp. 64f., of a split-up of "the enlarged Gal'aza province" after 690 B.C.E., appears tenuous both textually and geographically. No "province of Ṭab'el" or "territorial administrative unit" named Gidir is known from Assyrian sources, Nimrud letter ND. 2773 notwithstanding. This undated document speaks of Ṭab'el and Gidir in the most general terms; both locations are defined merely by the logographic determinative KUR *mātu*, "land." Besides, Oded's geographic deliniations would have us draw overlapping borders, especially with reference to Hamat and Gidir. If Hamat "covered roughly the same area as Solomon's district of Mahanaim" (p. 181), then it would have included both Gidir and Ṭab'el. See Kallai, *Tribes of Israel*, pp. 55f.

It seems better to maintain the traditional view of Assyrian administration in Israelite Trans-Jordan: one province, Gal'aza, with its capital at Ramoth-Gilead or Hamath. Cf. Aharoni, *The Land of the Bible*, p. 331 n. 114 and especially the critique of A. Alt, KS 2, p. 204.

[11] Cf. works of Aharoni and Tadmor, cited in n. 7, for elaboration.

[12] Cf. 2 Kgs 15:30; Rost, *Tigl. III*, III R 10, 2, 17-18; ND. 4301 +, rev. 10′-12′ (=*Iraq* 18 [1956], 126.) Oppenheim, ANET, p. 283b, incorrectly supplies the name [Menahem] in this Assyrian inscription, rather than that of Hanno, the Gazaite. Cf. Tadmor, "Campaigns," p. 264, and Wiseman in D. Winton Thomas, *Documents from Old Testament Times* (London: Thomas Nelson and Sons, 1958), p. 55.

[13] The chronology in this section follows that of H. Tadmor in his comprehensive study of the fall of Samaria in *JCS* 12 (1958) 33-40.

[14] 2 Kgs 17:4 tells of messengers sent by Hoshea to "So, king of Egypt." The identification of So with Sib'u, the Egyptian military commander mentioned in inscriptions from Sargon's reign, long acknowledged by historians (e.g., Noth, *History*, 262 n. 3; Bright, *History*, 258; Tadmor, in *JCS* 12 [1958] 38 n. 144, summarized the pertinent literature), has been recently subject to criticism.

Borger, *JNES* 19 (1960) 49-53, proved that the name Sib'u should be read Re'e (=SIB́-'*e*), the logographic writing reflecting a scribal pun on the commander's behavior in battle. We are told that: *kī rē'u* (LÚ.SÍB) *ša ṣēnašu ḫabta ēdānuššu ipparšidma* (Lie,

Hoshea's early capture during the ensuing Assyrian reprisals, Samaria did not surrender until the fall of 722, after a three-year siege.[15] Shalmaneser's death shortly thereafter left matters in Samaria unsettled. The new Assyrian king, Sargon II, determined to put an end to Samaria's continuing insurrection.[16] In 720 he retook the city, deported 27,290 of its residents,[17] and reorganized it as a royal provincial center.[18]

Only scattered details are known of Samaria's history under Assyrian rule. Assyria's holdings in Israel may have been consolidated around the new Samerina province,[19] from which foreign governors[20] and administrators[21] exacted "tax and tribute"[22] from the mixed population resettled in Israel. After Sargon's

Sargon, 55), "like a shepherd whose flock had been stolen, he fled alone." Cf. ANET, p. 285 n. 7. Following this demise of Sib'u, Goedicke, BASOR 171 (1963) 64-66, identified the Egyptian conspirator who aided Hoshea as Tefnakhte, whose residence was the city of Sais, in Egyptian *S ꜣ w* and in Hebrew *Soʾ*. W. F. Albright wrapped up these discussions in a small note, *BASOR* 171 (1963) 66, in which he reconstructs the Hebrew text behind the present one: 2 Kgs 17:4 — *ʾl sʾ* <*ʾl*> *mlk mṣrym*, "to So <to> the king of Egypt."

[15] Cf. 2 Kgs 17:4-5, 18:9-10. According to Tadmor (En. Miq. 4, cols. 287-89, *s.v.* "Chronology"), the seige lasted two calendar years.

[16] Samaria, "governed by the generals of the army or by the city elders" between 724/3-720 B.C.E. (so, Tadmor, *JCS* 12 [1958] 37), joined the Assyrian provinces in north Syria in rebellion upon Sargon's accession. See Nimrud Prism D, col. 4:25-29 (= Gadd, *Iraq* 16 [1954] 179).

[17] Variant: 27,280.

[18] The full text of Sargon's re-organization is discussed above, pp. 49-51.

[19] Y. Aharoni thinks that the Du'ru-Dor province was re-united with Samaria after 720 B.C.E., since no independent eponym from Dor is known. Moreover, a fragmentary Esarhaddon inscription (Borger, *Asarhaddon*, § 76, 16) associates the coastal territories with Samaria, as was the case in pre-Assyrian times. The mention of Dor in a late list of imperial centers (cf. Forrer, *Provinzeinteilung*, pp. 52ff.) may mean that Dor continued to serve as a secondary administrative district within the larger Samerina province. These speculations are developed in Aharoni, *The Land of the Bible*, 334. The Esarhaddon text, at the base of Aharoni's study, reads, in Borger's edition: *āl Apqu ša paṭi māt Samen[a* · x (?)], "Aphek, which belongs to the territory of Samen[a] (Simeon ?? Samaria ??)" The designation Simeon must be excluded from consideration; the tribal territory of Simeon in the Negev (at some distance from Aphek) was absorbed by the Judah tribe at an early date (cf. Kallai, *Tribes of Israel*, p. 295). Tadmor collated the line in question (November, 1963) and kindly informs me that the reading, in this "badly written draft of an inscription," is definitely: *sa-me* <*ri-*> ⌜*na.*⌝

[20] Two Samaritan governors appear as eponyms: Nabū-kīna-uṣur in 690 B.C.E. (cf. *RLA* 2, 451) and Nabū-šar-aḫḫēšu in 646 B.C.E. (cf. M. Falkner, "Die Eponymen der spätassyrischen Zeit," AfO 17 [1954-55] 113-14, 118).

[21] In addition to the *šaknu*-official appointed by Sargon (see above, p. 50), a Samarian LÚ.GAL.URU.MEŠ, *rab alāni*, "overseer of several cities or estates" (cf. CAD A 1, 389f.) named Aya-aḫḫē is known from a tablet fragment discovered at Samaria. See, G. A. Reisner, C. S. Fisher, and D. G. Lyon, *Harvard Excavations at Samaria* 1 (Cambridge: Harvard University Press, 1924), p. 247, and vol. 2, pl. 56b. Alt speculated on the nature of the transaction recorded on this payment note in "Briefe aus der assyrischen Kolonie in Samaria," *PJB* 37 (1941) 103f.

[22] The Sargon annals record: *biltu mandattu kī ša Aššurī ēmidsunūti* (Lie, *Sargon*, 17;

initial colonization in 720, new refugees were periodically transferred to Samaria,[23] either in replacement of men impressed into military service[24] or in an attempt to discipline restive colonists.[25] The upshot of these incessant transfers was a shift in the ethnic make-up of north Israel in favor of the foreign settlers. While our sources do not tell of a systematic Assyrian depopulation of the Ephraimite hill country, it seems clear that the native Israelites left on the land were not, as Noth contended, "numerically much greater" than the "foreign upper class" settlers.[26] The opposite was the case. Sargon's exile of 27,290 Israelites from Samaria was but the final stage in a bitter four-year struggle to subdue the rebellious city.[27] This extended engagement of the Assyrian army, meanwhile, must have had a devastating effect on the Samarian countryside — a fact inferable from the annal report of Sennacherib's campaign, of shorter duration, against

cf. above, p. 50), "I imposed tax and tribute upon them just as if they were Assyrians." The Sargon Display Inscription refers to the impost as *biltu šarri maḫrê ēmidsunūti* (Winckler, *Sargon*, 100.24-25), "I imposed the tax of the(ir) former king upon them." Of the two formulaic expressions, the former annal remark is no doubt historically more reliable. Reorganization of Samaria must have included revision of the former tax structure, so as to assess both new and foreign settlers and those Israelites not deported.

[23] Assyrian annals tell of one additional deportation to Samaria in Sargon's seventh year of "Tamudi, Ibadidi, Marsimani, and Hayapa — distant, steppe-dwelling Arabs" (Lie, *Sargon*, 120-123).

Biblical sources record that both Esarhaddon (Ezra 4:2) and Asnappar–Ashurbanipal (4:9f) brought additional settlers (on the identification of Asnappar, see B. Mazar, En. Miq. 1, cols. 480-81). Likewise, an anonymous "king of Assyria" settled people from Babylon, Cutha, Avva, Hamath and Sepharvaim in Samaria (cf. 2 Kgs 17:24). This king cannot be identified with Sargon, considering that Sargon styled himself a patron of Babylonian culture. See Tadmor, in *History of the Jewish People* 1 (Tel-Aviv: Dvir, 1969), p. 137. Either Sennacherib (so, Tadmor, *loc. cit.*) or Ashurbanipal (so, Winckler, *Alttestamentliche Untersuchungen*, 98-101; Olmstead, *Western Asia*, 73 n. 39; and Streck, VAB 7, ccclxiv and ccclxviii) may be the Biblical "king of Assyria," both monarchs having exiled Babylonians in large numbers after their respective conquests in 689 B.C.E. and 648 B.C.E. Other views are given by Burney, *Notes on the Hebrew Text of the Books of Kings* (reprint; New York: *KTAV*, 1970) 333ff.; and Montgomery, *Kings*, 472.

That settlers were brought to Samaria from scattered locations throughout Assyria's domain, including southern Babylonia, Elam (?) (cf. G. R. Driver, EI 5 [1958] 19*ff.; and En. Miq. 5, col. 739, *s.v.* "Nibḥaz"), and Syria (on the identification of Sepharvaim with Sibra'in in Ezek 47:16, cf. Albright, *ARI*[5], 222 n. 116; Mazar, *Yᵉdiot* 12 [1945] 99 n. 63), suggests that the deportations listed in 2 Kgs 17:24 resulted from several Assyrian campaigns during the reigns of more than one monarch. On other signs of this listing being part of a late composition, see discussion below, p. 109 n. 75.

[24] ABL 1009, in what looks to be an Assyrian army personnel report, mentions: 4 LÚ.BAN *Samernāya* ᵐ[ ] 1 LÚ.BAN *Samernāya* . . . (rev. 3f.), "4 Samarian archers . . . 1 Samarian archer" among the army units.

[25] See our remarks above, p. 69 n. 25.

[26] Noth, *History*, 262. Noth followed, in part, Alt's formulation (KS 2, 320-23): the Samarian community, a closed political, social and economic unit, was composed solely of foreign upper class elements.

[27] See Kaufmann's earlier observations, to similar effect, *Tolᵉdot* 4, 187 n. 43.

Judah, which claims over 200,150 (!) persons displaced.[28] Furthermore, that the Samarian province served as the reception center for countless deportees—including persons other than "foreign upper classes," as, e.g., Arab tribesmen[29]—means that areas outside the capital city were availible for resettlement, i.e., cleared of their former residents.[30]

With the last stage of its incorporation into the Assyrian empire accomplished in 720 B.C.E., Israel perished as an independent state, not to be restored even after the withdrawal of Assyria a century later. Whether Israelite territory was actually annexed to Judah during Josiah's rule or not,[31] the impress of Assyria's long rule in Samaria persisted; a Samarian satrapy was established in the territory of the old Neo-Assyrian Samerina province during the Neo-Babylonian and Persian periods.[32]

Accordingly, two distinct phases in Israel's political relations with Assyria are distinguishable: (1) a short period of vassalage, 745-720 B.C.E., during which Israel suffered substantial territorial losses, followed by (2) a century of provincial incorporation which effected the demise of the Israelite polity. If the policies of Assyrian administration executed in Judah were followed in Israel, then vassal Israel should have been free from imperial interference in its cultic

[28] OIP 2, 33:24-27. This remarkable number of exiles was explained away by Ungnad as an attempt by an Assyrian scribe to express "2,150." This smaller number, in turn, supported Ungnad's contention that Sennacherib's campaign to Judah was "seemingly unsuccessful." See, "Die Zahl der von Sanherib deportierten Judäer," ZAW 18 (1942-43), 199-202. But this fails to explain the occasion for such unusual numerical notation, unexampled in other Assyrian annals. While some exaggeration may be suspected at this point, that Sennacherib deported vast numbers of people to perform forced labor on his new capital at Nineveh is creditable. See the remarks of D. Oates, *Studies in the Ancient History of Northern Iraq* (London: British Academy, 1968), 57.

[29] Lie, *Sargon*, 120-123. Cf. above, n. 23. Eph'al doubts that this transfer was accomplished by means of an extensive campaign to the desert reaches, a feat nowhere claimed by Sargon. Rather, a mutually beneficial agreement, re-routing part of the Arabian spice trade to the inner-mountain roads of Palestine, brought nomadic tribesmen to settle the new Assyrian colony. See, *Nomads*, 77f., for the detailed case.

[30] Note that in the Sargon cylinder inscription, the area of resettlement is not limited to the city of Samaria alone (see above, n. 23); *māt bīt Ḫumria*, "Omriland" in its entirety was open to the nomads. See Lyon, *Sargon*, p. 4, line 20. See further Kaufmann's thoroughgoing critique of both Alt and Noth, *Tol^edot* 4, 172-74. Alt had failed to consider the Assyrian reports of mass exiles, from sundry locations, set to constructing new ports and cities, often for their own resettlement. Cf. von Soden's remarks, AO 37 (1938) 38, attributing the eventual downfall of the empire to this extensive deportation policy.

[31] See above, p. 71.

[32] Neo-Babylonian administration in Palestine as discussed by A. Alt, in "Die Rolle Samarias bei der Entstehung des Judentums," KS 2, 327-31, posits Samarian control of large areas of Judah, so as to explain the friction between Samaria and Jerusalem in the Persian period. Cf. also Noth, *History*, 288f.; and Bright, *History*, 324 and 347; and the criticism of Y. Kaufmann, *Tol^edot* 4, 177ff. Samaria under Persian rule may have experienced some revisions in its local autonomy; see K. Galling, "Syrien in der Politik der Achämeniden," AO 36/3-4 (1937), 9-27.

life, while provincial Samaria should have experienced the introduction of foreign cults. We proceed to investigate these suppositions.

Religion in North Israel

Little information concerning Israelite religion during the quarter century of Israel's Assyrian vassalage is available from the data reported in 2 Kings. The editor of Kings relentlessly rehearsed the historic "sins of Jeroboam, son of Nebat," i.e., rebellion against the Davidic dynasty and abandonment of the Jerusalem sanctuary (cf. 1 Kgs 12.25-33), as the sin of all of Israel's kings, save the last one, Hoshea, son of Elah. Of him alone are we told: "He did what was displeasing to YHWH, but not as the kings of Israel who preceded him (2 Kgs 17.2)." The basis for this lenient evaluation of Hoshea can no longer be determined;[33] information on Hoshea's religious activities has apparently been suppressed by the editor.[34] Significantly, however, tradition did record that Hoshea, despite subjection to the Assyrian aegis, exhibited YHWHistic loyalties, however measured.

There is no evidence of Assyrian interference in the Israelite cult prior to the 720 B.C.E. annexation of Samaria. John Gray claims that the service of the heavenly host recorded in 2 Kgs 17.16 is an Assyrian astral cult imposed upon Menahem and Hoshea as a token of Israel's subjection to Assyria.[35] But 17.16, part of an exhaustive Deuteronomistic indictment of Israel (2 Kgs 17.7-23), cannot be considered a true reflection of Israelite practice prior to annexation. The catalog of offenses bears little relation to what is narrated about north Israel throughout Kings. Several of Israel's sins (e.g., 17.17) appear here for the first time and resemble the offenses of Judah's Ahaz and Manasseh. The parallel developments in Judah (17.13), leading to its destruction (17.19-20), are cited as another example of YHWH's justifiable wrath. Finally, unlike other sections of the Deuteronomistic history in which the monarchy bears exclusive responsibility for Israel's doom, these verses denounce popular faithlessness in tones reminiscent of late prophecies. In all, this long passage stands out as an exilic addition to Kings,[36] questionable evidence for pre-720 B.C.E. Israelite practice.

[33] According to T. B. Giṭṭin 68a, "Hoshea abolished those guard-posts which Jeroboam (1) had placed on the roads (to Jerusalem) to prevent Israel from making pilgrimage." Kaufmann, *Tol^edot* 2, 266, conjectures that the verse refers to the removal of the Beth-el calves, since they were absent from their shrines at the time of the Josianic reforms (cf. 2 Kgs 23:15). On the whereabouts of the calves, cf. our alternate suggestions below, pp. 104f.

[34] Cf. Montgomery, *Kings*, 464f. Gray's supposition that this "mitigation of regular criticism" stems from Hoshea's neglect of cultic matters due to his over-involvement in politics, can hardly be correct (*Kings*², 641). The Kings historian would not have excused inattention to religious duties, one of his criteria for evaluating a monarch's reign.

[35] J. Gray, *Kings*², 648.

[36] Similar conclusions are reached by Montgomery, *Kings*, 470; Noth, *Überlieferungsgeschichtliche Studien*, 6 and 85; Eissfeldt, *Introduction*, 301; and Gray, *Kings*², 649f.

But even if we were to allow that the allusion to astral cults in Israel (2 Kgs 17.16) derived from reliable information, Assyrian imposition would still not be its source. Prior to Assyria's move into Syria-Palestine under Tiglath-pileser III, the prophet Amos had already inveighed against Israelite veneration of Mesopotamian stellar deities, Sakkut and Kaiwan (Amos 5.26).[37] The Amos citation has been unjustly suspect of being "either very late, i.e., after 722 B.C., or a late redaction of an earlier text which had become unintelligible."[38] Israel's reassertion of political dominion over Damascus and Hamath during the final years of Jeroboam II (cf. 2 Kgs 14.28)[39] exposed Israel anew[40] to mid-eighth century B.C.E. Aramaean culture, a culture suffused with Mesopotamian elements.[41] We suspect that astral cults popular in north Syria penetrated Israelite practice through Aramaean mediation,[42] as was the case a century later in Judah.[43] Consequently, as an independent vassal state, Israel was free of any cultic obligations.

The first direct cultic influence exerted by Assyria upon Israel can be noted after Samaria's capture and occupation. As with other localities, Sargon reports that in Samaria:

ilāni tiklīšun šalla[*tiš*] *amnu*[44]
I counted the gods in whom they trusted as spoil.

Gadd, in his publication of the Nimrud annal text, found these words to be "interesting evidence for the polytheism of Israel."[45] One need not wonder, however, at Sargon's presuming that some of the images removed from Samaria were gods of the city. Certainly the prized calves of the Beth-el sanctuary, considered by Israel to be "the visible pedestal on which the invisible Yahweh

It would appear that in formulating this passage on Israel's sins, the exilic editor was inspired by his own description of Judah's (i.e., Manasseh's) sins.

[37] Early discussion on the identification of these gods is summarized in Harper, *Amos and Hoshea* (ICC, 1905) 139-41; cf. also E. A. Speiser, "A Note on Amos 5:25," BASOR 108 (1947) 5-6; and T. L. Fenton, En. Miq. 5, col. 1037, *s.v.* "Sikkut." The earliest identification of Kaiwan as an astral deity is found in Ibn Ezra's comment, *ad loc.*

[38] Harper, *Amos-Hosea*, 138; similar evaluations in Fenton (see preceeding note); and Kaufmann, *Tolᵉdot* 3, 73 n. 27.

[39] On dating this event, see M. Haran, "Rise and Fall of the Empire of Jeroboam Ben Joash," VT 17 (1967), 278-84.

[40] Benjamin Mazar briefly touches upon "the influence of the eclectic culture of the Armaean empire" in Israel during the last half of the ninth century B.C.E. in Bib Arch *Reader* 2, 143; see his citations in n. 30.

[41] E.g., the parties to the Aramaic Sefiré treaty invoke at least five pairs of Mesopotamian deities, along with other West-Semitic deities. Cf. KAI 222 A, 8-10; J. A. Fitzmyer, *Aramaic Inscriptions of Sefîre*, 33-38, for identifications of deities and literature.

[42] See H. Tadmor, En. Miq. 3, col. 777.

[43] Cf. above, p. 87. As in Judah, Israel's newly-imported star-gods were probably incorporated into native astral cults. See above, pp. 85f.

[44] *Iraq* 16 (1954) 179, col. 4:32-33.

[45] *Ibid.*, p. 181.

stood,"[46] could easily have been mistaken by the Assyrians for Israelite gods.[47] The routine Assyrian annal remark might be better interpreted as the realization of Hosea's dire prediction:

> The dwellers of Samaria will fear for
> the calves of Beth-aven. . . .
> Even as it is carried off as tribute
> to Assyria, to the "great" king.[48]

Cultic changes, beyond the pillage of the Beth-el sanctuary, were especially felt in Israel with Sargon's reorganization of Samaria as a royal center. Expert supervisors trained the new provincials in the duties of Assyrian citizenship—the payment of tax and tribute and the "reverence of god and king."[49] But lest we suppose that the Samaritans henceforth undertook the exclusive worship of "Ashur and the great gods," the biblical narrative in 2 Kgs 17.24ff. shows otherwise. Even though the account exhibits a late Judahite disdain for Samaritan practice, we have no reason to doubt that its description of the religious situation in the Samarian province is "essentially correct."[50]

> Now the king of Assyria brought people from Babylon, Cutha, Avva, Hamath and Sepharvaim, and settled them in the towns of Samaria in place of the Israelites. They took possession of Samaria and lived in its towns. At the start of their settlement there, they did not revere YHWH, so YHWH sent lions against them, killing a number of them. They sent word[51] to the king of Assyria: The nations whom you have deported and settled in the towns of Samaria are not acquainted with the customs of the local god.[52] So, he sent lions against them, and now they are killing a number of them; because they are not acquainted with the customs of the local god.
>
> So the king of Assyria ordered: Transfer one of the priests whom you deported

[46] See W. F. Albright, *From the Stone Age to Christianity* (Garden City: Doubleday Anchor, 1957), 299 and discussion there; cf. also, Kaufmann, *Tol^{e}dot* 2, 260-61.

[47] Inasmuch as excavations at Beth-el have uncovered no eighth and seventh century B.C.E. destruction, the city must have peacefully surrendered to Sargon. Cf. Kelso, "The Second Campaign at Bethel, BASOR 137 (1955) 5-9, and IDB 1, 392. Nonetheless, earlier statements concerning the violent Assyrian takeover of Beth-el, e.g., Albright, *ARI*^{5}, 165f., are now incorporated in the final excavation report. See AASOR 39 (1968) 37; cf. p. 51. The archaeological evidence is apparently capable of equivocal interpretation.

[48] Hos 10:5-6. On Beth-aven as a pejorative for Beth-el, cf. Medieval commentaries *ad loc.* and Harper, *Amos-Hosea*, 263. On rendering *mlk yrb* as " 'Great' king," a title of Assyrian royalty, cf. Harper, 277f.; and H. W. Wolff, *Hosea* (BK, 1961) 222, who points to *mlk rb* in Sefiré. See Fitzmyer, *Sefiré Inscriptions*, 61.

[49] The full Sargon text concerning Samaria is presented and discussed above, pp. 49-51. (Gray's revised commentary *Kings*^{2}, 644, still presents the dated translation of this passage found in older textbooks.)

[50] So James D. Purvis, *The Samaritan Pentateuch and The Origin of the Samaritan Sect* (Cambridge: Harvard University Press, 1968), p. 94. Purvis' study contains a comprehensive survey of the conflicting Samaritan and Jewish claims relating to the sect's origins. See, especially, pp. 8 n. 12, and 88-118. For suggested date of composition of 2 Kgs 17:24ff., cf. n. 75 below.

[51] Lit. "they said;" cf. Burney, *Notes on Kings*, p. 336, "Impersonal; 'it was told.' "

[52] Lit. "god of the country."

from there. Let him[53] go and live there, and instruct them in the ways of the local god. Accordingly, one of the priests who had been deported from Samaria came to live in Beth-el; he instructed[54] them how to revere YHWH.

Now each nation made its own gods. They set (them) up in the shrines of the cult sites which the Samaritans had built, each nation in the towns in which they lived. The people of Babylon made Succotbenot; the people of Cutha made Nergal; the people of Hamath made Ashema. The Avvites made Nibhaz and Tartak; and the Sepharvites burn their children in fire to Adrammelek and Anammelek, gods of Sepharvaim. They (also) revered YHWH; so they made some of their number[55] priests who sacrificed for them at the shrines of the cult sites. Thus, they revered YHWH and (at the same time) worshiped their own gods after the custom of the countries from where they had been deported.

Early in the Assyrian occupation of north Israel,[56] the foreign settlers in Samaria, made fearful by the ravages of wild beasts in the desolated countryside, which they ascribed to the anger of the local god, set out to adopt the cult of the Israelite YHWH. Under royal mandate, a former Israelite priest re-established the sanctuary at Beth-el,[57] which was to survive Assyria's rule in Israel.[58] As Paul recently pointed out, the language of the royal order repatriating the Beth-el priest — "let him go . . . and instruct them in the ways of the local god" (2 Kgs 17.27) — is strikingly reminiscent of the original Assyrian decree concerning the city's resettlement — "I had them trained in proper conduct," i.e., "to revere god and king" — and argues for the credibility of the biblical narrative.[59] But this terminological similarity will not support Paul's suggestion that the biblical order shows that Sargon was "effecting a religious homogenization of the disparate elements of the populace" based upon "the correct cult of the native gods."[60] If anything, it was the original Assyrian resettlement order charging

[53] Hebrew: "them." On the alternation in numbers in the Hebrew text and the versions, cf. Montgomery, *Kings*, 473 and 479.

[54] Cf. Joüon, *Grammaire de l'hébreu biblique* (Rome: Pontifical Biblical Institute, 1923), § 121, gN for the paraphrastic verbal constructions in vss. 25, 28, 29, 32, 33 (a feature of late Hebrew).

[55] For this rendering of *miqṣōtām*, cf. Gen 47:2; and E. A. Speiser, *Genesis* (AB, 1964), *ad loc.*; A. Ehrlich, *Mikrâ* 1, 125.

[56] As pointed out above, n. 23, the list of deportees in 2 Kgs 17:24 is a composite record, reflecting the activities of several Assyrian kings. In the post-Sennacherib age, Esarhaddon exhibited particular toleration for foreign cults. See above, pp. 38-39. If the responsive Assyrian king referred to in 2 Kgs 17:26 be Esarhaddon, then the indeterminate wording "at the start of their settlement" (17:25) would refer to the period between 689-680 B.C.E.

[57] Did this restoration at Beth-el include the return of pillaged images (e.g., the calves), as was the practice of Assyrian kings in so many instances? Cf. above, pp. 74ff. It is certain that Josiah, a half-century later, did not encounter the calves; had they been in place, a notice in 2 Kgs 23:19 would have been in order. Cf. the remarks of H. W. Wolff, "Das Ende des Heiligtums in Bethel," in *Archäologie und Altes Testament, Festschrift für Kurt Galling* (Tübingen, J. C. B. Mohr: 1970), 289.

[58] See 2 Kgs 23:15.

[59] S. M. Paul, "Sargon's Administrative Diction in 2 Kings 17:27," JBL 88 (1969), 73.

[60] *Ibid.*, p. 74. Similar conclusions seem to have been reached by H. Tadmor, *History*

disciplined Assyrian citizenship (i.e., "proper conduct") which attempted this kind of homogeneity.[61] Rather, the biblical passage accords with liberal Assyrian religious policies, which demanded of deportees acknowledgment of the superiority of Ashur but which, all the while, took little or no offense at private or public worship of other deities.[62]

Once granted leave by the Nineveh authorities, a motley of Assyrian, Aramaean, and Israelite cults sprang up among the settlers in Samaria,[63] though only the activities of strict YHWHists merit the attention of the biblical historians from this point on. We hear of north Israelites from the Galilean tribes of Asher, Manasseh, Zebulun, and Issachar — "the remnant that has escaped from the hands of the Assyrian kings" — accepting Hezekiah's invitation to join in the passover ceremonies in Jerusalem (2 Chr 30.1-11, 18).[64] Ephramite

of the Jewish People 1, 137. We have dealt with the problem of identifying the "Assyrian king" in 2 Kgs 17:24, assumed by Paul to be Sargon, above in n. 23.

[61] Paul's discussion overlooked the Assyrian text concerning Samaria altogether, relying solely upon the Dūr-Sharruken passage; see above, pp. 49ff.

[62] Our interpretation of 2 Kgs 17:24ff. obviates Albright's suggestion (*ARI*[5], 166) that the Assyrians saw the restored Beth-el sanctuary "as a check" to revived interest in the Jerusalem Temple. Cf. Albright, *Biblical Period*, 77 and 80; and adoptions by Bright, *History*, 266; J. Myers, *II Chronicles*, xxf. This view would have us assume that Assyria considered Hezekiah's cultic reforms (2 Kgs 18:3-6) a threat to its rule in Samaria. But Assyrian texts evidence no antagonism towards foreign cults, and political activity hostile to the empire was always countered with military force, not religious activism. Besides, in 2 Kgs 17:24ff., the initiative for a YHWH cult proceeded from the local residents, not the king.

[63] Perhaps we should include local Canaanite cults in this listing; note the reported presence of an Asherah pole in Beth-el, 2 Kgs 23:15.

Porten summarizes the scholarly attempts at identification of the gods worshipped at Samaria in *Archives from Elephantine*, 171-73. To his bibliography add, G. R. Driver, "Geographical Problems," *EI* 5 (1958) 18*-20*; J. T. Milik, *Biblica* 48 (1967) 556ff.

[64] Myers, *II Chronicles*, 177f., points to Sargon's preoccupation with rebels to the north and east as providing the opportune time for Hezekiah's appeal to Israel. E. W. Todd, in "The Reforms of Hezekiah and Josiah," *SJTh* 9 (1956) 288f., justifies Hezekiah's move into Israel by reviving T. H. Robinson's earlier suggestion (*History*, 380 and 398) that Sargon had ceded parts of Israel's southern territory to Judah after 720 B.C.E. as reward for "the fidelity of Ahaz" to the empire.

Explications of this sort labor under the assumption that Assyria would have taken offense at native religious activities. On the contrary, so long as Hezekiah remained a loyal vassal and with Samaria firmly under Assyrian control (note the settlement of Arab tribes in Samaria in Sargon's seventh year; Lie, *Sargon*, 120), there is no reason to suppose that Assyria would have shown concern. Moreover, Robinson's conjecture in unfounded. He found evidence for Judah's northern expansion in the large number of cities — 46 — taken by Sennacherib from Hezekiah in 701 B.C.E. But we know little concerning the tally procedures of Assyrian scribes. The number of cities captured in Urartu during Sargon's eighth campaign are no less startling. E.g., cf. TCL 3, 239, 272, 286, 305. Cf. additional remarks of Thiele, *Mysterious Numbers of the Hebrew Kings*[2], 150-52.

On the unusual one-month postponement in celebrating the passover, see Talmon's suggestive remarks concerning Hezekiah's "concession" to north Israelite cult traditions in "Divergencies in Calendar-Reckoning in Ephraim and Judah," *VT* 8 (1958) 58-63.

contributions count in the financing of the temple repairs undertaken in Josiah's eighteenth year (2 Chr 34.9; cf. 2 Kgs 22.4). Josiah carries his cultic reforms to Samaria and its towns (cf. 2 Kgs 23.15, 19-20; 2 Chr 34.6).[65] Even after Jerusalem's fall, eighty mourning men from Shechem, Shiloh, and Samaria set out to offer gifts at the site of the destroyed YHWH temple (Jer 41.5).[66] Nowhere is the suggestion made that the Israelite remnant adopted foreign cults during the Assyrian occupation, [67] nor do we hear anything further as to the development of syncretistic Samaritanism.

This silence is astonishing considering the friction which developed in the fifth century B.C.E. between the returning Judahite exiles and their Samaritan neighbors. The Samaritans present themselves as religiously akin to the Judahites, but are rebuffed in their efforts to join in rebuilding the YHWH temple (cf. Ezra 4.1-3). Scholars explain this rejection of the Samaritans as based upon the returnees' religious antagonism toward the "mixed breed" (cf. 2 Kgs 17.24-41) who were "not true worshipers of Yahweh."[68] Passages in Chronicles critical of northern Israel before the exile allegedly reflect the same postexilic antagonism.[69] But the foreign cults of 2 Kings 17 never become an issue for rejection in the Ezra-Nehemiah documents; that the Samaritans "look to" YHWH as their God is never disputed. Moreover, the Chronicler addresses north Israelites as "brothers" of the Judahites (cf. 2 Chr 11.4; 28.8), who, having strayed from "the god of their fathers" (30.7), are called upon to return to YHWH. How can fifth century B.C.E. Samaritans, considered "outsiders" excluded from Israel's community, be thought to be lurking behind the Chronicler's account?[70]

Martin Noth's explanation for the Samaritan repulse proves to be equally unfounded. Noth postulated:

> The old antithesis between north (Israel) and south (Judah) continued below the surface (throughout the exilic period) and broke out again when plans were made

[65] H. W. Wolff would see 2 Kgs 23:4 as evidence for the desecration of the Beth-el altar among the earliest acts of Josiah in the North. See Wolff, *Das Ende des Heiligtums in Bethel*, 289f. But Wolff pays insufficient attention to the verbal peculiarities in clause 4b; on which see GKC § 112 pp. and n. 3, and the comments of Montgomery, *Kings*, 529 and Gray, *Kings*², 732.

[66] M. Noth observes (*The Laws in The Pentateuch and Other Studies* [Philadelphia: Fortress Press, 1967] 264) that this passage "surely implies that even before the catastrophe" Israelites considered "the Jerusalem sanctuary as the official central sanctuary," thus authenticating the Chronicler's information.

[67] Josiah's purge in Samaria was directed at established Israelite heterodoxies; e.g., Jeroboam's altar (2 Kgs 23:15); rural cult sites "built by Israel's kings (23:19)," not newly-imported cults.

[68] So, J. Myers, *Ezra-Nehemiah* (AB, 1965) 35; cf. also Galling, *Chronik*, 194.

[69] Cf., for example, Rudolph, *Chronikbücher*, 300; Galling, *Chronik*, 160; Bright, *History*, 266; and von Rad, *OT Theology* 1, 348 n. 3: "It is a very obvious assumption that Chronicles was interested in the delimitation of the community from the Samaritans, and that it wanted to prove that the cultic community at the Jerusalem Temple was the true Israel."

[70] See the remarks of Kaufmann, *Tolᵉdot* 4, 185-88.

for the rebuilding of the sanctuary in Jerusalem. . . . The inhabitants of the neighboring provinces, in which the foreign upper classes had gradually been absorbed or were in the process of being absorbed by the local Israelite population, were regarded by the Judaeans, who had had no foreign upper class imposed on them, as cultically unclean.[71]

But the Samaritans did not present themselves to Zerubbabel as descendants of the old indigenous Israelite population. By their own admission, they were foreigners (cf. Ezra 4.2). The Samaritan sect ultimately did lay claim to an ancient pedigree dating back to premonarchic Israel; but nothing in Samaritan tradition points to its acquaintance with or development from pre-exilic north Israelite traditions.[72] After all, Israel's majority status, along with the hegemony of the Israelite cult, effectively had come to an end with the Assyrian occupation,[73] leaving the hodge-podge of foreign settlers in Samaria[74] to come upon YHWH-ism in a most unconventional manner.

Yehezkel Kaufmann explains the disappearance of pagan Samaritanism as the effect of two hundred years of settlement in the land of Israel which led to the "Judaization" of the Assyrian deportees' formal cultic practices. That they were nonetheless rejected by the returnees Kaufmann accounts for by the fact that with respect to their national-historical identity, the Samaritans remained non-Israelites (cf. Ezra 4.2). As religious converts, the Samaritans appeared on the scene with their demand for equal recognition within the Jerusalem cult community prior to Israel's systemization of a procedure for religious conversion.[75] Alternatively, M. Weinfeld[76] has argued that the rejection of the Samar-

[71] Noth, *History*, 353, cf. 291-92.

[72] See the independent, complementary analyses of Kaufmann, *Tolᵉdot* 4, 188, and Purvis, *The Samaritan Pentateuch and the Origin of the Samaritan Sect*, 92-94.

[73] The hostile reception Hezekiah's Passover call received in Ephraim (cf. 2 Chr 30:10-11) may reflect the predominantly foreign ethnic make-up of the Samarian province. The Galilean Israelites, left intact by Tiglath-pileser III (cf. above, p. 99), looked to Jerusalem to provide the cultic continuity upset by the loss of Beth-el; while the Israelite minority left in Samaria responded with scorn to the Judahite invitation — apparently an indication of their prompt absorption by the more numerous colonists.

[74] Cf. our remarks above, p. 101. Alt's attempt to identify the *ʿam hāʾāreṣ* in the post-exilic documents as foreign "ruling classes" (KS 2, 321 n. 2; followed by Bright, *History*, 349 and 354; and Myers, *Ezra-Nehemiah*, xxvii), is refuted by Kaufmann, *Tolᵉdot* 4, 184f., 519f.; and now, Tadmor, *JWH* 11 (1968) 66-68.

[75] Kaufmann, *Tolᵉdot* 4, 197-207. At this point, we would venture a date for the 2 Kgs 17:24-33 account. The last Assyrian settlement noted is that of Ashurbanipal, *ca.* 643 B.C.E. (see above, p. 101 n. 23); while the latest date for the presence of a syncretistic cult in Samaria must be set prior to the return of the exiles, *ca.* 538 B.C.E. Only one occasion during this hundred-year period seems appropriate for expressing the animus towards Samaritanism as found in 2 Kgs 17:24ff. — the reforms of Josiah. The exceptional slaughter of north Israelite rural priests (contrast 2 Kgs 23:5 and 19) may indicate an intemperate handling of pagan Samaritans after the manner of the *ḥerem* extirpation of the aboriginal Cannanites. 2 Kgs 17:24ff. precedes Josiah's purge, but not by much. On 2 Kgs 23:19, cf. Montgomery, *Kings*, p. 534; and Kaufmann, *Collected Works*, pp. 165f.

[76] M. Weinfeld, "Universalism and Particularism in the Period of Exile and Restoration" [Hebrew], *Tarbiz* 33 (1964) 228-42.

itans (and Ezra's later expulsion of foreign wives)[77] stemmed not from Israel's unpreparedness to receive converts, but from the exclusivist ideology of strict "Torahists," who laid stress upon Israel's election as YHWH's "holy people."[78]

For our purposes, the adoption by the Samaritans of the Israelite cultus to the ultimate exclusion of both private and state pagan cults is significant, for it indirectly confirms what we have described as liberal Assyrian religious policies. Samaria's provincial annexation and century-long occupation successfully dismembered the Israelite body politic, so that Israel as an independent state did not reappear even after the withdrawal of Assyrian troops and the collapse of the empire. The rump Israelite cult, on the other hand, reintroduced into Samaria to serve the needs of the Assyrian colonists and unhampered by imperial structures, endured the occupation, eventually supplanting diverse pagan cults.[79]

[77] Cf. Ezra 9-10; Neh 13:1-3.

[78] Weinfeld, "Universalism," 237-38. Weinfeld identified a second ideological party within post-Exilic Judaism: prophetic universalists, who anxiously announced salvation to all pagan converts. But the demarcation between the exclusivists and the universalists apparently was not as sharp as Weinfeld would have us believe. Some priests and levites did not hesitate marrying foreign women (cf. Ezra 9:1, 10:18ff.), and at least one prophet, Malachi, urged their expulsion (cf. Mal 2:11; see the remarks of Kaufmann, *Tolᵉdot* 4, 370-71).

Note, too, that the exclusivist demands all issued from recent repatriates to Judah, e.g., Zerubbabel (Ezra 4:3), Ezra and Nehemiah. Perhaps the rigors of the exilic experience engendered a degree of ethnicism among these early "Zionists," which, however, seems to have dissipated once restoration was accomplished.

[79] No small part in converting the Samarians to YHWHism is due to the continued presence of the Jerusalem sanctuary and Judah's royal interest in the affairs of the former Israelite state.

SUMMARY AND CONCLUSIONS

A new picture of Neo-Assyrian imperial policy concerning religion and cult emerges from this investigation, superseding the older one drawn from the juxtaposition of Assyria and the manner of imperial Rome: *cuius regio eius religio* ("as to the master, so to his religion") (see above, pp. 2-4).

"Ashur and the great gods" were not the only divine authors of Assyria's victories; the Assyrian conqueror acknowledged that local foreign gods, in control of the destinies of their adherents, were also active in Assyria's behalf. The traditional Mesopotamian literary motif of divine abandonment was incorporated in annalistic boasts that disaffected gods of the enemy had stopped protecting their devotees, thus exposing them to the onslaught of Assyrian armies.[1] Rather than vaunt the impotence of foreign gods before the might of Ashur — to the additional discomfiture of defeated populations — Assyria was satisfied with the political submission of its subjects; it did not interfere with the continued performance of local cults (see above, pp. 11-21).

The literary motif of divine abandonment was translated into reality by the transfer of the divine images of defeated nations to Assyria.[2] Such transfer did not effect an abrogation of local cults; for once the native priesthood managed to rationalize the destruction and take-over of its homeland, the interrupted cult was resumed, with or without the exiled cult statue (see above, pp. 33-34). Public recognition of Assyria's political suzerainty by the vanquished, which took the form of ceremonious surrender and the avowal of subject status, was usually sufficient to obtain the restoration of the exiled statues to their shrines (see above, pp. 34-37).

[1] Biblical tradition recounts a striking illustration of the Assyrian utilization of the abandonment motif in the first of Rabshakeh's speeches to the men of Jerusalem (2 Kgs 18:25): "Moreover, is it without YHWH that I have come up against this place to destroy it? YHWH said to me: Go up against this land and destroy it." Childs, *Isaiah and the Assyrian Crisis*, 84, finds the Rabshakeh's argument reflective of a theology "so peculiar to Isaiah and so foreign to any Near-Eastern pattern that the issue of dependency upon Isaianic tradition cannot be avoided." However, our identification of Assyrian propagandistic use of native rationalizations of defeat furnishes an adequate Assyrian background to this speech.

The biblical citation is the only example known so far of the abandonment motif employed in Assyrian diplomatic disputation. But then, our knowledge of the disputation pattern is limited to a single cuneiform reference; cf. Saggs, *Iraq* 17 (1955) 23ff. (cited by Childs, *op. cit.*, pp. 80-81).

[2] See above, pp. 22-25. Capture of statues was evidently selective, affecting only the enemy's principal shrines.

There is no evidence, textual or pictorial, to suggest that Assyria subjected native cults to regulation or that it interfered in any way with customary rites. On the contrary, Esarhaddon boasted of housing numerous divine statues in comfortable quarters "befitting their divinity," until he could complete plans for their repatriation. Only in the case of the Arab statues did we find cuneiform inscriptions, proclaiming the might of Assyria's god and king, engraved on foreign cult objects (above, pp. 35-37). But these very same Arab gods were the beneficiaries of handsome gifts from both Essarhaddon and Ashurbanipal—"studded red-gold stars" sent in gratitude to the Arabian Ishtar, Atarsamain. There are even suggestions that Assyria's rulers endowed sacrifices to non-Assyrian gods, to be offered by local rulers in the name of the overlord, in all likelihood accompanied by invocations of divine blessing upon Assyria (see above, pp. 39-40).

While Nineveh extended official recognition to foreign gods (above, pp. 46-49, esp. nn. 37-38), it also required subject peoples to acknowledge the majesty of Assyria's "great gods." However, only in territories formally annexed as provinces was an Assyrian cult introduced, the planting of "Ashur's weapon" in the provincial center serving as its focal point (above, pp. 53-55). Provincials were expected to bear the tax burdens for the upkeep of palace and temple, just as if they were native-born Assyrians. Unfortunately, our sources give no indication of the role provincials played in the imported Assyrian cults; though whatever that role may have been, native cults seem to have remained unaffected (above, pp. 55, 105-107). We may suppose that with the expansion of the Assyrian empire, Ashur's domain expanded as well, so that in areas "made over into Assyria," Ashur became the recognized head of a pantheon that now encompassed new foreign gods.[3]

Such cultic impositions obtained only within the territorial confines of the Assyrian state; vassal states bore no cultic obligations whatsoever (see above, pp. 55-56). Alliance with Assyria demanded of vassals unwavering loyalty in political and economic matters, and any trespass of loyalty oaths (*adû*) incurred immediate punishment. But there is no record of the imposition of Assyrian cults upon vassal states. The occasional presence of the royal stele in these territories merely served to mark the outer reaches of Assyria's political influence and did not signify the inauguration of a royal cult, an idea itself foreign to Assyria (see above, pp. 56-60).

[3] Whether foreign gods were identified as manifestations of Assyrian gods is not certain. See our remarks above, p. 20 n. 52 and p. 40 n. 110.

Earlier, New Kingdom Egypt had not only experienced the penetration of cults of Syrian gods who had "supported" its Asiatic conquests, but also identified Asiatic gods with their Egyptian counterparts. After several centuries of contact, even mythical concepts freely cross-fertilized the two distinct divine realms. See the latest survey discussion by Rainer Stadelmann, *Syrisch-Palästinensische Gottheiten in Ägypten, Probleme der Ägyptologie* 5 (Leiden: E. J. Brill, 1967).

The Neo-Assyrian empire, on the other hand, may have been too short-lived for such divine fusion to have fully developed.

Biblical narratives of the Neo-Assyrian age provide complementary evidence of the tolerant Assyrian religious policies, both in the provinces and in vassal states. Judah, for the better part of a century (*ca.* 740-640 B.C.E.), bore the onerous yoke of Assyrian vassalage (see above, pp. 65-72), but never experienced the imposition of Assyrian cults. The foreign innovations reported of the reigns of Ahaz and Manasseh are attributable to the voluntary adoption by Judah's ruling classes of the prevailing Assyro-Aramaean culture. Pagan cults, whether of Mesopotamian origin (as, e.g., horse dedications to the sun; see above, pp. 86-87) or of Aramaean derivation (as, e.g., Molech child sacrifice; above, pp. 77-83), seem to have reached Palestine through Aramaean mediation, where they were then wedded to local pagan practice. In Judah, disenchantment with YHWHistic tradition, which apparently could not account for the grievous state of affairs after Hezekiah's defeat in 701, abetted the assimilation of such foreign ritual (see above, pp. 94-96).

North Israel was not much different. As with Judah, Israel's short term as an Assyrian vassal passed without the imposition of foreign cults. Even before Assyria's arrival in Palestine, Mesopotamian deities had found their way to Israel's shrines, following upon renewed Israelite contact with the Aramaeans of north Syria during the early eighth century B.C.E. (above, pp. 103-104).

All this changed with the annexation of Samaria in 720 and its transformation into an Assyrian province. The penetration of foreign cults was accelerated, this time at the hands of the Assyrian colonists resettled in Samaria, though once again we found evidence of the non-coercive imperial policy. In addition to displaying the habits of good Assyrian citizenship — "reverence of god and king" — the Samaritans continued to worship their native gods alongside the local YHWH (see above, pp. 105-110).

Once the contention that Assyrian imposition of state cults was the source of Israelite idolatry falls, then several other popular notions are likewise discredited:

(1) The cult reforms of Hezekiah and Josiah can no longer be thought of as expressions of political rebellion directed against Assyrian rule.[4] Nor can Manasseh's reform, according to the Chronicler's report (in itself spurious), be characterized as a "nationalistic revolt . . . accompanied by nationalistic religion."[4a] We may, therefore, reconsider their stated intent as "religious reform," and look for their motivation in what Kaufmann has termed "the spirit of repentance and soulsearching" which took hold in Judah during the recurring crises of the eighth century B.C.E.[5]

[4] Cf., e.g., the remarks of M. Noth, quoted above, p. 4, and the earlier observations of Olmstead, *Assyria*, 214 and 632; *Palestine-Syria*, 464 and 500; and Bright, *History*, 265 and 298.

[4a] So Olmstead, *Palestine-Syria*, 485. Olmstead paid no attention to the literary and historical problems of this episode (2 Chr 33.15-16), and, by inverting the given order of events, re-wrote his source to serve his case. Cf. above, p. 67 n. 15.

[5] See Kaufmann, *Tolᵉdot* 2, 265-67. This is not to deny that political events had an effect upon religious movements. E.g., Samaria's fall served as an object lesson for the

(2) The assumption of Neo-Babylonian cultic impositions on the analogy of supposed Assyrian models[6] is no longer tenable. A cursory reading of NB historical documents turned up no evidence of such impositions, but a separate study is in order.

Finally, our investigation calls into question critical discounting of the Deuteronomist's charge that Manasseh alone was responsible for Judah's fall. Von Rad, following the earlier formulations of Martin Noth, put it succinctly:

> The Deuteronomist's sole concern is a theological interpretation of the catastrophes which befell the two kingdoms. Consequently, he examined past history page by page with that in view, and the result was quite unambiguous: the fault was not Jahweh's; but for generations Israel had been piling up an ever-increasing burden of guilt and faithlessness, so that in the end Jahweh had had to reject his people.[7]

Manasseh appears, therefore, as merely that Judahite king who, culminating "an almost unbroken series of breaches of the revealed will of God," tipped the scales in favor of the "long-due judgment."[8]

Frank M. Cross rejects this view of the Deuteronomistic historian:

> Before the pericope of Manasseh there is no hint in the Deuteronomic history that hope in the Davidic house and in ultimate salvation is futile. The very persistence of this theme of hope in the promises to David and his house requires that . . . the Deuteronomist . . . was writing a sermon to rally God's people to the new possibility of salvation, obedience to the ancient covenant of Yahweh, and hope in the new David, Josiah.[9]

Cross contends (p. 18) that "the attribution of Judah's demise to the unforgivable sins of Manasseh" is the product of an exilic editor (*ca.* 550 B.C.E.), "tacked on and not integral to the original structure of the [Kings] history."

But are the passages condemning Manasseh really "tacked on?" Or was Manasseh merely the most recent and therefore the best remembered idolator in Judah's past? I think not. The Deuteronomistic historian viewed the age of Manasseh as unprecedented both in the nature and scope of its "apostasy." Our literary and archaeological study has confirmed this evaluation; it was indeed an age of unprecedented abandonment of Israelite tradition. Heretofore royal "apostates" had been blamed for straying from the Mosaic law for known causes;

reform-minded Hezekiah (cf. 2 Chr 30:7); and the decline of Assyria during Josiah's regency must have certainly encouraged a national revival.

[6] E.g., A. Weiser, *Jeremia* (ATD, 1956), 75, has claimed that the astral cults in Jeremiah refer to the honoring of "Babylonian . . . state gods" introduced after the 605 B.C.E. Babylonian take-over of Judah. (On the non-official, popular character of these cults, see our discussion, pp. 84-86).

[7] Von Rad, *Studies in Deuteronomy* (SBT 9, 1961) 77.

[8] Von Rad, *OT Theology* 1, 340f.

[9] Cross, "The Structure of the Deuteronomic History," in *Perspectives in Jewish Learning* 3 (Chicago: College of Jewish Studies Press, 1967), 17.

foreign wives instigated both Solomon and Jehoram to idolatry.[10] But all previous idolators had been punished.[11] Only Manasseh's apostasy was "groundless" and unexpiated. The feeling that such enormities as described in 2 Kgs 21:1-16 could only be expiated through destruction and exile need not be late exilic rationalization. After Israel's collapse in 720 B.C.E., the threat of exile hung over Judah. When the hopes for YHWH's grace were dashed by Josiah's untimely death in 609, the presentiment of doom may have set in (cf. Jer 15:4). Manasseh's dubious distinction, therefore, need not be ascribed to schematized historiography, nor is it peripheral to the Deuteronomistic history. It expresses the resignation of those Judahites who, having sponsored the Josianic reforms, now anticipated YHWH's final judgment.[12]

[10] Cf. 1 Kgs 11:4-5; 2 Kgs 8:18, and our comments above, p. 84 n. 103, and p. 91.

[11] The juxtaposition of the accounts of idolatry during the reigns of Solomon (1 Kgs 11:1-6), Jehoram (2 Kgs 8:18), and Ahaz (2 Kgs 16:1-4) and the accounts of the successive diminution of the David empire (cf. 1 Kgs 11:11-13; 2 Kgs 8:20-22, 16:6) points to their causal relationship, *viz.*, trespass leads to YHWH's punishment. Note the Chronicler's express linking of two of these events; cf. 2 Chr 21:10, 28:19.

[12] The formulaic critcism levelled at all post-Josianic kings (see 2 Kgs 23:32, 37; 24:9, 19) may be the Deuteronomist's way of saying that no justification could be found to stave off the divine sentence. On the question of the witness of these verses to the religious state of affairs after 609 B.C.E., see now M. Greenberg, "Prolegomenon" to C. C. Torrey, *Pseudo-Ezekiel and the Original Phophecy* (reprint; New York: KTAV, 1970) xxviii-xxiii.

APPENDIX 1
ISRAELITE CAPTURE OF FOREIGN GODS

BIBLICAL sources record two spoliations by Israel of the gods of a defeated enemy, both events causing consternation to later writers aware of the Israelite ban on idolatory:

(1) 2 Sam 5:21 reports that after successfully routing the Philistines at Baal Perazim, David and his men carried off (*wayyiśśāʾēm*) the idols left behind by the retreating Philistines. The parallel account in 1 Chr 14:12 exonerates[1] David for non-compliance with the laws of *ḥerem* (Deut 7:5, 25), which dictated proscribement of all Canaanite images, by midrashically parsing the verb *wayyiśśāʾēm*, "carried off," as "set fire."[2]

That David actually despoiled Philistine images is seemingly the plain sense of the text. In a later battle at Rabah, David is victoriously crowned with the studded gold crown of Milkom, the Ammonite god (2 Sam 12:30).[3] These accounts of Davidic spoliation bear the marks of early Israel in their inattention to the later Deuteronomic concern for ensnarement by pagan cult objects (Deut 7:25).

(2) The second account of spoliation, preserved in 2 Chr 25:14-16, concentrates on the aftermath of the Judahite victory over Edom in the early eighth century B.C.E. "Now after Amaziah returned from defeating the Edomites, having brought back the gods of the Seirites, he set them up as gods. He would bow down before them and would offer incense to them" (25:14). A prophet arrives to rebuke Amaziah for worshiping the Edomite gods, who had been proven impotent by Judah's very victory.

[1] Cf. e.g., Curtis, *Chronicles*, 209.

[2] A noun, *maśʾēt*, "signal-fire," is known in biblical Hebrew, e.g., Judg 20:38, 40; Jer 6:1; and Lachish Letter 4:10 (= KAI, 194). Radak (at 2 Sam 5:21) suggests that the verbal forms of *nāśāʾ* in Nah 1:5 and Job 32:22 be similarly interpreted. Cf. T. B. Avodah Zara 44a. The verbal literalness of the Chronicles' interpretation is missed by most moderns, e.g., Smith *Samuel* (ICC, 1899), 291, "The Chronicler adds that David burned them . . ."

Whether the Chronicler's *Vorlage* of Samuel already displayed evidence of this "burning" as argued by Lemke (HTR 58 [1965], 351f.) is of little consequence in understanding the midrashic nature of the interpretation discussed. On the primacy, though, of the first half of the Chronicles verse, see Smith, *Samuel*, p. 290 and Seeligman, Tarbiz 25 (1956), 121.

[3] The Massoretic vocalization of the Hebrew text avoids association with a foreign god by revocalizing *Milkom* to read *Malkām*, "their king;" but compare already Rashi and all modern commentaries *ad loc.* The story is deleted in its entirety by the Chronicler.

No satisfactory explanation has yet been proffered for Amaziah's veneration of foreign images.[4] The Chronicler himself may have been puzzled, for while worship of non-Israelite gods proven in battle was readily understandable (cf. 2 Chr 28:23), the attraction of the defeated Edomite gods seemed utterly foolish. Most commentaries note, therefore, that the Chronicler "used"[5] this tale to set the stage for a defeat which was to overtake Amaziah — a defeat rationalized by his infidelity to YHWH (see 25:20).

Yet against the background of Assyrian practice (discussed above, chs. 1-2), Amaziah's act is intelligible. Amaziah saluted the gods of Edom for their help to Judah by abandoning their adherents. To the Chronicler, however, any recognition of foreign gods was interpreted as abandonment of YHWH, and so deserving of punishment.[6]

[4] Cf. Rudolph, *Chronikbücher*, 283; Elmslie, *Chronicles* (Camb. B.², 1916), 282, who finds the same policy pursued by Solomon in 1 Kgs 11:7.

[5] Rudolph, *loc. cit.* Does he mean "invent" as did Wellhausen (*Prolegomena*, 206f.)?

[6] In a later passage, 2 Chr 28:23, the Chronicler reported that Ahaz thought Aramaean gods capable of extending him aid. While most other biblical writers avoided ascribing real activity to foreign gods, outside of contexts where a pagan is addressed (e.g., Judges 11:24), the Chronicler readily admitted that certain renegade Israelites held such thoughts, to their eventual discomfiture at YHWH's hand. Cf. the remarks of Kaufmann, *Tolᵉdot* 1, 276-79.

APPENDIX 2
A TRIBUTE LIST FROM THE DAYS OF SARGON II

THE most recent addition to the small number of instances in which Judah is mentioned in NA sources is found in ND. 2765, published by H. W. Saggs.[1] The reverse of the tablet, containing a supplementary message to the main body of the letter, is presented here in a new transcription and translation:

33.	45 ANŠE.KUR.RA.MEŠ *ša* ⸢ x⸣*at?-ta-mu*[*r*]	45 [ ] horses, I inspected.
34.	LÚ.MAḪ.MEŠ KUR ⸢*Mu-ṣur*⸣-*a-a*	The chieftains[2] of the Egyptians,
35.	KUR *Ḫa-za-ta-a-a* KUR *Ia-ú-du-a-a*	Gazaites, Judahites,
36.	KUR *Ma-'a-ba-a-a* KUR *Ba-an-am-ma-na-a-a*	Moabites, Ammonites
37.	UD.12.KAM *ina* URU *Kal-ḫi e-tar-bu-u-ni*	arrived in Kalḫu on the 12th (of this month)
38.	⸢*ma*⸣ *-da-na-*[*te!*]*-šú-nu*[3] *ina* ŠU^{11}-*šú-nu*	with their tribute.
39.	23 ? ANŠE.KUR.RA.MEŠ	He had 23 horses
40.	*ša* KUR *Ḫa-za-ta-a-a ina* ŠU^{11}-*šú*	from the Gazaites.
41.	KUR ⸢*Ú-du-mu*⸣ *-a-a* KUR [*As-du-*]*da-a-a*[4]	The Edomites, [Ashdo]dites,
42.	KUR *An-*[*qa-*]*ru-na-a-a*[5] [ ] x	E[q]ronites
43.	[x LÚ.EN (?) x]*-a-a*	[..........]ites
44.	[ ] x x *ú-ṣa-a*	come forth.

The inclusion of Egypt, along with a number of Philistian cities, among the tribute-bearers suggests that this document be dated to the period immediately following Sargon's victory in the Ashdod campaign of 712 B.C.E., a unique era of Egyptian recognition of Assyrian suzerainty.[6]

[1] *Iraq* 17 (1955) pl. xxxiii (= no. 16), 134-35. The text, as published by Saggs, has been reproduced without modifications by Donner in MIO 5 (1957) 159ff.

[2] Saggs did not transcribe the ideogram LÚ.MAḪ, but simply noted that it was not to be identified with the usual Akkadian *maḫḫu*, "ecstatic," but "seems to be used of emissaries, particularly those bringing tribute, of states which were not under Assyrian administration" (p. 135, note to line 34). CAD Ṣ, 213, now reads LÚ.MAḪ as *ṣīru/ṣīrāni*, "(foreign) chieftain," following Martin, StOr 8/1 (1936) 26f.

[3] Saggs' suggested reading ⸢*i*⸣*-da-na-aš* (?)*-šú-nu* is both textually and grammatically incorrect. The signs are better read as a plural noun, *maddanātu*, "tribute;" cf. AnSt 11 (1961) 152, 57.

[4] Cf. Tadmor, "Campaigns," 272.

[5] Saggs read *a*[*k*(?)*-r*]*u-na-a-a*. But Assyrian transcriptions of the name of biblical 'Eqron always appear in the dissimilated form, e.g., *Am-qar-ru-na*; *Am-qar-u-na*; *Am-qa-ar-ru-na*; cf. El-Amin, *Sumer* 9 (1953) 37-40. This Assyrian form of the city-name is to be explained as a dialectical variant of *Aqqaron. For details, see A. Hurvitz, *Lĕšonénu* 33 (1968) 18-24. Our reading follows this form. Cf. the reading on the tribute tag published in *Iraq* 27 (1965) 16: *An-qar-u-na-a-a*.

[6] Cf. Saggs, 152-53; Tadmor, JCS 12 (1958) 39ff. For a somewhat earlier dating, see Donner, MIO 5 (1957) 181. Other instances of Egyptian tribute payments rendered in horses were collected by Weidner, AfO 14 (1941-44) 44 n. 14.

TABLE 1

SPOLIATION OF DIVINE IMAGES

Ruler	Geographic Area	Destination	Term	Source
Tiglath-pileser I	Qummuḫ		*našû*	AKA, p. 41, II.31-32
(1115-1077 B.C.E.)	Ḫaria		*našû*	AKA, p. 57, III.81
	Lower Zab		*šûṣû*	AKA, p. 58, III.102-IV.3
	Kirḫu		*šûṣû*	AKA, p. 61, IV.23f.
	Muṣru		*našû*	AKA, p. 79, VI.8f.
	Suḫu	*ana ālīya* ᵈ*Aššur*	*našû* *wabālu*	KAH 2, 71.43
Adad-nirari II	Ḫanigalbat		*šalālu*	KAH 2, 84.69-72
(911-891 B.C.E.)		*ana ālī[ya . . .]*		KAH 2, 83.rev.4f.
Tukulti-ninurta II (890-884 B.C.E.)		*ana Ni[nu]a*	*wabālu*	Scheil, obv. 7f.[1]
Ashurnasirpal II (883-859 B.C.E.)	Bīt-Ḫalupē		*šalālu*	AKA, p. 283, I.85-89
	Laqē		*turru*	AKA, p. 357, III.40
Shalmaneser III (858-824 B.C.E.)	Bīt-Adini		*nasāḫu*	Iraq 21 (1959), p. 38, 6; Iraq 25 (1963), p. 54, 26-28
		ana ālīya Aššur	*wabālu* *turru*	WO 2/2 (1955), p. 146, 48-50; 2/5, 414, III.5f.
	Namri	*ana māt Aššur*	*wabālu* *šalālu*	WO 2/2, (1955) p. 152, 94f.; Sumer 6 (1950), p. 16, IV.19
	Bīt-Ḫaban	*ana māt Aššur*	*nasāḫu* *wabālu*	WO 2/2 (1955), p. 156, 126
Shamshi-adad V	Babylonia		*šalālu*	KB 1, p. 184, IV.17; 21; 33
(823-811 B.C.E.)		*ana libbi mātīya*	*wabālu*	KB 1, p. 184, IV.6-8, cf p. 202 IV.6-8 and AfO 9 (1933-34) p. 92, III 42-48

(Continued on next page)

[1] Olmstead, *Assyria*, 77, interprets this passage as self-imposed exile to Assyria on the part of the son of Ammibali. But the mention of *šallatu*, "booty," as part of the items brought to Tukulti-ninurta speaks out against such a view. See V. Scheil, *Annales de Tukulti-Nimip II Roi d'Assyrie 899-844*, *Bibliothèque de l'École des Hautes Études*, IVᵉ section, No. 178 (Paris, 1909), *loc. cit.*

TABLE 1 (CONTINUED)
SPOLIATION OF DIVINE IMAGES

Ruler	Geographic Area	Destination	Term	Source
	Nairi		*šalālu*	KB 1, p. 178, II.27-29
Adad-nirari III (810-783 B.C.E.)				KB 1, p. 202, IV. 17
Tiglath-pileser III (744-727 B.C.E.)	Babylonia		*šalālu*	Rost, *Tigl. III*, Thontafel, 17, 18,
	Gaza		?	21; Rost, *Tigl. III*, Kleine Ins., I, 10.
			abāku	Baby. Chron. I, 5
	Arabia		?	*Iraq* 18 (1956), p. 126, rev. 18
Sargon (721-705 B.C.E.)	Israel		*šallatiš manū*	*Iraq* 16 (1954), p. 179, IV.32f.
	Philistia		*ana šallati manū*	Winckler, *Sargon*, p. 116, 105; Lie, *Sargon*, 259f.
	Urartu		*šallatiš manū*	Winckler, *Sargon*, p. 112, 76f.
			šalālu	TCL 3, 350
	Dūr Yakin		*šalālu*	*Iraq* 16 (1954), p. 186, VI.61f.
Sennacherib (704-681 B.C.E.)	Philistia	*ana māt Aššur*	*nasāḫu warū*	OIP 2, 30.62-64
	Til-Garimmu		*šallatiš manū*	OIP 2, 63.12
	Bīt-Yakin		*šalālu*	OIP 2, 38. 41; 75.99
		ana māt Aššur	*warū*	OIP 2, 87.25f.
	Uruk		*ḫabātu ekēmu*	Babyl. Chron. III, 1-3
			šalālu	OIP 2, 87.31-33
Esarhaddon (680-669 B.C.E.)	Bāzu	*ana qereb māt Aššur*	*šalālu*	Borger, *Asarhaddon*, § 27, Ep. 17.71f.
	Arabia	*ana qereb māt Aššur*	*šalālu*	Borger, *Asarhaddon*, § 66, 18-19
	Egypt		*abāku*	Baby. Chron. IV, 25
Ashurbanipal (668-627 B.C.E.)	Egypt		?	Iraq 7 (1940), pp. 106f., no. 33. 8-9
	Elam	*ana māt Aššur*	*šalālu*	Thompson, *Prisms* 5, 3-4; Asb. Rm.V.59-62; 119; VI.44-47

(Continued on next page)

TABLE 1 (CONTINUED)
SPOLIATION OF DIVINE IMAGES

Ruler	Geographic Area	Destination	Term	Source
			šūṣū	K.2631+, rev. 4
			šallatiš	(Streck, VAB 7,
			manū	p. 184)
	Tyre	*ana māt Aššur*	*šalālu*	Asb. Rm.IX.121
	Arabia	*ḫarrān māt*	*šēpūšun*	Asb. Rm.IX.3-8
		Dimašqa	*šuškunu*	
			qātā	Asb. Rm.IX.3-8
			kašādu	
	Babylonia		*abāku*	ABL 259, rev. 2

TABLE 2[1]

ADŪ VIOLATIONS REPORTED IN NA HISTORICAL INSCRIPTIONS

1. Rebellion against or removal of local officials loyal to Assyria
   1) *šēṭūtu* PN *šarri bēlīšunu ilqū imīšū ardūssu*[2]
      They showed disregard[3] for PN, the king, their lord and neglected his service.
   2) PN_1 PN_2 *irdudūma ana* PN_3 *išpurū epēš ardūti*[4]
      PN_1 expelled PN_2 and sent to PN_3 to be his vassal.
   3) PN_1 *ša šūt rēšīya irdudūma* PN_2 *elīšunu urabbū*[5]
      PN_1, who expelled my official, elevated PN_2 (to a position) over themselves.
2. Plotting and inciting insurrection
   1) *ittīya ušam/nkirma ikṣura tāḫāza*[6]
      He induced them to rebel against me, and prepared for battle.
   2) PN_1 PN_2 *ittīya ušbalkitma*[7]
      PN_1 induced PN_2 to rebel against me.
   3) *zērāti māt Aššur iltapparū ilqū šēṭūtu*[8]
      They dispatched hostile messages concerning Assyria and showed disregard.
   4) *itti* PN_1 *šādid nīrīya šitnuntu idbubūma ana* PN_2 *ittaklū*[9]
      They plotted hostilities against PN_1, who bears my yoke, and trusted in PN_2.
   5) *ana* PN *idbubū napādiš*[10]
      They plotted to cut off PN.[11]
   6) *ana* PN_1 *ekēme miṣrīya išpur*[12]
      He wrote to PN about seizing my territory.
3. Armed attack against Assyrian territory and/or vassal states
   1) *ummānšu karāssu idkēma ana* PN *ardu dāgil pānīya nītu ilmešuma iṣbatu mūṣāšu*[13]
      He mobilized his troops and camp, and laid seige[14] to PN, my faithful vassal, thus blocking his exit.
   2) *iḫtabbata/iḫtanabbatū ḫubut miṣir mātīya/māt* GN[15]
      They continually plundered border regions of my country / of GN.

(Continued on next page)

[1] NA annal and dedicatory literature, the basis for the present compilation, is far from being repetitive and tiresome, as is commonly held (e.g., Olmstead, *Assyria*, 203). Our reading of the texts found an obvious stylistic attempt to vary elements in describing similar events. Equivalent phrases are interchanged and substituted in multifarious combinations, alleviating monotony.

[2] TCL 3, 80.

[3] On the meaning of *šēṭūtu*, cf. TCL 3, 15 n. 9; Lie, *Sargon*, 11 n. 13; AHw 545, 6e "Misachtung." On the verb *šēṭu*, see E. Ebeling, B. Meissner, and E. Weidner, *Die Inschriften der Altassyrischen Könige* (Leipzig: Quelle and Meyer, 1926) 116 n. 1; Asb. IT.142-43 and Borger, *Asarhaddon*, § 65, rev. 34.

[4] Lie, *Sargon*, 96-97.

[5] Lie, *Sargon*, 167.

[6] Lie, *Sargon*, 266; cf. also 80.

[7] Lie, *Sargon*, 85; cf. OIP 2, 61.64-65.

[8] *Iraq* 16 (1954) 183, 51-52; cf. Lie, *Sargon*, 73, 208, 250f. (var. *išpurma*).

[9] Lie, *Sargon*, 59-60.

[10] Lie, *Sargon*, 77.

[11] See AHw 732a. Otherwise in CAD D, 11, "secretly (?)."

[12] Lie, *Sargon*, 199f.; *Iraq* 16 (1954) 182, 20-24.

[13] Borger, *Asarhaddon*, § 27, ep. 4, 41ff.

[14] See AHw 798b.

[15] Asb. Rm.VIII.51; Asb. B.VIII.5.

TABLE 2 (CONTINUED)
ADŪ VIOLATIONS REPORTED IN NA HISTORICAL INSCRIPTIONS

3) *ana miṣir Aššur uṣammir lemutti ašar tibki iḫṭi ana miṣir Aššur*[16]
He plotted evil against the border regions of Assyria, and at the site of (oath-) libation,[17] he trespassed the border.
4) *ana miṣirīka ibbalkitu ṣalti ittīšunu īpuš*[18]
He crossed your border and fought with them.
5) PN_1 *itti* PN_2 *sarrāti idbubma* 22 *birātēšu ēkimšu*[19]
PN_1 spoke treacherously against PN_2 and took 22 of his fortresses away from him.
6) *ummānātēšu idkamma*[20]
He mobilized his troops.
7) *igrānni ana* [*epēš*] *qabli* . . .[21]
He became hostile toward me, to do battle . . .
8) *ištene''a lemuttu ana kašād ummānātīya*[22]
He contrived evil to capture my troops.
9) *ittīya ittabalkit*[23]
He rebelled against me.
10) *ana emūq/ṭēm ramānīšu ittakil*[24]
He trusted in his own strength/judgement.

4. Joining an enemy coalition
1) PN_1 *itti* PN_2 *iškuna/ittadin pīšu*[25]
PN_1 came to an agreement with PN_2.
2) *ana kitri/rēṣūti* PN *illikamma*[26]
He came to the help/aid of PN.
3) *ana emūq aḫāmeš ittaklū*[27]
They trusted in each other's strength.
4) *ša* PN_1 *ana dannūtīšu iškunu ittaklu ana* PN_2 PN_3[28]
(He was the one) who set PN_1 as his stronghold and trusted in PN_2 (and) PN_3.

(Continued on next page)

[16] Asb. IT.157-58; cf. *Iraq* 30 (1968), 109, 26′.

[17] *Adū* oaths are known to have been sworn in solemn ceremony, which oft-times included libations. Cf. Borger, *Asarhaddon*, § 27, ep. 2, 50f., ***adē māmīt ilāni rabūti ana naṣār šarrūtīya ina mē u šamni itmū***, "They took a solemn oath by the great gods, by water and oil, to guard my rule." For additional references to water ceremonies in oaths, see VTE, 155; Craig, *Assyrian and Babylonian Religious Texts* 1 (Leipzig: Hinrichs, 1895) 24, rev. 9. Our passage probably refers to the place where previous oaths of loyalty had been undertaken. For an alternate suggestion regarding the use of oil as a medium of oath sanction, see K. R. Veenhof, Bi Or 23 (1966), 312f.

[18] ABL 1380, 8ff.

[19] Lie, *Sargon*, 101.

[20] Asb. IT.146f.; Asb. B.V.42 (*ummānšu*).

[21] Lie, *Sargon*, 19; cf. VAB 7, 212, 15.

[22] Asb. Rm.V.23-24; Asb. F.III.72-74.

[23] Rost, *Tigl. III*, Nimrud I, 20-21; Annals, 235-36 (broken) and 43 (*ibbalkitu*); Lie, *Sargon*, 110.

[24] Asb. B.I.56; Asb. Rm.I.157; Asb. IT.146f.

[25] Asb. Rm.VIII.48-49, 69; Asb. F.III.8; Asb. IT.142-43; Rost, *Tigl. III*, Nimrud I, 20-21, Thontafel, obv. 19.

[26] Asb. B.VII.49-50; Asb. F.III.14ff.

[27] Rost, *Tigl. III*, Annals, 62.

[28] Asb. Rm.VII.20ff.; Asb. IT.108.

TABLE 2 (CONTINUED)
ADŪ VIOLATIONS REPORTED IN NA HISTORICAL INSCRIPTIONS

5) *ša ana* (*šar*) *māt* GN *ittaklu*[29]
(He,) who trusted in (the king of the) land of GN.
6) *ana rēṣūti aḫāmeš iššaknū nīš ilānīšunu itti aḫāmeš izkurū ana emūqi ramānīšunu ittaklū*[30]
They agreed upon mutual defense, took an oath with one another by their gods, and trusted in their own strength.

5. Withholding tribute and gifts
1) *ana lā našē bilti iršā* [*elīya*] *nīd aḫi*[31]
He became negligent as regards tribute payment.
2) *maddattu iklāmma*[32]
He held back his tribute.
3) *mandattu* ᵈ*Aššur nadān šattīšunu iklū*[33]
They withheld Ashur's tribute, their yearly gift.[34]
4) *ana paḫātīšunu lā sanqū lā inamdinū mandattu nadān mātīšun*[35]
They did not obey their governor and did not hand over their country's tribute.
5) *iklā tāmartuš*[36]
He withheld his gifts.[37]

6. Disobedience to royal orders; failure to send greetings
1) *amat šarrūtīya lā iṣṣurū lā išmū zikir šaptēya*[38]
They did not keep my royal order; they did not obey my command.
2) *mēriḫēte ištanappara*[39]
He was constantly sending me insolent messages.
3) *dabāb surrāte ittīya idbubma*[40]
He spoke treacherously against me.
4) *rakbušu adi maḫrīya ul išpuramma šulum šarrūtīya ul išāl*[41]
He did not send his messenger to me to inquire after my royal well-being.
5) *ana ša'āl šulmēya šēpēšu iprusma*[42]
He held back from inquiring after my well-being.

(Continued on next page)

29 Asb. IT.106; Asb. B.VI.19-20; Lie, *Sargon*, 59-60; TCL 3, 81; Borger, *Asarhaddon*, § 76, 12.

30 Borger, *Asarhaddon*, § 27, ep. 6, 26-27.

31 Lie, *Sargon*, 68, cf. 250f.; *Iraq* 16 (1954) 179, 25-28.

32 Lie, *Sargon*, V.4-2; Asb. Rm.VII.90 (*maddattašu kabittu*).

33 *Iraq* 16 (1954) 177, 45-46.

34 See comments above, p. 51.

35 Asb. Rm.IX.117ff.

36 Lie, *Sargon*, 266; *Iraq* 16 (1954) 180, 52-53, and 185, 21; Asb. B.VIII.3. See also EI 8 (1967) 243, frag. 3, 1.4.

37 On *tāmartu*, see discussion of vassal gifts above, pp. 55f.

38 Asb. B.II.42f.; Asb. Rm.I.51; Asb. IT.81; cf., Borger, *Asarhaddon*, § 27, ep. 5, 65ff.; § 57, 6.

39 Asb. B.IV.97; cf. Borger, *Asarhaddon*, § 76, 12.

40 Asb. Rm.VIII.68; cf. Lie, *Sargon*, 79.

41 Borger, *Asarhaddon*, § 27, ep. 4, 49-50; cf. Asb. B.VII.48; Lie, *Sargon*, V.4-2.

42 Asb. B.VIII.2.

TABLE 2 (CONTINUED)
ADŪ VIOLATIONS REPORTED IN NA HISTORICAL INSCRIPTIONS

6) *lā ūṣūnimma lā išālū šulum šarrūtīya*[43]
   They did not come out to inquire after my royal well-being.

7. Disregard of previous royal favors
   1) *ṭābti ēpussunūti imšūma*[44]
      They forgot the favors I did for them.
   2) *ṭābti abi bānīya imšūma*[45]
      They forgot the favors of my father, my begetter.
   3) *ṭābti lā iṣṣurma*[46]
      He showed no regard for the favors.
   4) *epšēt dameqtīya libbašun lā iḫsusma*[47]
      He disregarded my kind acts.
   5) *damiqtu ēpušuš ša ašpuru rēṣūtu imšima*[48]
      He forgot the favor I did for him by sending help.

[43] Asb. Rm.IV.133-34; Asb. F.III.49-50.

[44] Asb. Rm.I.119.

[45] Asb. E.II.30ff.; Asb. B.IV.19 (*lā ḫassu*); Asb. Rm.VIII.66.

[46] Asb. B.VIII.1.

[47] *Iraq* 16 (1954) 183, 48-52; cf. Asb. B.VII.5-6; Asb. F.III.8; Borger, ***Asarhaddon***, § 27, ep. 4, 41ff.

[48] Asb. Rm.V.23-24; Asb. F.III.72-74.

ABBREVIATIONS

AAA *Annals of Archaeology and Anthropology*

AASF B *Annales Academiae Scientiarum Fennicae* (Series B)

AASOR *The Annual of the American Schools of Oriental Research*

AAWB *Abhandlung der Königlichen Akademie der Wissenschaften zu Berlin, philosophisch-historische Klasse*

AB *Anchor Bible.* Garden City: Doubleday

ABL Harper, Robert F. *Assyrian and Babylonian Letters Belonging to the Kouyunjik Collection of the British Museum.* 14 vols. London and Chicago: University of Chicago Press, 1892-1914.

ADD Johns, C. H. W. *Assyrian Deeds and Documents.* 4 vols. Cambridge: Deighton Bell and Co., 1898-1923.

AfO *Archiv für Orientforschung*

AHw Von Soden, W. *Akkadisches Handwörterbuch.* Wiesbaden: Harrassowitz, 1959- .

AJSL *American Journal of Semitic Languages and Literatures*

AKA King, L. W., and Budge, E. A. Wallis. *Annals of the Kings of Assyria,* I. London: British Museum, 1902.

AnBib *Analecta Biblica* (Rome)

AnOr *Analecta Orientalia* (Rome)

AnSt *Anatolian Studies*

ANEP Pritchard, James B. *The Ancient Near East in Pictures Relating to the Old Testament.* Princeton: Princeton University Press, 1954.

ANET Pritchard, James B. *Ancient Near Eastern Texts Relating to the Old Testament.* 2nd ed. Princeton: Princeton University Press, 1968; and, *Supplement*, 1969.

AO *Der Alte Orient*

AOAT *Alter Orient und Altes Testament.* Neukirchen-Vluyn

AOS *American Oriental Series.* New Haven: American Oriental Society.

ARAB Luckenbill, D. D. *Ancient Records of Assyria and Babylonia.* 2 vols. Chicago: University of Chicago Press, 1926-1927.

ARM *Archives royales de Mari.* Paris: Imprimerie nationale, 1950- .

ARU Kohler, J., and Ungnad, A. *Assyrische Rechtsurkunden.* Leipzig: Pfeiffer, 1913.

AS *Assyriological Studies.* University of Chicago.

- 5. Piepkorn, A. C. *Historical Prism Inscriptions of Ashurbanipal I*, 1933.
- 16. *Studies in Honor of Benno Landsberger on his Seventy-Fifth Birthday*, 1965.

ASAW *Abhandlungen der Sächsichen Akademie der Wissenschaften, philologisch-historische Klasse*

Asb. Ashurbanipal historical texts, quoted according to:

- Rm. = Streck, VAB 7
- B = Piepkorn, AS 5
- C = Bauer, Theo. *Das Inschriftenwerk Assurbanipals.* Leipzig: J. C. Hinrichs, 1933.

D	= Piepkorn, AS 5
E	= Piepkorn, AS 5
F	= Aynard, J.-M. *Le Prisme du Louvre AO 19.939*. Paris: Librairie Ancienne Honore champion, 1957.
H	= Millard, A. R. "Fragments of Historical Texts From Nineveh: Ashurbanipal." *Iraq* 30 (1968), 98-120.
IT = (Ishtar Text)	= Thompson, R. C. "The British Museum Excavations at Nineveh, 1931-32." AAA 20 (1933), 71-127.
ATD	*Das Alte Testament Deutsch*. Göttingen: Vandenhoeck and Ruprecht
BA	*Beiträge zur Assyriologie und semitischen Sprachwissenschaft*
BASOR	*Bulletin of the American Schools of Oriental Research*
BDB	Brown, F., Driver, S. R., and Briggs, C. A. *A Hebrew and English Lexicon of the Old Testament*. Oxford: Clarendon Press, 1952.
BFCT	*Beiträge zur Förderung christlicher Theologie*
BibArch	*Biblical Archaeologist*
BIN	*Babylonian Inscriptions in The Collection of J. B. Nies*
BiOr	*Bibliotheca Orientalis*
BK	*Biblischer Kommentar: Altes Testament*. Neukirchen-Vluyn: Neukirchener Verlag
BM	Museum signature of the British Museum
CAD	*The Assyrian Dictionary of the Oriental Institute of the University of Chicago*
CAH	*Cambridge Ancient History*
Camb. B.	*The Cambridge Bible for Schools and Colleges*. Cambridge: at the University Press.
CBQ	*Catholic Biblical Quarterly*
CT	*Cuneiform Texts from Babylonian Tablets in The British Museum*
DN	Divine name
EI	*Eretz Israel*
En. Miq.	*Encyclopedia Miqrāʾīt*. (Hebrew.) Jerusalem: Mosad Bialik, 1955- .
GAG	Von Soden, W. *Grundriss der akkadischen Grammatik*. AnOr 33 (Rome, 1952),
GKC	*Gesenius' Hebrew Grammar*. Edited by E. Kautzsch. Translated by A. E. Cowley. Oxford: Clarendon Press, 1910.
GN	Geographic name
HAT	*Handbuch zum Alten Testament*. Tübingen: J. C. B. Mohr
HS	*Die heilige Schrift des Alten Testaments*. Bonn: Peter Hanstein
HTR	*Harvard Theological Review*
HUCA	*Hebrew Union College Annual*
IB	*The Interpreter's Bible*. New York: Abingdon
ICC	*International Critical Commentary*. Edinburgh and New York: T. & T. Clark and Scribners.
IDB	*Interpreter's Dictionary of the Bible*. Nashville: Abingdon, 1962.
IEJ	*Israel Exploration Society*
JAOS	*Journal of the American Oriental Society*
JBL	*Journal of Biblical Literature*
JCS	*Journal of Cuneiform Studies*
JNES	*Journal of Near Eastern Studies*
JRAS	*Journal of the Royal Asiatic Society of Great Britain and Ireland*
JSOR	*Journal of the Society of Oriental Research*
JWH	*Journal of World History*

K.	Museum signature of Kouyunjik Tablet Collection in the British Museum
KAH	*Keilschrifttexte aus Assur historischen Inhalts*
KAI	Donner, H.-Röllig, W. *Kanaanäische und Aramäische Inschriften.* Wiesbaden: Harrassowitz, 1962-1964.
KAV	*Keilschrifttexte aus Assur verschiedenen Inhalts*
KB	*Keilinschriftliche Bibliothek*
KHAT	*Kurzer Hand-Commentar zum Alten Testament.* Tübingen.
KUB	*Keilschrifturkunden aus Boghazköi*
LSS	*Leipziger semitistsche studien*
MA	Middle Assyrian
MAOG	*Mitteilungen der Altorientalischen Gesellschaft*
MDOG	*Mitteilungen der Deutschen Orient-Gesellschaft*
MIO	*Mitteilungen des Instituts für Orientforschung der deutschen Akademie der Wissenschaften zu Berlin*
MVAG	*Mitteilungen der Vorderasiatischen Gesellschaft*
NA	Neo-Assyrian
NB	Neo-Babylonian
ND.	Signature for Nimrud documents (London and Baghdad)
OB	Old Babylonian
obv.	obverse
OECT	*Oxford Editions of Cuneiform Texts*
OIP	*Oriental Institute Publications.* Chicago: University of Chicago Press. 2. Luckenbill, D. D. *The Annals of Sennacherib*, 1924. 26. May, H. G. *Material Remains of the Megiddo Cult*, 1935.
OLZ	*Orientalistische Literaturzeitung*
Or	*Orientalia, New Series*
OTL	*Old Testament Library.* Philadelphia: Westminster.
OTS	*Oudtestamentische Studiën*
PJB	*Palästinajahrbuch*
PN	Personal name
PSBA	*Proceedings of the Society of Biblical Archaeology*
I-V R	Rawlinson, H. C. *The Cuneiform Inscriptions of Western Asia.* 5 vols. London: 1861-1884.
RA	*Revue d'assyriologie et d'archéologie orientale*
RB	*Revue Biblique*
rev.	reverse
RLA	*Reallexikon der Assyriologie*
Rm.	Rassam. Museum signature of Kouyunjik Tablet Collection in the British Museum.
SBAW	*Sitzungsberichte der Bayerischen Akademie der Wissenschaften, philosophische-historische Abteilung*
SBT	*Studies in Biblical Theology*
SH	*Scripta Hierosolymitana*
SJTh	*Scottish Journal of Theology*
StOr	*Studia Orientalia*
s.v.	under the entry
T.B.	Talmud Babli
TCL	*Textes cunéiformes du Louvre*
ThStKr	*Theologische Studien und Kritiken*
TZ	*Theologische Zeitschrift*
UM	Gordon, Cyrus H. *Ugaritic Manual.* AnOr 35 (Rome, 1955).

VAB	*Vorderasiatische Bibliotek.* Leipzig: J. C. Hinrichs. 2. Knudtzon, Weber and Ebeling. *Die El-Amarna Tafeln*, 1915. 3. Weissbach, F. H. *Die Keilschriften der Achämeniden*, 1911 4. Langdon, S. *Die Neubabylonischen Königsinschriften.* 1912 7. Streck, M. *Assurbanipal und die letzten Assyrischen Könige bis zum Untergange Nineveh's*, 1916.
VAS	*Vorderasiatische Schriftdenkmäler Königlichen Museen zu Berlin*
VAT	Museum signature of Staatliche Museen, Berlin
VT	*Vetus Testamentum*
WM	Haussig, H. W. *Wörtenbuch der Mythologie*, 1ste Ab. Die Alten Kulturvölker; Band 1: *Götter & Mythen im Vordern Orient.* Stuttgart: E. Klett, 1965.
WO	*Die Welt des Orients*
WVDOG	*Wissenschaftliche Veröffentlichung der Deutschen Orientgesellschaft*
WZKM	*Wiener Zeitschrift für die Kunde des Morgenlandes*
Y^{e}diot	*Yediot Bahaqirat Eretz-Israel Weatiqoteha* continuing the *Bulletin of the Israel Exploration Society* (New Series)
YOS	*Yale Oriental Series*
ZA	*Zeitschrift für Assyriologie und Verwandte Gebiete*
ZAW	*Zeitschrift für die alttestamentliche Wissenschaft*

Index of Biblical Sources

Books are listed according to the order of the Hebrew MT.

Index of Words and Terms Discussed

Index of Authors Cited

Italic type indicates location of full bibliographic citations.